Northern Ireland

Aspects of Political Economy

Series Editor: Geoffrey Harcourt

Published

A. Asimakopulos, *Investment, Employment and Income Distribution*
Pat Devine, *Democracy and Economic Planning*
Richard M. Goodwin and Lionello F. Punzo, *The Dynamics of a Capitalist Economy*
Marc Jarsulic, *Effective Demand and Income Distribution*
Peter Nolan, *The Political Economy of Collective Farms*
Bob Rowthorn and Naomi Wayne, *Northern Ireland*
Christopher Torr, *Equilibrium, Expectations and Information*
Warren Young, *Interpreting Mr Keynes*

Forthcoming

Paul Dunne, ed., *Quantitative Marxism*
Grazia Ietto-Gillies, *Causes and Effects of International Production*
Ravi Kanbur, *Risk Taking, Income Distribution and Poverty*
Heinz Kurz, *Capital, Distribution and Effective Demand*
Jose Salazar, *Pricing Policy and Economic Development*
Ian Steedman, *From Exploitation to Altruism*

Northern Ireland
The Political Economy of Conflict

Bob Rowthorn
and
Naomi Wayne

Polity Press

First published in 1988 by Polity Press
in association with Basil Blackwell.

Reprinted 1988

Editorial Office:
Polity Press, Dales Brewery, Gwydir Street,
Cambridge CB1 2LJ, UK

Basil Blackwell Ltd
108 Cowley Road, Oxford, OX4 1JF, UK

British Library Cataloguing in Publication Data

Rowthorn, Bob
  The political economy of Northern Ireland.
  —(Aspects of political economy).
  1. Northern Ireland. Economic development.
  Political aspects
  I. Title   II. Wayne, Naomi   III. Series
  330.9416′0824
  ISBN 0-7456-0535-4
  ISBN 0-7456-0536-2 Pbk

Typeset in 11 on 12½pt Plantin
by Downdell Limited, Oxford
Printed in Great Britain by
T.J. Press Ltd, Padstow

Contents

Acknowledgements

The authors and publishers are grateful to the following for permission to quote previously published material:
The Ulster Political Research Group for extracts from its pamphlet 'Common Sense' (Appendix 5); Sinn Féin for extracts from its discussion document 'A Scenario for Peace' (Appendix 5); the BBC for its 'News and Current Affairs Index – Coverage of Matters affecting Northern Ireland' (Appendix 6).

In producing this work we have benefited from extensive discussion in both Ireland and Britain, with people of very diverse religious persuasions and political views. All have given their time generously and we are most grateful to them. Many do not wish to be identified and it would be invidious to name the rest. We are also grateful to Lucia Hanmer for her valuable research assistance, and to Diana Day and Indira Dhokalia for computing and secretarial help.

Bob Rowthorn and Naomi Wayne

Introduction

In the late 1960s Northern Ireland exploded on to the world's television screens. What had been a very small and distant corner of the United Kingdom, about which few people, including the people of mainland Britain, knew anything at all, suddenly became a focus of political attention.

Centuries earlier Britain had conquered Ireland, dispossessed the native Catholic population and garrisoned the island with Protestant settlers brought over from the mainland. In 1921, following a bitter war, Britain partitioned Ireland and withdrew from all but the north-eastern corner. This remaining territory was retained for the Protestant settlers as their own separate statelet and was given the name Northern Ireland. However, within the boundaries of this statelet many Catholics were left behind. With British acquiescence, the Catholics in Northern Ireland were systematically excluded from political power and deprived of their economic and civil rights. At the end of the 1960s a section of the Catholic community finally rebelled, and for the past 20 years Britain has been struggling to put this rebellion down.

For many British people the sudden outbreak of strife in Northern Ireland led to a belated discovery that there was a part of the United Kingdom where a community was routinely subjected to massive and naked discrimination because of its members' religious affiliation. No longer could people in mainland Britain claim they did not know that Northern Ireland Catholics were denied access to jobs, housing, and even to equal voting rights in local elections. The law too, it turned out, was different in Northern Ireland. Ordinary British domestic standards of law enforcement and of civil liberties did not apply; instead, for nearly half a century, this supposedly integral part of the

United Kingdom had been governed by a unique system of 'emergency' legislation.

Briefly, this discovery was traumatic – as also was the experience of being pilloried on the world political stage for having allowed such a situation to exist unchecked for so long. However, after 50 years of colluding with oppression and discrimination in Northern Ireland, the British government was not to be easily moved. And as it failed to take the drastic steps needed to tackle the Catholic community's grievances, rebellion in Northern Ireland turned into open warfare. Civil rights marches gave way to bitter armed conflict; and demands for an end to the very existence of Northern Ireland as a separate political entity – in other words, for political reunification of the island of Ireland – began to compete with appeals for an end to discrimination alone.

As unrest and violence grew, Britain's response proved ever more wanting. Amongst the major political parties, bipartisanship became the order of the day. Successive Labour and Tory governments denied the political nature of Northern Ireland's tragedy, characterizing it instead as yet another example of modern day 'terrorism'. Reforms were grudging, limited and always too late, while priority was given to a military solution – crushing the 'men of violence' and thus restoring Northern Ireland to 'normality'.

Media attention, too, focused more and more on the 'mindlessness' of the 'terror' and less and less on the political causes of the conflict. That Northern Ireland was a problem without a solution, a primitive tribal hangover, an impenetrable mystery that defied rational analysis, rapidly became the received wisdom. Unsurprisingly, it was not long before British popular interest and concern had waned almost to vanishing point. However, in the mid-1980s this near uniformity of unconcern has itself started to break up. Both in Britain and elsewhere, for a number of reasons, there has been a rebirth of interest in Northern Ireland's affairs.

The Republican hunger strikes of 1981 and Sinn Féin's successful entry into constitutional politics, employing their new strategy of the armalite *and* the ballot box, has made Britain's denial of the political roots of the Northern Ireland conflict ever less tenable. Simultaneously, there has been substantial criticism from within the United States over Britain's failure to tackle the continuing phenomenon of employment discrimination against Catholics in Northern Ireland. This has not only helped to put the issue of discrimination against Catholics firmly back on to the political agenda; even more significantly, it has, to the British government's evident annoyance, internationalized the whole question of the conflict in Northern Ireland. Finally, there has been the Anglo-Irish Agreement: a high-profile political initiative on the part of both the British and the Irish governments, and the first of its kind for a decade.

In this context, when even the British government's approach to the unrest in Northern Ireland is taking on something of a political dimension, a growing number of people are beginning to ask long-overdue questions. What kind of place is Northern Ireland? Why does conflict continue there? What are the origins of this conflict? Is it inevitable that it should go on for ever? And, most notably, is there a strategy which Britain could and should adopt, not merely to contain the conflict militarily, but to bring it to a lasting and just political conclusion? In this welcome atmosphere of resurgent interest and concern, this book is intended as a contribution to the public debate about the future of Northern Ireland and its people.

The political economy of Northern Ireland

In spite of the patchy and erratic media and public interest, Northern Ireland has still managed to spawn a vast literature. However, this literature is uneven in coverage and very compartmentalized. Thus, history is far more extensively treated than economics. Indeed, in the case of the latter, relatively little is produced outside the confines of official publications. While much of this economic writing is useful as far as it goes, it is very narrowly focused. Missing is any consideration of economic questions in their socio-political context. Meanwhile, most other writings about Northern Ireland do not consider economic questions at all or give them a mere passing reference.

One of our main purposes in writing this book is to remedy this defect. Economic questions are discussed at length against the background of the social and political factors which influence them.

Central to this is our examination of the issue of religious discrimination and Catholic disadvantage, which we seek to rescue from the civil rights ghetto to which it is presently confined. In conventional economic literature such issues, if considered at all, usually appear under the euphemistic heading, 'geography of industrial location'. In this book, discrimination and Catholic disadvantage are given the centre stage, not only as a historical phenomenon, but in our analysis of politics and the economy.

British withdrawal

Another feature of the literature on Northern Ireland is the complete absence of any serious discussion of British withdrawal. In conventional writings this option is normally dismissed out of hand as unthinkable or utterly impractical. In Republican literature an equally cavalier approach is taken, with, at most, a page or two of hopeful assertion devoted to the subject.

The second major purpose of this book is to examine extensively the question of British withdrawal. Here we argue both for the desirability of withdrawal and for its practicality. We recognize that many of the fears surrounding withdrawal are genuinely felt and deserve to be taken seriously. However, in this book we seek to demonstrate that though not entirely unfounded, these fears are greatly exaggerated and that the supposedly dire consequences of a British decision to withdraw are by no means a foregone conclusion.

We discuss at length how the outcome of any decision to withdraw would depend crucially on the way such a decision was implemented. We focus in particular upon Northern Ireland's overwhelming economic dependence on Britain. Without British support the province could not survive on its own for more than a few weeks. Consequently, if Britain were, in Pontius Pilate fashion, simply to wash its hands and abandon Northern Ireland entirely, the result would be catastrophic. The already bankrupt economy of the province would finally disintegrate and full-scale civil war would be a real possibility. This is the doomsday scenario which the opponents of withdrawal claim would be inevitable were Britain to leave. If these opponents are right, their case is unanswerable. However, in this book we argue that the Pontius Pilate approach to withdrawal is not the only option. Despite the loss of its empire, Britain is still a powerful country with considerable economic and military strength. We show in detail how this strength could be used constructively, both to avoid economic chaos following withdrawal and to facilitate a comparatively peaceful transition to a united Ireland.

We do not suggest that such a transition would be completely trouble free and without violence. However, we do claim that withdrawal could be organized in such a way as to minimize the scale of violence and contain it at a level which is both morally and politically acceptable. Any bloodshed which might accompany a properly organized transition to a united Ireland, although tragic in itself, would be less than the cumulative deaths and injuries arising from an indefinite continuation of the current conflict. Those who oppose withdrawal on the grounds that it would lead to a bloodbath exaggerate the risks of such a catastrophic outcome, while failing to appreciate the suffering involved in decades of the present low intensity warfare.

British responsibilities

A central theme of this book is that Northern Ireland is a British problem. Britain is responsible for the present situation there, and only Britain can find a solution. It was Britain which first conquered the island of Ireland; and Britain which partitioned this island in 1921. It was Britain which created the statelet of Northern Ireland, whose main reason for existence was the preservation of Protestant privilege. It was Britain which allowed Protestants within this new statelet to oppress its Catholic inhabitants. And for the last two decades it has been Britain which has been trying to put down Catholic rebellion and maintain Northern Ireland in being. Finally, it is Britain's refusal to leave Northern Ireland which perpetuates the present violence and killing.

Most British people perceive Britain as acting as healer and policeman, helping to bring Northern Ireland's Catholics and Protestants together and controlling the extremists on both sides. In fact, as we will show in this book, its role there is deeply divisive. What Britain actually does is continually to harass the poorer and most discontented sections of the Catholic population. At the same time, Britain exacerbates intercommunal strife by deploying local Protestant security forces to suppress rebellious Catholics. Moreover, Britain's all-pervasive control of Northern Ireland both makes constructive political activity almost impossible, and removes the incentive for serious dialogue between Catholics and Protestants.

So much for the past and present. For the future, Britain has the chance to make restitution - and the responsibility for doing so. It has a responsibility to work for a stable and just peace which will end the bloodshed once and for all. Such a peace is impossible while Britain remains in Northern Ireland. Thus, to start out on the road to peace, Britain must end its military and political control of Northern Ireland. While not in itself guaranteeing peace, this is an essential first step.

Britain's next step must be to ensure that this withdrawal is accompanied by a speedy and orderly reunification of the two parts of Ireland. To bring this result about, Britain must use its still considerable powers to minimize the amount of economic disruption and violence during the transition to a united Ireland. Moreover, for some years following reunification, it will have to provide sufficient financial aid to allow the people of Northern Ireland - both Catholic and Protestant - to live in reasonable comfort and rebuild their shattered economy. This is the least Britain can do, given its responsibility for the condition the Province is now in.

Quite apart from these general considerations, Britain also has specific obligations to the separate communities in Northern Ireland. To the native Catholics Britain has a responsibility to reverse the historic injustice of partition, which separated them from their fellow Catholics in the rest of Ireland and institutionalized their subordination to Northern Protestants. Britain also has a responsibility to the Protestant community, whose loyalty she has both encouraged and exploited. Protestants in Northern Ireland have given their lives generously in two world wars to defend Britain's interests, and in more recent years hundreds have been killed and thousands injured while serving in the British security forces inside the province. It would be quite wrong simply to abandon them without some provision for their future. During the negotiations preceding withdrawal, Britain must insist that adequate guarantees are given regarding their economic, civil and religious rights within a united Ireland. And following withdrawal Britain must use its economic strength to ensure these guarantees are honoured.

In the end it may be that some Protestants would simply not be prepared in any circumstances to live in a united Ireland. In the event of British withdrawal, they could, perhaps, be given financial aid to help them establish new lives elsewhere. However, this should be seen as a very last resort. Everything possible should be done to reassure the Protestant community, and to persuade its members to stay. They have an enormous amount to offer to a united Ireland, and it would be a tragedy for everyone concerned if there was a mass exodus of Northern Protestants following reunification.

No monopoly

One point we wish to emphasize at the very outset is that neither community in Northern Ireland has a monopoly of suffering in the present conflict. Amongst both Catholics and Protestants, hundreds have been killed and thousands injured, lives have been ruined and homes wrecked.

In relative terms it is undoubtedly the Catholics who have suffered the most, for it is against them that the main weight of repression has been directed. Most of the vast number of people imprisoned over the years for so-called 'terrorist' (i.e. political) offences have been Catholics, and most of the victims of sectarian assassination have also been Catholics. But hundreds of Protestants have also been shot or blown to pieces, and thousands more have been seriously injured. Moreover, in recent years, the balance of suffering has begun to shift and the Protestant share of casualties has been rising. One reason for this is the policy of Ulsterization, whereby the task of repressing the Catholic rebellion has been given over mainly to local Protestants instead of British soldiers. Such a policy saves British lives, but it means more casualties for the Protestant community. It also means greater inter-communal bitterness and makes reconciliation between Catholics and Protestants even more difficult.

No community in Northern Ireland has a monopoly of justice on its side either. Amongst both Catholics and Protestants there are many people who oppose sectarianism and genuinely seek reconciliation. Indeed, desire for reconciliation can be found in what may appear the most unlikely quarters. For example, leaders of some paramilitary organizations have made serious efforts in recent years to confront the problem of sectarianism and to find a solution which can permit the two communities to live in harmony.

On the Republican side, leaders of Sinn Féin have become increasingly vocal in their condemnation of sectarianism and have explicitly recognized the need for constitutional guarantees to safeguard Protestant rights in a united Ireland (see the document *A Scenario for Peace* which is reproduced in Appendix 5). At the same time, the organization's military wing, the IRA, has made more attempts to reduce civilian casualties among Protestants in recent years (though such attempts, it must be said, have not prevented some terrible occurrences such as the Enniskillen bombing in 1987). These developments on the Republican side, though at times uneven, represent a reassertion of traditional Republican history and ideology. Republicanism traces its origins back to the eighteenth-century Protestant-led United Irishmen, and at an official level has always been in favour of religious tolerance.

More striking, given their history of overtly sectarian violence, is that similar sentiments are sometimes to be found amongst Protestant paramilitaries. Prominent leaders of the Ulster Defence Association (UDA) have made several appeals calling for reconciliation between Catholics and Protestants. They have also gone on record in support of power sharing between Catholics and Protestants, within the framework of local self-government for Northern Ireland as a region of the UK (see the document *Common Sense*, also reproduced in Appendix 5). These pronouncements should not be accepted uncritically. Despite its official commitment to reconciliation, the UDA retains links with another organization, the notorious Ulster Freedom Fighters (UFF), which is still engaged in the assassination of Catholic civilians. In addition, as we explain in chapter 9, power sharing within the UK does not provide a viable solution to the present conflict, and it is doubtful if the scheme proposed by the UDA would ever get off the ground. Yet despite these qualifications, there is no doubt that the leaders of the UDA have made an impressive effort to rethink their position and to find a compromise acceptable to Catholics. This in itself is a sign of hope. It indicates the potential for realism and compromise amongst the Protestant paramilitaries. It also suggests that, faced with the *fait accompli* of British withdrawal, they would accept the inevitability of Irish unity, and not provoke the bloody civil war which many fear.

Structure and content

The book is organized as follows.

Chapter 1 provides a brief opening note intended to assist readers through the terminological tangle which inevitably colours writing about Northern Ireland.

In chapter 2 a rapid survey is made of Irish history from early colonial days to partition. Here we treat as the central - indeed the defining - characteristic of this history the conflict between Ireland's Catholic natives and its Protestant settlers. We see how, especially in the north-eastern corner of Ireland, where Protestants formed a majority, the struggle of working-class Protestants to maintain a privileged position over Catholics overlaid and largely submerged any common class interest the two communities would otherwise have shared. We emphasize that, neither in this, nor in the early part of chapter 4 do we make any claims to originality. Both these sections cover ground which has, from a variety of standpoints, been extensively traversed already; our purpose in including them is to locate our subsequent economic and political discussion within a historical context.

Chapter 3 gives an outline of the major ways in which discrimination against Catholics was built into the very fabric of the Northern Ireland state. In this chapter we examine Northern Ireland's unique constitutional and political relationship to the rest of the United Kingdom. We consider the key issues of electoral gerrymandering; unequal employment access for Catholics and Protestants; discrimination in housing; and Protestant domination of the administration of justice. For evidence we look both to the explicit statements of some of the leading Protestant protagonists, and to statistics. In particular, we draw heavily on the Report of the Cameron Commission, which was set up by the British government to investigate the civil disorders of the late 1960s.

Another historical survey is made in chapter 4, this time of the developments within Northern Ireland from the civil rights marches to the current stage of the conflict. In this chapter we describe the way civil rights gave way to militant republicanism in the face of Britain's consistently inadequate responses to Catholic grievances. We show also how British governments, both Labour and Conservative, sought to deny the political nature of the conflict by criminalizing its participants. We then examine how this strategy rebounded, bringing Catholic paramilitaries into constitutional politics in a manner hitherto unprecedented. This development provided the impetus for the Anglo-Irish Agreement which is examined in depth in chapter 9.

Chapter 5 provides an account of the human cost of the conflict in Northern Ireland. We describe the imprisonment, injury and deaths which have occurred on an enormous scale over the last two decades. We also show how civil liberties, already limited for nearly 50 years under Northern Ireland's 'emergency legislation', have been cut back and abused ever further. We argue that one of the more serious effects of the conflict has been the persistent censorship and manipulation of the news media, with its very damaging implications for British democracy.

A review of Northern Ireland's economy, from the foundation of the state up to the present day, is given in chapter 6. In this chapter we describe the huge transformation which occurred during the 1950s and 1960s when local industry was run down and the province became dominated by multinational firms. However, in the last 20 years this process has gone into reverse, with multinationals reducing their activities or pulling out altogether. The result has been a severe crisis in the local economy: with unemployment now extremely high, and only huge subsidies from the British government keeping the province afloat. Though this crisis cannot be blamed simply on the present armed conflict, the conflict has greatly exacerbated it and made the province's economic situation much worse. We also show how, despite

Northern Ireland's economic difficulties, some people have done extremely well and have experienced a marked rise in their standard of living over the past 20 years. Thus, the picture is not one of unrelieved poverty, but of a widening gap between the haves and the have-nots. The chapter concludes with a brief look at the Irish Republic. We argue that, despite its numerous problems and high unemployment, the Republic has a much stronger economy than Northern Ireland and its long-term economic prospects are much better.

In chapter 7 a comparison is made between the economic situation of Catholics and Protestants. We describe in detail the immense economic disadvantage suffered by the Catholic community in Northern Ireland. While poverty and insecurity are widespread amongst the working class of both communities, the situation is considerably worse for Catholics. We show how most of the best jobs are held by Protestants and how Catholics are crowded into lower-paid, less skilled and less secure occupations.

In chapter 8 we briefly discuss the political implications of Northern Ireland's economic dependence on Britain, and the importance of establishing peace if an upturn in the province's economy is to be achieved. We argue that a sustained recovery in the local economy is almost inconceivable while the present conflict continues. Though not the only factor responsible for the crisis, the conflict is the single most important obstacle to a genuine recovery. Peace would not, in itself, guarantee such a recovery, but is an essential prerequisite.

An extended examination of the various ways in which an end to the conflict in Northern Ireland might be secured is made in chapter 9. It commences with a detailed account of the thinking behind and the implications and content of the Anglo-Irish Agreement. Here we recognize the tactical lessons, at least, that have been learned since the last great attempt at constitutional reform – the 1974 Sunningdale experiment. But we argue, too, that the agreement is inherently and fundamentally flawed: its essence is compromise and the maintenance of a delicate balance, in a situation whose resolution demands, by contrast, a decisive breach with the past. After reviewing other options, chapter 9 presents a detailed discussion of the feasibility and the actual mechanics, legal, military, political and economic, of a British withdrawal from Northern Ireland.

Chapter 10 briefly concludes with a summary of the main reasons which are normally given for opposing British withdrawal from Northern Ireland, and we explain why we consider these reasons to be erroneous.

To make this book accessible to the widest possible readership we have dispensed with footnotes. However, much of the relevant evidence which we rely on is contained in Tables and Appendices, and there is also an annoted Bibliography. Among the appendices there is an analysis of the religious composition of the Northern Ireland population, together with a discussion of likely changes in the future. We list statistics concerning matters such as incidence of deaths and injuries; numbers interned, detained and charged with 'terrorist' offences. Also included are policy documents from two of the main paramilitary (or paramilitary-associated) protagonists: Sinn Féin and the Ulster Defence Association (UDA). We reproduce these partly because they will be less accessible to a general readership than the statements of the constitutional parties, and partly because they represent some of the most open-minded thinking on either side of the communal divide.

1 The Words We Use
A Note on Terminology

One of the difficulties in talking about the present situation in Northern Ireland is choosing the right language. Very often even the words people use depend on their politics and on their religious affiliations. This means that frequently it is quite impossible to find a 'neutral' expression. In the glossary below we explain which words are generally used by which section of the community in Northern Ireland, and which we use here.

The people

There are about 1.5 million people in Northern Ireland. Around 60 per cent are Protestant and virtually all the rest Catholic.

Unionists
Most of the Protestants wish to see Northern Ireland remain legally united with Britain. They describe themselves as loyal to the Crown and in favour of keeping the Union with Britain. So they are often called 'Unionists' or 'Loyalists'. Broadly speaking, Loyalists are the more militant Unionists, those more willing to use physical force. Here we mainly use the term *Unionists* as it covers a wider range of people who all share a desire to remain part of the United Kingdom.

Nationalists
Most of the Catholics want Northern Ireland and the Republic of Ireland to be united into one national state. They are often called 'Nationalists' or 'Republicans'. Broadly speaking, Republicans are the more militant Nationalists, those more willing to use physical force,

and also often those with more radical social policies. We mainly use the term *Nationalists* as it covers a wider range of people who all share a desire to see a united Ireland.

The territory

Ireland is an island, divided geographically in several different ways: into 32 counties, four provinces and two states.

Éire
This is the Gaelic term for Ireland and the name on the Republic's stamps. However, it is a name rarely heard in the Republic; more commonly it is used by people in Northern Ireland who are strongly opposed to a united Ireland as it makes the Republic sound foreign.

Free State
This was the legal name of the Republic until 1949. Today it is quite often used by both Catholics and Protestants in Northern Ireland, but rarely by people in the Republic.

Northern Ireland
This is the legal name for the territory north of the border. It is the nearest to a neutral term and is the one we use. Northern Ireland is sometimes said to be a state and sometimes a *province*. We mainly use the latter term.

Republic of Ireland
This is the legal name for the territory south of the border. It is the nearest to a neutral term and is the one we use.

Six Counties
This is a name often used by Nationalists. It refers to the fact that six out of Ireland's 32 counties are north of the border.

Twenty-Six Counties
This is a name often used by Nationalists to describe the Republic.

Ulster
From the map we can see that the province of Ulster is partly north and partly south of the border. However, Unionists often use the name 'Ulster' to refer to Northern Ireland alone.

MAP 1   The Provinces and Counties of Ireland

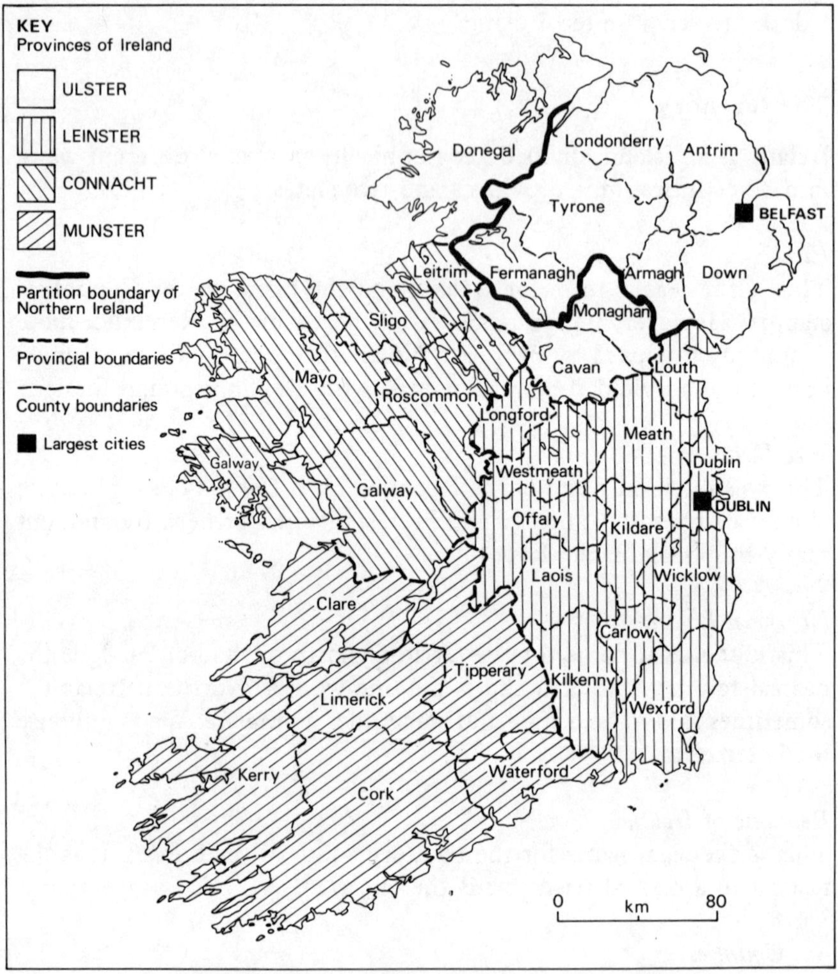

United Kingdom
This is the legal name of Great Britain (England, Scotland and Wales) plus Northern Ireland. It is a term frequently employed by Unionists to emphasize the constitutional relationship between Britain and Northern Ireland. Nationalists very rarely use it. We use the term 'United Kingdom' as the legal name when we are discussing Great Britain and Northern Ireland together.

Special place names

Derry

Northern Ireland's second city is called either 'Derry' or 'London-derry'. Catholics always use the original name, Derry. Protestants who live in the city usually say Derry too – there is even a local Unionist organization called 'the Apprentice Boys of Derry'. Other Protestants call it Londonderry, the name the city was given after a famous battle in 1689. There is no neutral, or even nearly neutral term.

A few years ago, the Nationalist local council changed the legal name of the city council from Londonderry to Derry. However, the name of the city itself remains Londonderry. We use the name *Derry* except when quoting from official government statistics. To further complicate issues, the county where Derry is situated is still called Londonderry. We use the name *Londonderry* to refer to the county.

2   How Did It All Begin?

The setting

At one time the whole of Ireland was a British possession, ruled from Westminster. However, as a glance at the map will show, modern Ireland is now divided into two parts. This division dates back to partition in 1921-2, when 26 of Ireland's 32 counties were granted independence after a guerrilla war against British rule. The remaining six counties in the north-east, around Belfast, kept their link with Britain, and from them a new region, with the name Northern Ireland, was created.

Although technically still part of the United Kingdom and subject to the Parliament at Westminster, this region was given a separate parliament of its own - Stormont - and extensive powers of self-government. These powers were so great that Northern Ireland was, in terms of domestic policy, in many respects an independent country. However, following massive civil unrest, Stormont was abolished in 1972, and since then Northern Ireland has been administered directly from Westminster.

The 'Irish Question'

At the present time, the total population of Ireland as a whole is around 5 million, of which about 3.5 million live in the Republic and 1.5 million in Northern Ireland. The population is divided into two main religious groupings: Catholics and Protestants. However, their geographical distribution is very uneven. The great majority of Protestants are in Northern Ireland where they outnumber Catholics in a ratio of 60 to 40. By contrast, the Republic's population is overwhelmingly Catholic - about 93 per cent.

This population distribution, the way it came about, and the different experience of the two religious groups has led to the 'twin minority' problem. In Ireland as a whole, the Protestants make up a fifth of the total population. In Northern Ireland, however, they form the majority. If Ireland were to be reunited as the nationalists want, Northern Protestants would become a minority, subject, they fear, to the will of the Catholic majority. This helps to explain why most of them are opposed to a united Ireland. On the other hand, should self-government be restored to Northern Ireland, as most unionists want, Northern Catholics would once again be subject to the will of a Protestant majority, as they were between 1921 and 1972.

Natives and settlers

To understand the situation in Ireland today, and in particular why religious affiliation is so important, we have to go back to the seventeenth-century 'Plantation', when waves of settlers were sent over from Britain. At that time Ireland was already a British possession, having been conquered by Henry II in the twelfth century. However, this conquest was never complete, and large parts of the country had remained under native control. Moreover, some of the earlier invaders from Britain had 'gone native', adopting the Gaelic language and customs and intermarrying with the local population. They also shared the same Catholic religion, and like the original native Irish, were in a state of sporadic revolt against the Crown. In short, they had become Irish themselves.

Thus, though supposedly a British possession, Ireland had become a serious problem to British rulers. Not only were the Irish constantly rebelling, but the country was a useful base for foreign armies, and a convenient haven for any British rebels who needed somewhere to flee and to regroup from. Ireland was therefore seen as a strategic threat by Britain; the Plantation was designed to solve the 'Irish problem' and eliminate this threat once and for all. The idea of the Plantation was simple. Ireland would be filled with Protestant, English-speaking settlers from Britain, who would provide a loyal garrison to subdue the natives and safeguard British interests. In return for their loyalty, they would receive land and other benefits, together with military aid from Britain should the need arise.

This plan reached its most extreme form under Oliver Cromwell. Great numbers of Catholic Gaelic-speaking natives were driven out of the east and centre of the country and resettled in the infertile west.

Their land was seized, and under an Act for the settlement of Ireland passed in 1652, anyone who resisted was made liable to the death penalty. Given that resistance was widespread, this penalty, fully applied, would have wiped out around 80,000 people – about half the Catholic adult male population.

As it was, Cromwell's policy was only very partially implemented. At most, hundreds not thousands were executed. In addition, settlers did not come over in such large numbers, nor were Catholics driven out on the scale originally envisaged. However, what *was* highly successful was land seizure: by 1700 around 90 per cent of all land in Ireland was owned by Protestants, compared with less than 10 per cent a century earlier. At the same time, tough 'Penal Laws' were passed against the Catholic religion, and restrictions were imposed on the use of the Gaelic language and customs.

The overall effects of Cromwell's policy were patchy. In most of Ireland the incoming Protestants provided only a thin upper crust of landlords and administrators, while below them there remained a vast mass of Catholic labourers and tenant farmers. This meant that there emerged a well-defined class difference between settler and native, such that most settler–native conflicts were also class conflicts. However, in one part of the country, the north-east, the situation was radically different. This was the one area which did receive a large influx of settlers during the seventeenth century. Great numbers of Presbyterians were brought in from nearby Scotland, together with Episcopalians and other Protestants from England.

Even so, there were not enough of the settlers to expel the native Catholics altogether. The result was a mixed population of settlers and natives, living side by side in roughly equal numbers, and competing with each other for the same land or the same jobs. On average, the Protestant settlers were considerably better off than the Catholic natives, and most of the rich were – and still are – Protestant. However, from the outset there have always been many poor Protestants. This has meant that in the north-east the settlers have been spread across all social classes.

As a consequence, the conflicts which developed in this part of Ireland between Catholic native and Protestant settler were often *within* the same social class. They involved farmer against farmer, worker against worker, with lower-class settlers struggling to establish or maintain their superiority over natives in the same class. Such a situation is not unique to Northern Ireland. It has occurred wherever a country has been colonized on a mass basis. An obvious example is

Algeria, where the relatively poor formed a significant element of the settler community.

Seeds of modern Ireland: 'Orangeism' and Republicanism

The Plantation was accompanied by great violence. Many Catholics were killed, while Catholic resistance meant that the Protestants who settled the land lived under seige and often lost their lives too. In total, over 100,000 settlers and troops died in battles over the Plantation. 40,000 Irish people left to serve in European armies and another 100,000 were transported to Britain's other colonies as slaves.

Towards the end of the seventeenth century, a last ditch effort was made to return Ireland - and Britain - to Catholic rule. In 1689 the Dutch Protestant Prince William of Orange became King of England. The previous king, James II, a Catholic, fled to Ireland, hoping to get the backing of France and Ireland to restore him to the English throne. His troops trapped 35,000 Protestants in Derry for 15 weeks. The starving city was eventually saved by the arrival of the British fleet. The next year, 1690, William took his army to Ireland and defeated James at the Battle of the Boyne.

When, a hundred years later, in 1795, the Protestants formed an organization to campaign to keep Ireland a British colony, they called it the 'Orange Order' in memory of King William's victories. The Order still survives today, as do the memories. Every year, Northern Ireland Protestants commemorate these defeats of the Catholics with the 'Orange Marches' held in July and August.

Yet neither the Plantation, nor William's victory had solved the 'Irish problem' for Britain. Rebellion and revolt continued. Most famous of all was the rising of the United Irishmen in 1798 which was inspired by the ideals of the American and French Revolutions. While the great majority of the United Irishmen were Catholics, the rising was led by Protestants, many of them Presbyterian manufacturers and tenant farmers from Ulster who also suffered economic and political discrimination.

The United Irishmen were the first modern Republicans: they aimed to establish an independent republic of Ireland in which Catholics and Protestants would live in harmony. As the Protestant Wolfe Tone put it:

To subvert the tyranny of our execrable government, to break the connection with England, the never failing source of all our political evils, and to assert the independence of my country - these were my objects. To unite the whole people of Ireland, to abolish the memory of all past dissensions and to substitute the common name of Irishman in place of the denominations of Protestant, Catholic and Dissenter - these were my means. (Quoted in Sean Cronin, *Irish Nationalism*)

However, the rising was opposed by the majority of Protestants in Ireland, and was totally crushed by the British Army, with the help of a local militia recruited from the Protestant Orange Order. Two years later, under the 1800 Act of Union, Ireland was legally integrated into the United Kingdom. The Irish parliament was abolished and the Irish were given the right to send MPs to Westminster.

Union

The aims of the Act of Union were complex. Clearly it was intended to prevent any further uprisings and to tie Ireland more firmly to Britain. However, it also had another and, it may be considered, more ambitious purpose.

The old Protestant settler parliament, despite the more liberal views of some of its members such as Henry Gratton, had consistently opposed equal rights for Catholics. The Act of Union was designed to undermine the power of the Protestant settlers, for it was to be accompanied by reforms intended to win Catholic acceptance of British rule. Indeed the Catholic church gave its support to the Act of Union, having been persuaded by the promise of Catholic emancipation.

In the event, vigorous lobbying in Westminster by Protestant settlers was able to obstruct change for thirty years. Not until 1829 was the Catholic Emancipation Act passed. By this time nationalist sentiment amongst the Catholic population was widespread, and more well organized than it had ever been. Reforms which, in 1800, *might* have won Catholic acceptance of union with Britain, were no longer sufficient. Indeed, every reform merely fuelled nationalist self-confidence.

As the nineteenth century wore on, there was growing conflict over economic and social issues. Poverty, hunger and frustration sent the now ever-present anger of the native Irish boiling over. Huge sums in rent to Protestant absentee landlords were pouring out of the country. Successive failures of the potato crop - which formed the bulk of the peasants' diet - were leading to mass starvation, while the corn which the peasants grew for their landlords continued to be exported. A million died in the 'Great Famine' of the 1840s. Agitation over land reform became ever more bitter and intense, as the native Irish fought to recover their property. At the same time an immense nationalist movement for self-government was growing. It had become clear that Britain's aim to absorb Ireland into the United Kingdom had failed.

Home Rule

The new nationalist movement was divided over both aims and methods. On the one hand were those who sought Home Rule. This was a form of limited self-government, under which Ireland would have a parliament of its own, but would remain within the British Empire and recognize the British monarch as head of state. On the other hand were the Republicans, who wanted complete independence for Ireland outside the Empire.

As to method, the Home Rulers preferred peaceful agitation and achievement of reform through Parliament, while the Republicans were more inclined to armed struggle. However, the dividing lines were not always clear: there were times when the Republicans supported the Home Rule movement, while the Home Rulers always had a violent undercurrent. Indeed, many saw the choice between Republicanism and Home Rule as a largely tactical question.

The great majority of Irish nationalists in the nineteenth century were Catholics. However, a number of Protestants came to support Home Rule as the century wore on. This was especially so in the south where many of the old settler class now thought of themselves as Irish. Indeed, some of the most famous nineteenth-century leaders of Irish nationalism were Protestants; and at the time of the first Home Rule Bill in 1886, the Irish Parliamentary Party at Westminster was led by a southern Protestant, Charles Stewart Parnell. In the north there was also some Protestant support, especially among radical socialists. However, such people were both few in number and virtually without influence among the Protestant population, the overwhelming majority of whom were passionately opposed to Home Rule. This opposition was rooted in the inequalities between Protestant settlers and Catholic natives that had remained and taken on new forms in the years since the Plantation.

Inequality

The original basis for settler–native strife concerned the ownership of land. Following the Plantation the economic development of Ireland created new inequalities.

Ireland's industrial revolution was confined largely to the north-east, what is now Northern Ireland. Here a huge linen industry developed in the eighteenth and nineteenth centuries. Then came thriving ship-building and engineering towards the end of the nineteenth century. The area around Belfast had, by 1900, become one of the most indus-trialized places in the world, and one of the most prosperous regions of the United Kingdom. By 1911 a half of all industrial jobs in Ireland were located in its north-eastern corner, while one in five were in Belfast alone.

In contrast, the rest of Ireland was still an underdeveloped country. It was rural and poor, with most of its population working on the land, and with only a small industrial sector based mainly on food processing.

With the industrialization of the north-east, Belfast and the sur-rounding area became an island of prosperity in a sea of poverty. It attracted thousands of Catholic peasants who streamed from the countryside desperate for work. Faced with this tide of cheap labour, the Protestant workers of the city fought to keep the best paid and most secure jobs for themselves. In part they did this by direct physical force. But much more importantly, they depended on securing prefer-ential treatment from Protestant employers. In many instances this involved Protestant employers practising open discrimination in favour of Protestant workers. However, there were also more subtle means available, which meant that blatant discrimination was fre-quently unnecessary. For example, many Protestant employers and Protestant workers belonged to the Orange Order. This functioned as a private labour exchange, ensuring that many jobs could be filled without ever coming on to the open market. In addition, some trade unions, especially in shipbuilding and engineering, either excluded Catholics from membership altogether or kept them out of the best work.

As a result of all these factors, it became virtually impossible for a Catholic to obtain skilled employment in certain industries. Thus, by 1911, though Catholics made up about 30 per cent of the population of Belfast, only 5 per cent of all skilled workers in the Belfast area were Catholic.

Protestant fears

In every respect, therefore, Northern Protestants had acquired a highly privileged position by comparison with the Catholics. They had secured most of the better jobs and occupied most of the best land. Even the poorest Protestants were generally better off than the poorest Catholics. It is hardly surprising that their chief reaction to the idea of a self-governing Ireland was one of fear: in a society where Catholics were in a majority Protestants could only lose.

This fear clearly had a degree of justification. Some of the more naked forms of discrimination against Catholics would simply not have been possible in a self-governing state, and therefore some privilege would certainly have been lost. In addition, the Protestants were frightened of retribution. This too was not surprising – throughout the nineteenth century, Catholics had been badly mistreated. Like other settlers in later colonial situations this century (Kenya, Rhodesia, etc.) the Protestants assumed that once the native community was in control it would want to get its own back. But there were also some special features of the Irish situation.

The conflict was not just about Protestant privilege; it also had a purely religious dimension. The Unionist slogan 'Home Rule is Rome Rule' expressed a genuine anxiety that Protestants would be persecuted for their religious beliefs in an independent Ireland. Given the conservative and intolerant mood of the Catholic church at the end of the nineteenth century, this fear was understandable.

Another special aspect of the situation concerned the economy. Most colonies on the verge of independence have had no significant manufacturing industry: their economies are usually based on agriculture, mining or a combination of the two. In Ireland, however, there was a large manufacturing sector located in the north-east, which was mostly owned and worked in by Protestants. Most of this sector's output was exported to Britain and to other parts of the British Empire. To remain prosperous and successful, this industry needed continuing access to British and Empire markets.

A common theme of Home Rule campaigners was the need for protection against British goods, so as to foster the development of Irish industries. Northern Protestants were afraid that were Home Rule achieved, it would be followed by an economic war with Britain in which their exports (linen, ships, engineering goods, etc.) would suffer. There might, of course, be a compensating gain for Ireland as a whole, in the form of new industries and new jobs. But they assumed, probably reasonably, that many of these industries would be located in the south and most of the jobs would go to Catholics.

A few Protestants, mostly socialists, argued that lower-class Protestants should throw in their lot with lower-class Catholics and try to achieve a radically new Ireland from which both communities would benefit. But this appeal seemed more like a pipe-dream than a real alternative to most Protestant workers; as far as they could see, independence, or even Home Rule, threatened all of their basic interests and offered them nothing in return.

Partition

By the early part of this century, after many years of agitation, it appeared that Home Rule would finally become a reality. Faced with this prospect, the Unionists of the North mobilized to prevent it. They formed a militia called the Ulster Volunteer Force, smuggled in thousands of rifles from abroad and prepared for action. They even threatened to declare independence and set up their own breakaway state in the North should Home Rule go through. They were supported by large sections of the British establishment: the Tory Party and many at all levels of the British Army and Civil Service. These supporters had a double motivation. They regarded Home Rule as a terrible betrayal of their Protestant friends. They were also appalled by the threat to Empire that Home Rule for Ireland represented. For if Ireland, which was actually part of the United Kingdom itself, were allowed independence, who knew which colonies might follow.

Many decades later something similar happened in Algeria, where French settlers took up arms to block independence and sections of the army threatened a military coup. France's President de Gaulle simply dumped the settlers and pulled out of Algeria. But Britain's Prime Minister Lloyd George was no de Gaulle. He surrendered to Unionist threats and abandoned his original scheme of Home Rule for the whole of Ireland. By 1919 the British army were locked in a fierce guerrilla war with nationalist forces. When a truce was eventually agreed in 1921 Lloyd George proposed the following compromise.

Ireland would be partitioned into two separate countries with the border between them very carefully drawn. It would separate off the six north-eastern counties where, in total, there was a Protestant majority, and keep them within the United Kingdom but with a parliament of their own. The remaining 26 counties, where most of the population was Catholic, would be given independence within the Empire. This arrangement would divide up the province of Ulster: the three of its counties which had large Catholic majorities would be left in the southern state.

Initially all the nationalists rejected partition. They had many

MAP 2 Ireland at the time of partition

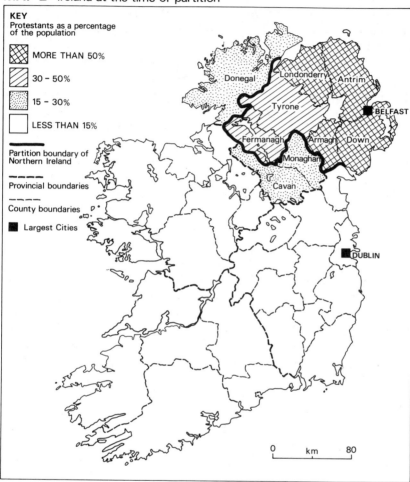

KEY
Protestants as a percentage
of the population

MORE THAN 50%

30 - 50%

15 - 30%

LESS THAN 15%

Partition boundary of
Northern Ireland

Provincial boundaries

County boundaries

Largest Cities

Donegal · Londonderry · Antrim · Tyrone · BELFAST · Fermanagh · Armagh · Down · Monaghan · Cavan · DUBLIN

0   km   80

NOTE: *for clarity this map omits the names of non-Ulster counties (all of which were less than fifteen per cent Protestant at time of partition)*

reasons: partition would only give partial independence; it would leave the great bulk of the country with virtually no modern manufacturing industry; it would also mean a sizeable minority of Catholics being marooned in a Protestant statelet, in an area where, for decades, Catholics had suffered the most severe discrimination. However, eventually a section of the guerrilla forces came to the conclusion that no better deal could be won and signed a treaty with Britain. What followed was a bitter civil war whose scars have lasted to this day. Eventually the pro-Treaty side defeated the anti-Treaty forces and by mid-1923 the Irish Free State was firmly established. In 1949, 27 years on, the Free State left the British Commonwealth and became the Republic of Ireland.

Politics in the Republic today are still conditioned by this history. The Irish Constitution, adopted in 1937, declares that the territory of the state includes all 32 counties of Ireland. The political party that supported the treaty became the modern Fine Gael while the anti-treaty forces split. One section remained as the militant Sinn Féin; the other became Fianna Fáil, which, since the 1930s, has been the Republic's single largest political party. All of the major political parties are verbally still in favour of a united Ireland, though they have no credible strategy for achieving this aim.

The new Northern Ireland

From the time of its birth, the new Northern Ireland state was profoundly divided. The Catholics who lived there were treated as dangerous outsiders. In the first couple of years frequent attacks were mounted on Catholic workers. The already limited number of Catholics employed in the shipyards were assaulted and driven out. In Belfast 500 Catholic businesses were wrecked and 10,000 Catholic workers forced to leave their jobs. As time went by, outright violence against Catholics diminished. But as we shall see, what was left was a society where discrimination against Catholics was a fact of life.

At the same time, the Official Unionist Party, which had formed Northern Ireland's first government, had massive support throughout the Protestant community. Though even more reactionary than the British Tories, the Official Unionists had taken the votes of the overwhelming majority of Protestants of all classes. In the decades to come, they continued to command huge cross-class Protestant support. The result was permanent one-party Protestant government – 50 years of uninterrupted Official Unionist rule – and rule which was practically free from any intervention by the government in Britain. For though Northern Ireland was – and is – constitutionally part of the United Kingdom, and financially supported by Britain, its relationship to the rest of the UK has always been unique. Unlike England, Scotland and Wales, for 50 years Northern Ireland's domestic affairs were shaped by its own parliament and government. Within the financial framework set by Britain, the province's parliament and government had virtually complete freedom to run matters as they saw fit.

Indeed, until 1968, Northern Ireland's affairs were dealt with by a department of the Home Office whose other ragtag and bobtail responsibilities comprised the regulation of British summer time, liquor licensing, London taxicabs, and the protection of birds and animals. Between 1964 and 1969, the British home secretary spent a total of no more than half a day in Northern Ireland.

Meanwhile, the Northern Ireland government's legal freedom to do much as it liked internally was reinforced by a British parliamentary convention not to discuss any internal Northern Ireland affairs at Westminster. This convention was supported just as much by Labour as by the Tories. Yet at the same time, MPs from Northern Ireland were (and still are) elected to Westminster, and have always taken as full a part as they have wished in all the British parliament's activities. Most of the province's parliamentary representatives at Westminster have been Unionists, whose voting patterns have paralleled those of the Tories.

A few British MPs, chiefly Labour members, did retain an interest in and concern about Northern Ireland. However, their attempts to put it on the British political agenda were universally rebuffed. By agreeing not even to talk about Northern Ireland much less intervene in its affairs, all the major political parties in Britain were able to avoid thinking about the province and gaining any knowledge about it. In the next chapter we examine what kind of society existed in Northern Ireland while, for nearly half a century, Britain closed its eyes.

3 What Kind of Place? Fifty Years of the Northern Ireland State

By 1922 the Northern Ireland state was established. Then the Unionist government took steps to strengthen its own position in power and to ensure the continued support of the whole Protestant population, regardless of class. Chief among these steps were the reorganization of the local government electoral system, and the introduction of a Special Powers Act. Though described as an emergency measure, the Act stayed in force for nearly 50 years.

The result of the government's measures was a society where religious discrimination was built into the very system: in voting, the allocation of housing, the allocation of jobs and the administration of justice. Much of the time discrimination was simply 'the way things worked'. But sometimes, as we shall see, it was open, admitted, and even advocated.

In 1969, in response to agitation by the civil rights movement and civil disorder, the British Labour government set up the Cameron Commission to investigation the causes. While many books and articles have been written about discrimination in Northern Ireland, the most influential and respected has been the Cameron Commission's report. In a very careful, low-key document, the Commission concluded that evidence of discrimination was widespread and could not be doubted. It stated (para. 127):

The weight and extent of the evidence which was presented to us concerned with social and economic grievances or abuses of political power was such that we are compelled to conclude that they had substantial foundation in fact and were in a very real sense an immediate and operative cause of the demonstrations and consequent disorders.

Much of what follows here is drawn directly from the pages of the Cameron Commission report.

Local government

At partition both parts of Ireland contained distinct religious minorities whose voting generally reflected their religion. Britain bequeathed to both the Republic and Northern Ireland a voting system - proportional representation - which would have given some protection to those minorities. For example, in an area which was 40 per cent Catholic and 60 per cent Protestant, Catholics could expect about 40 per cent of the council seats under this system. Under Britain's own 'first past the post' electoral system, Catholics in such an area might have ended up with no seats or very few, depending on the population breakdown of each ward.

In 1920 the operation of proportional representation meant that Nationalists won control of 25 out of 80 councils in the area then covered by Northern Ireland. Such a result was not repeated, for in 1922 the Unionist government in Northern Ireland abolished PR. At the same time it set up an electoral commission to redraw the local government boundaries. There were Unionists who were willing to spell out exactly what was intended by these moves. Unionist MP for Fermanagh and Tyrone, William Miller, said:

When the government of Northern Ireland decided to do away with proportional representation the chance that they had been waiting for so long arrived and they took advantage of it . . . they divided the country in the way they thought best. (*Northern Whig*, 13 July 1923)

The redrawn boundaries were said to have been *gerrymandered*. In Catholic areas the ward boundaries were fixed so that Nationalist seats were won with huge majorities, thus 'wasting' Nationalist votes. Unionist majorities were small, but sufficient to give them control.

The result was dramatic. After the 1924 elections Nationalists controlled only two out of nearly 80 local councils. To take but one specific example, in the area covered by Omagh Rural Council the population was 61.5 per cent Catholic. In 1920 the Nationalists won with 26 seats to 13. In 1924 the Unionists were victorious with 21 seats to 18. Though the 1924 results were somewhat exaggerated, because many Nationalists boycotted the elections, in later years, when they took part again, the pattern of Unionist victories still continued.

The gerrymander was underpinned by the restricted franchise: only ratepayers and their wives could vote. In 1945 the Labour government had introduced universal suffrage for local elections in Britain. A year later, instead of following suit, the Northern Ireland government passed a law narrowing the franchise still further by taking away votes from lodgers who were not ratepayers. This resulted in about a quarter of the adult population being excluded from voting. Catholics, who were poorer and less likely to have tenancies, were particularly hard hit: in 1969 three-quarters of those who were disenfranchised were Catholic. At the same time, the company directors' vote was retained: limited companies could have up to six votes depending on their rateable value. Most of the company votes were Unionist.

The Cameron Commission investigated the operation of the local government electoral system in those towns where major disturbances had arisen in 1968: Londonderry, Armagh, Newry and Dungannon. It also examined the situation in the town of Omagh, and in the County of Fermanagh. It was sharply critical (para. 134):

In each of the areas with Unionist majorities on their council the majority was far greater than the adult population balance would justify. In Londonderry County Borough, Armagh Urban District, Omagh Urban District and County Fermanagh a Catholic majority in the population was converted into a large Unionist majority on the Councils. In the two Dungannon councils a very small Protestant majority held two thirds or over of the seats on the councils. The most glaring case was Londonderry County Borough where 60% of the seats on the Corporation were held by Unionists ... In Londonderry County Borough there was the following extraordinary situation in 1967.

	Catholic voters	Other voters	Seats
North Ward	2530	3946	8 Unionists
Waterside Ward	1852	3697	4 Unionists
South Ward	10047	1138	8 Non-Unionists
Total	14429	8781	20

This Unionist control of local government had the following effects.

1 It put overwhelming power over local authority housing and jobs into Unionist hands.
2 It meant there were very few contested local elections as the results were a foregone conclusion. (Thus, between 1923 and 1955 the

average of uncontested seats was: rural councils 96 per cent, county councils 94 per cent and urban and borough councils 60 per cent.)
3 It left Catholics feeling very bitter and aggrieved. In particular, it led many of them to conclude that they had no hope of improving their situation through constitutional politics.

Local authority housing

In 1944 a Northern Ireland government survey showed that 39 per cent of all houses in the province were in urgent need of replacement. County Fermanagh was the worst affected, with 43.7 per cent needing replacement in the town of Enniskillen and over 50 per cent in most of the rural districts. This was because no houses had been built at all between 1921 and 1945. In the next 22 years the council built 1,048 houses. In this majority Catholic area, where Catholics were also poorer and in greater need of rehousing, 195 (18 per cent) of the new houses went to Catholics and 853 (82 per cent) to Protestants.

The gerrymander not only meant that Unionist councils had the power to deny Catholics housing; where their majorities were tight they had a positive incentive to do so, as the tenancy of a local authority house brought with it the right to vote. Thus, the ruling Unionist members of Omagh Rural Council (an area 62 per cent Catholic) wrote for advice to the Unionist Whip in the Northern Ireland government:

We would point out that in some districts cottages are required by Unionist workers but we hesitate to invite representations as we know there would be a flood of representations from the Nationalist side and our political opponents are only waiting the opportunity to use this means to outvote us in divisions where majorities are close. (Quoted in 'One Vote Equals Two', the Mansion House Anti-Partition Conference, Dublin 1949)

Like County Fermanagh, many councils simply did not build houses for years. When they did, they allocated Catholics houses in Catholic areas only.

The Cameron Commission was blunt in its findings here (paras. 139–40):

Council housing policy has been distorted for political ends in the Unionist controlled areas to which we specially refer. In each houses have been built and allocated in such a way that they will not disturb the political balance. In Londonderry County Borough a vast programme has been carried out in the South Ward – and Catholics have been rehoused there almost exclusively. In

recent years housing programmes declined because the Corporation refused
to face the political effects of boundary extensions even though this was
recommended by all its senior officials.

In Omagh and Dungannon Urban Districts Catholics have been allocated
houses virtually in the West Wards alone. Conversely Protestants have been
rehoused in Unionist wards where they would not disturb the electoral
balance. . . . We have no doubt also, in the light of the mass of evidence put
before us, that in these Unionist controlled areas it was fairly frequent for
housing policy to be operated so that houses allocated to Catholics tended, as
in Dungannon Urban District, to go to rehouse slum dwellers, whereas
Protestant allocations tended to go more frequently to new families. Thus the
total numbers allocated were in rough correspondence to the proportion of
Protestants and Catholics in the community; the principal criterion however
in such cases was not actual need but maintenance of the current political
preponderance in the local government area.

Local authority jobs

The Cameron Commission reviewed the mass of allegations put to it
concerning Catholic underrepresentation in local authority employment. It stated it was completely convinced that Unionist councils
'have used and use their power to make appointments in a way which
benefited Protestants'.

Using the figures available for October 1968 it reported (para. 138):

Only 30% of Londonderry Corporation's administrative, clerical and technical employees were Catholics. Out of the ten best posts, only one was held
by a Catholic.

In Dungannon Urban District none of the Council's administrative, clerical
and technical employees was a Catholic.

In County Fermanagh no senior council posts, (and relatively few others)
were held by Catholics: this was rationalised by reference to 'proven loyalty'
as a necessary test for local authority appointments. In that County, among
75 drivers of school buses at most seven were Catholics.

The Commission also examined the situation in predominantly Catholic Newry. It said:

It is fair to note that Newry Urban District employed very few Protestants.
But two wrongs do not make a right: Protestants who are in the minority in
the Newry area, by contrast to the other areas we have specified, do not have
a serious unemployment problem, and in Newry there are relatively few
Protestants, whereas in the other towns Catholics make up a substantial part
of the population. (Cameron Report, para. 138)

Other employment

In great tracts of the public sector - for example, the fire service, the ambulance service and electricity supply - Catholics in Northern Ireland were either absent or massively underrepresented. This was also the case throughout Northern Ireland's civil service, but it was particularly marked at the technical and higher levels. In 1969, out of 213 people employed in the technical and professional grades, only 13 were Catholics. Of the 319 employed in the higher administrative grades, 23 were Catholics. The exclusion of Catholics was sometimes openly admitted. In 1934, Lord Craigavon said in the Northern Ireland parliament: 'The appointments made by the Government are made, so far as we can manage it, of loyal men and women . . .'

The private sector was also encouraged to discriminate. Sir Basil Brooke, parliamentary secretary to the Northern Ireland government, who later served for 20 years as Northern Ireland prime minister, was reported thus by the *Fermanagh Times*, 13 July 1933:

There were a great number of Protestants and Orangemen who employed Roman Catholics. He felt he could speak freely on this subject as he had not a Roman Catholic about his own place. He appreciated the great difficulty experienced by some of them in procuring suitable Protestant labour but he would point out that Roman Catholics were endeavouring to get in everywhere. He would appeal to Loyalists therefore, wherever possible, to employ good Protestant lads and lasses.

A year later, when he had become minister of agriculture, he said:

I recommend those people who are Loyalists not to employ Roman Catholics 99% of whom are disloyal; I want you to remember one point in regard to the employment of people who are disloyal . . . You are disenfranchising yourselves in that way . . . You people who are employers have the ball at your feet. If you don't act properly now, before we know where we are we shall find ourselves in the minority instead of the majority. (*Londonderry Sentinel*, 20 March 1934)

In 1950 Tom Teevan, chairman of Limavady Rural Council and subsequently Unionist MP for West Belfast returned to the same theme. He complained:

In Londonderry City and County, where we should have been on our guard, our majority has dropped from 12,000 to a perilously low figure. How did that come about? Through the ruinous and treacherous policy, pursued unwittingly perhaps, of handing over houses owned by Protestants to Roman Catholics. It is also caused by the great employers of Labour in the North of Ireland employing Roman Catholic Labour. (*Londonderry Sentinel,* 19 January 1950)

At the start of the 1960s, the Unionist newspaper the *Newsletter,* 6 March 1961, reported Unionist barrister Robert Babington, who later became a MP, urging publicly:

Registers of unemployed Loyalists should be kept by the Unionist Party and employers invited to pick employees from them. The Unionist Party should make it quite clear that the Loyalists have the first choice of jobs.

And as late as 1964 Senator J. Barnhill, quoted verbatim in 'The Plain Truth', Campaign for Social Justice in Northern Ireland, stated: 'Charity begins at home. If we are going to employ people we should give preference to Unionists.'

The mechanics of discrimination

The main ways in which Catholic job opportunities were restricted were largely unchanged since the nineteenth century. They were as follows:

1 Much industry was located in places which were difficult or dangerous for Catholics to reach.
2 Catholics who sought employment were less likely to be hired.
3 Once companies acquired the reputation of not hiring Catholics, Catholics stopped bothering to apply.
4 Some trade unions acted as hiring agents and constituted a hidden but effective barrier to Catholic recruitment.
5 There was frequently no public recruitment. Employers relied on word-of-mouth hiring through existing staff (who told relatives and friends of vacancies) and through other social contacts (e.g. the Orange Order).

The result was a striking unevenness of Catholic distribution across industries. (See table 3.1.) We can see that very few Catholics were to be found in the growing banking, finance and insurance industries. Many were in low-pay sectors such as construction, clothing and footwear, but they were largely absent from the better paying areas, most notably engineering. For example, in 1970 there were about 400 Catholics amongst the then 10,000 workers in shipbuilders Harland and Wolff. Shorts, the aircraft manufacturers, had a few

Table 3.1 Distribution of Catholic and Protestant workers in industry, 1971

Industrial category	% Catholic	% Protestant	% Not stated
Shipbuilding	4.8	89.5	5.7
Vehicles	11.7	79.5	8.8
Gas, electricity, water	15.4	78.2	6.4
Mechanical engineering	16.0	77.0	7.0
Insurance, banking, finance	16.2	75.2	8.6
Metal manufacture	18.2	72.0	9.8
Electrical engineering	19.3	72.6	8.1
Public administration, defence	19.6	71.7	8.7
Instrument engineering	19.8	73.8	6.4
Food, drink, tobacco	21.4	60.9	7.7
Textiles	23.6	69.1	7.3
Construction	37.0	52.9	10.1
Leather, Leather goods, fur	39.8	50.7	9.5
Clothing, footwear	40.1	50.7	9.2

Source: Northern Ireland Population Census, 1971

hundred Catholic employees amongst 7,000. Mackies and Sirocco engineering companies, though both located next to Catholic ghetto areas, had virtually entirely Protestant workforces.

The law, the judges and the police

The law Though part of the United Kingdom, many of the civil liberties safeguards that are taken for granted in Britain were removed in Northern Ireland soon after the state was established.

In 1922 the Northern Ireland Unionist government passed the Special Powers Act. It gave the Northern Ireland minister for home affairs very extensive powers. At any time the minister could issue far-reaching regulations limiting citizens' legal rights. At various times between 1922 and the introduction of Direct Rule in 1972, the regulations included the following:

1 People suspected of crimes could be arrested and interned - that is, kept in prison without trial - for as long as the government wished.

2   The death penalty applied for some firearms and explosives offences.
3   It was an offence to refuse to answer questions put by a policeman.
4   The government could examine bank accounts and seize money deposited in accounts.
5   Newspapers could be prevented from printing certain reports or could be banned altogether.
6   Houses could be searched without a warrant.
7   Named individuals could be confined to particular areas of the province.
8   The authorities did not have to hold inquests on any dead bodies found in Northern Ireland.
9   People who committed offences connected with explosives, fire-arms, causing fires and blackmail, could be punished by flogging.

The Act also included the following 'catch all' clause, to cover any other actions at all:

If any person does any act of such a nature as to be calculated to be prejudicial to the preservation of the peace or maintenance of order in Northern Ireland and not specifically provided for in the regulations, he shall be deemed guilty of an offence against the regulations.

The mere existence of the Special Powers Act created a heavy atmosphere of repression. And in practice, it was extensively used – to ban organizations, newspapers, meetings and processions. In the early 1920s, and then again from 1938 to 1945 and 1956 to 1961, it was used to introduce internment, thus ensuring that many political and military opponents of the government were put out of circulation for lengthy periods.

In 1963, the South African minister for justice, Mr Vorster (who later became prime minister) was introducing a new Coercion Bill in the South African parliament. He commented that he 'would be willing to exchange all the legislation of that sort, for one clause of the Special Powers Act' (quoted in Michael Farrell, *The Orange State*).

The judiciary   During the lifetime of the Northern Ireland state, it has always been the case that the overwhelming majority of judges and magistrates have been Protestants. They have also frequently had close and open Unionist connections. Thus, in 1970, out of the seven High Court judges, three were former Unionist MPs and the fourth was the son of a Unionist Minister.

Interestingly, the first Lord Chief Justice of Northern Ireland was a Catholic. But he could not have been a more unusual one: he was the only Catholic Unionist MP ever in the British parliament, and during the War of Independence was the Attorney-General for the British administration.

The police To enforce the law there were two police forces: the Royal Ulster Constabulary (RUC) and the Ulster Special Constabulary, known commonly as the B Specials.

The Royal Ulster Constabulary was the regular police force. The great majority of its members were Protestants. When the RUC was established it was intended that Catholics would form a third of the force, but in 1922 they only made up a sixth, and the proportion fell as the years went on. By 1969 it had dropped to 11 per cent. To make up the shortfall of Catholics, the RUC recruited extra men from the B Specials.

The RUC was effectively a paramilitary force. Unlike the police in mainland Britain, its members were always armed and they trained with rifles, sub-machine-guns, machine-guns and armoured cars. It was inevitable that the RUC was very closely associated with the Unionist nature of the Northern Ireland state. For apart from its 'regular' policing duties, the RUC was frequently deployed to enforce the Special Powers Act: raiding houses, arresting internees, enforcing the bans on meetings and processions.

From the very beginning the B Specials were a Protestant force with close Loyalist connections. They drew many of their members from the Ulster Volunteer Force; indeed, whole UVF units became 'Special' platoons. No secret was made of their religious composition – in fact it was frequently and proudly asserted by leading Loyalists. Unionist MP William Grant's statement to the Northern Ireland parliament in 1936 is but one of many examples: 'I would like to point out that the Special Constabulary are composed entirely of loyal Protestant working men ... there are no Roman Catholics amongst the Special Constabulary' (NI Parliamentary Debates (Hansard), House of Commons, vol. 18 February 1936). Their affiliations with Loyalist organizations were also quite open, and indeed, the Cameron Commission noted that 'Until very recent years, for drill and training purposes, the Ulster Special Constabulary have made large use of Orange Lodges' (Cameron Report, para. 145).

The 'Specials' too were a paramilitary force. They were armed with rifles, revolvers, bayonets, and sub-machine-guns, which they kept in their homes. From the 1950s onwards they also had access to bren-guns and armoured cars. With their close knowledge of local people and conditions, they were a very effective machine for crushing resistance to the Unionist regime.

Most of the time the 'Specials' were used for part-time work such as manning road blocks and patrols. They were notorious amongst the Nationalist community for their harassing and often violent techniques: demanding proof of identity from known Catholic neighbours; rough searching and abuse of Catholics while waving Protestants on. In addition, they could be mobilized for full-time paramilitary duties at very short notice.

Describing the B Specials the Cameron Commission said (para. 145):

The recruitment of this force, for traditional and historical reasons, is in practice limited to members of the Protestant faith. Though there is no legal bar to Catholic membership, it is unlikely that Catholic applications would be favourably received even if they were made.

With their reputation for blatant Protestant partisanship, frequent violence and their open Loyalist connections, the 'Specials' were universally detested by Nationalists, whether of moderate or militant views. A year into 'the troubles', in October 1969, the 'Specials' were disbanded.

4 Civil Rights and Beyond
From 1968 to the Present Day

Since the late 1960s Northern Ireland has been in ferment. Much inspired by the slightly earlier American civil rights movement, a new civil liberties organization, consisting mainly of Catholics plus some liberal-minded Protestants, was formed. This organization, the Northern Ireland Civil Rights Association (NICRA), set out to challenge discrimination in the Northern Ireland state. In late 1968 it launched a campaign of civil disobedience: demonstrations, marches, squatting Catholic families in new council housing that had been earmarked for Protestants, etc.

NICRA's main demands were as follows:

1 The vote for everybody in local council elections, as in the rest of the United Kingdom.
2 An independent commission to redraw electoral boundaries so as to ensure fair representation.
3 Laws against discrimination in local government employment.
4 A compulsory points system for housing which would ensure fair allocation of housing.
5 The repeal of the Special Powers Act.
6 The disbanding of the B Specials.

What these demands amounted to was that Northern Ireland should be brought into line with the rest of the UK. Looked at from outside, they seem modest and reasonable aims. Within the province they were viewed very differently.

NICRA's first march in 1968, from Coalisland to Dungannon, passed off peacefully. But the next big march in Derry, which NICRA sponsored, was opposed by Unionists and violently broken up by the RUC and the B Specials. Three months later a newly formed radical

students organization, the People's Democracy, organized a march
from Belfast to Derry. Though the demonstration was both peaceful
and legal, the police joined crowds of Unionists in attacking it both on
Burntollet Bridge and outside Derry, and within the city itself.

The British government set up the Cameron Commission (see pages
28–32) to investigate the causes of these disturbances. In the chapter of
its report dealing with the performance of the police, the commission
began with a general observation: stretched to the limits, the majority
of the police behaved well. But then the commission became more
specific: 'in the heat of action a senior police officer temporarily lost
control of himself . . .' (para. 170). It went on:

there was unauthorised and irregular use of batons by certain unidentified
policemen . . . their use at that stage not warranted by the circumstances. It
was at this time - very early in the proceedings - that Mr Fitt MP and
Mr McAteer were struck by police batons. The baton charge . . . took place
after advice to disperse had been given, and while in fact a large proportion of
the demonstrators were in the act of dispersal . . . there seems to have been
neither reason nor excuse for the indiscriminate use of water cannon on
pedestrians . . . our investigations have led us to the unhesitating conclusion
that on the night of 4/5 January a number of policemen were guilty of mis-
conduct which involved assault and battery, malicious damage to property in
the streets in the predominantly Catholic Bogside area . . . and the use of
provocative, sectarian and political slogans. (Para. 171)

The Army

The summer of 1969 was marked by serious violence. When the
Protestant Apprentice Boys of Derry set out on their annual parade
through the city and around the walls overlooking the Catholic Bogside, they were met, not by the usual silent resentment of the Catholic
community, but by stones, petrol bombs and barricades. The police
reacted fiercely and there were two days of fighting until troops of the
British Army were sent in.

Two days later Protestants from Belfast's Shankill made armed
attacks on Catholics in the Falls area. Six people were killed and 150
Catholic homes were burned. Between July and September nearly
2,000 Belfast families fled their homes. Over 80 per cent of these
families were Catholic. This meant that 5.3 per cent of Catholic households and 0.4 per cent of Protestant households had been displaced.
Throughout this period, the police, especially the B Specials, had
shown themselves clearly to be on the side of the Protestants. So when

the British Army was finally sent in, it was not surprising that its soldiers were welcomed by many in the Catholic community as protectors.

Reform

Between 1969 and 1972 a number of reforms were introduced. These included

1 Universal adult suffrage in local elections.
2 Redrawing the local government electoral boundaries.
3 The appointment of a parliamentary ombudsman and a commissioner for complaints.
4 Disarming the RUC and establishing a new and more representative police authority.
5 Disbanding the B Specials and establishing the Ulster Defence Regiment, a new part-time regiment of the British Army.
6 Removing from the local councils all powers in connection with housing.
7 Establishing a housing executive to handle public authority house building and allocate public housing on an objective points system.

But it was too late; the reforms had taken too long. They also had major limitations. For example, though the B Specials who were hated by the Catholic community were disbanded, many former Specials were allowed to fill the ranks of the replacement Ulster Defence Regiment, and the Regiment was never other than overwhelmingly Protestant. Not until 1973 was anything done to tackle discrimination in employment. Then a purely *advisory* body – the Standing Advisory Commission on Human Rights – was established, to monitor discrimination and *recommend* measures to prevent it. Only in 1976, after eight years of 'the troubles', was the tiny Fair Employment Agency set up, with legal powers to start addressing the problem.

Most important of all, though Britain had sent in the Army, it had left untouched Northern Ireland's separate government and parliament. Thus, in charge of administering reforms intended to *undermine* discrimination, was the same one-party Unionist government that had *instituted and presided over rampant discrimination* for nearly half a century. And nothing had happened to give Catholics any faith that this Unionist government would dismantle the same discriminatory system it had itself created.

British half-heartedness fuelled a growing Catholic disillusionment with the usefulness of pressing for or even achieving reforms. At the same time, the confidence that many Catholics had initially felt in the British Army soon evaporated. In its place came bitter hostility, as the Army - being an Army - resorted to tough military-style methods rather than to ordinary police tactics to quell civil disobedience.

As Catholic disillusionment and bitterness mounted, civil disobedience and peaceful protest gave way to outright violence. The Irish Republican Army (IRA), an organization which had practically vanished, came back to life. In providing defence to the Catholic ghetto areas first against Protestant paramilitaries and the police, and then against the army, it secured a wide measure of support within the minority community. This gave it the base it needed to resurrect the demand for a united Ireland, and to initiate the campaign which has lasted to this day to overthrow partition by force.

Internment

It was internment which finally cemented Catholic cynicism about how far the province had really changed, and, in particular, their conviction that they could not trust the Unionist government. In August 1971, using its long-standing 'emergency' legislation, the Special Powers Act and with Britain's agreement, the Northern Ireland government suddenly introduced internment without trial. In the first dawn swoop, 342 men were picked up. Only two were Protestants, and both of these had Republican sympathies.

Internment also served to solidify the rift between the British troops and the Catholic community. For although it was the Northern Ireland government which introduced internment, and the RUC Special Branch which named the suspects, it was the British Army that was used to carry out the operation and pick people up.

By the end of 1971 the internment camps held over 700 people, none of whom had been charged with any offence. Before internment began in August, there had been 30 deaths in 1971. The wave of violence which followed left another 143 people dead by the end of the year.

Then, in January 1972, thirteen Catholics taking part in a march in Derry were shot dead by the British Army. In Dublin a massive protest demonstration against these 'Bloody Sunday' killings ended with the British Embassy being burned down. At the inquest in Derry the City Coroner said:

It strikes me that the army ran amok that day and they shot without thinking what they were doing. They were shooting innocent people. These people may have been taking part in a parade that was banned - but I don't think that justifies the firing of live rounds indiscriminately. I say it without reservation - it was sheer unadulterated murder. (Quoted in *The Troubles*, R. Broad et al)

At last the British Tory government led by Edward Heath reacted. In March 1972 the Northern Ireland parliament, Stormont, was suspended and Direct Rule from Westminster imposed. The number of internees was substantially reduced and internment without trial was largely replaced by the 'Diplock Courts'. These were a specially established system of trial by judge without a jury. Lastly, in recognition of the political situation and of the unusual judicial procedures being used, paramilitary prisoners, both Loyalist and Republican, were given 'special category status'. This meant they were kept in special prisons and were not required to wear prison clothing. They were even allowed to dress in paramilitary uniform. They were permitted to operate their own military discipline and parade in military formation. The prison authorities also recognized the paramilitary command structure by communicating all orders through the prisoners' paramilitary commanding officers. 'Special category status' was, in effect, prisoner-of-war status.

Power sharing

Direct Rule was only expected to be a temporary arrangement. No sooner was it introduced than work got under way to restore devolved (that is Northern Ireland-based) government to the province. Indeed, Northern Ireland's history since 1972 has been marked by a range of unsuccessful efforts in this respect. The first scheme to be tried was 'power sharing'. This was intended as a way of giving the Nationalist community some limited but direct role in Northern Ireland's government.

The power sharing experiment started in mid-1973 when a Northern Ireland Assembly was established, with a membership elected by proportional representation. Government authority was to rest with an Executive which was required to be 'widely acceptable throughout the community'. The Heath government aimed to ensure this acceptability by appointing the executive itself. The government picked a Unionist chief executive plus five other Unionists; a nationalist deputy chief executive from the Social Democratic and Labour Party; three more SDLP members; and one member of the Alliance Party.

Alongside power sharing there was to be machinery recognizing the links Catholics felt with the people of the Republic. In December 1973 in Sunningdale in Berkshire, the British and Irish governments, together with the executive, agreed to set up a Council of Ireland. This body, with members from north and south of the border, was intended to be purely consultative. Its advisory nature was emphasized by the government of the Republic, when it publicly declared that there could be no change in the status of Northern Ireland unless a majority of the Northern Ireland people wanted such a change. Direct Rule then ended and the new executive took office on 1 January 1974.

From the outset, power sharing faced massive opposition. For militant nationalists it feel well short of their aspirations, while for the majority of Unionists it went much too far. When, in February 1974, the miners' strike brought about a British general election, the Northern Ireland Unionists' election campaign focused wholly around the call to bring down the executive. All the Unionists who were elected - 11 out of Northern Ireland's then 12 MPs - were committed opponents of power sharing.

But it was not until May 1974 that the Unionist campaign came to fruition. Then the Unionist Ulster Workers Council called a general strike to protest against both power sharing and the Council of Ireland. While many were intimidated into joining the strike, there can be no doubt that it enjoyed mass backing from Protestant workers. Meanwhile the new Labour government made little attempt to save the power-sharing experiment. Though thousands of troops were in the province the government barely used them. In particular, while essential services were threatening to come to a halt, the Army was not deployed to keep them going. Lacking even a basic measure of support from the British government, the Unionist members of the executive resigned and the executive collapsed. It had lasted less than five months. Direct Rule resumed and has operated ever since.

Criminalization

Until the mid 1970s 'the troubles' were generally regarded as being political in origin, and therefore needing a political solution. This meant that though the conflict was not actually *described* in this way, up till then, it was *handled* as a war over Northern Ireland's political future, which was being waged between a guerrilla army and a regular army. The granting of 'special category status' for paramilitary prisoners was obvious evidence of the British government's political approach. So too were the periodic discussions it held with leaders of the IRA to try to work out some future for the province.

Now, demoralized by the failure of power sharing, the new Labour administration in Britain began to reshape official strategy towards Northern Ireland. It aimed to transform public perception of the conflict, so that 'the troubles' no longer appeared to be about politics at all. The last internees were released at the end of 1975. From then on, internment without trial was completely replaced by trial in the special no-jury 'Diplock Courts' which had originally been set up in 1972. At the same time, the government abolished special category status for anyone convicted of an offence committed after March 1976. This meant the paramilitary command structure within the prison system would no longer be recognized, and paramilitary prisoners would be held in ordinary prisons and would have to wear prison uniform. In other words, they were to be treated simply as ordinary criminals.

Meanwhile, as we shall see below, the government started 'Ulster-izing' Northern Ireland's security; that is, moving the main respons-ibility for security in the province from the British Army to the locally recruited security forces. These local forces consisted of the Royal Ulster Constabulary (RUC) and the Ulster Defence Regiment (UDR), both of which were overwhelmingly Protestant in membership.

The new twin strategies of 'criminalizing' the paramilitaries, and 'Ulsterizing' the security forces, marked a significant break. From now on, the government presented the conflict in the province not as a serious political problem, but solely as a matter of law and order.

Ulsterization

It was the regular British Army which spearheaded Britain's campaign against the IRA until the mid-1970s. The locally recruited security forces played only a supportive role. The shift of responsibility from the Army to the local police took place for three reasons.

To begin with, as we have already noted, while the Army was in the front line it was hard to maintain that the conflict was not political. Secondly, British soldiers were being killed in very large numbers. This was causing considerable concern and political discontent in mainland Britain. Lastly, Northern Ireland was becoming a drain on military resources. In particular, large numbers of troops were being

moved from the British Army on the Rhine to Northern Ireland. This
not only withdrew them from foreign duties, it also meant much of
their training was devoted to low-level security operations - i.e. anti-
guerrilla activities - rather than regular soldiering. Thus, the British
Army was perpetually short of manpower and, at the same time, the
troops were receiving the wrong training with respect to Britain's
wider military role.

The British government's solution to these problems was similar to
that adopted by the United States in Vietnam. Under its Vietnam-
ization policy, the USA transferred security from its own army to
locally recruited forces. In Northern Ireland, Ulsterization involved
greatly expanding and rearming the previously disarmed RUC. The
RUC then took over all but the most sensitive security operations and,
in effect, became a military force in its own right. The Army remained
to do most of the policing in the sensitive border areas like Crossmaglen
in South Armagh, and also certain parts of West Belfast. However,
even in these areas, the Army worked with the UDR which consists of
locally recruited Protestants.

Table 4.1   British security forces in Northern Ireland, 1969–84[a]

	Royal Ulster Constabulary (RUC)	Ulster Defence Regiment (UDR)	British Army	Total
1969	3,061	0	2,693	5,754
1972	4,409	644	17,183	22,236
1979	7,298	2,407	13,124	22,829
1984	10,296	2,669	9,516	22,481

[a] Full timers only

Source: Irish Information Partnership

This shift localized the conflict, bringing it from Britain back to the
province. Now it is people from Northern Ireland who are deployed to
do most of the controlling of other people from Northern Ireland.
Until recently this has chiefly meant Protestants controlling Catholics,
but with the Unionist protests against the Anglo-Irish Agreement it
has also begun to mean local Protestants controlling other Protestants.
Now too, when the security forces are attacked and killed, the victims
are far more likely to be local police and UDR members than British-
born soldiers.

Economic improvements

Alongside criminalization and Ulsterization, Britain had a third strand
to its Northern Ireland policy. As we shall see in detail in chapter 6,
from the mid-1970s to the advent of Thatcher, the government also set
out to raise the living standards of the local population, especially the
Catholics. It improved the 'social services' such as health and education; created great numbers of public-sector jobs; and built lots of new
community facilities such as leisure centres.

It was hoped that with these measures support for the IRA would
gradually wither away, things would gradually return to normal in the
Province, and there would be no need for any major political change.
However, as events were to show, Britain's strategy failed. More than
that, it had very unexpected results.

The hunger strike

Britain's plan to criminalize the paramilitary prisoners ran into
immediate opposition. For several years, IRA and other Republican
prisoners wore blankets only, rather than accept prison uniform. They
also went on a 'dirty protest', fouling their prison cells and refusing to
co-operate with the prison regime. When the British government, by
this time led by Margaret Thatcher, showed no signs of giving way, a
hunger strike began. Ten Republican prisoners died before the
campaign to restore special category status ended.

Though the Republicans eventually called off the hunger strike
without having achieved their specific objective, they secured something far more important. In the Catholic areas of Northern Ireland,
in the Republic and throughout the world, they won immense
sympathy. By their very willingness to starve themselves to death,
they persuaded people they were political prisoners.

Local Catholic support showed itself in a way that no one had
anticipated. Traditionally central to IRA strategy has been the
boycotting of the electoral process in both parts of Ireland – on the
ground that to participate is to accept partition. During the hunger
strike this strategy was partially suspended. To demonstrate the
strength of popular nationalist support for their cause, a number of
prisoners stood in elections. Though none were able, or willing, to
take their seats, one hunger striker, Bobby Sands, was elected to the
British parliament; and two other prisoners, one of whom was also a
hunger striker, were elected to the Irish parliament, Dáil Eireann.

These successes encouraged the rethink which had already started among Republicans. The IRA adopted a new dual strategy: electoral politics alongside armed struggle. Sinn Féin, the political wing of the IRA, proceeded to stand candidates for another short-lived Northern Ireland Assembly which James Prior had set up, and then for the British general election in 1983. In the General Election it won one Westminster seat and pushed its total vote up to 100,000, which was about 40 per cent of the Nationalist vote overall in the province.

Britain's attempt to depoliticize the Northern Ireland conflict had not only failed - it had backfired. Without abandoning the military road, the IRA had entered the world of conventional electoral politics. The conflict in Northern Ireland was now certainly a *political* issue in a way that it had not been for years. The shift in the IRA's strategy, and its considerable success, caused deep concern in government circles both in Britain and in the Republic. Out of this concern were born the most important political initiatives since the 1974 power-sharing experiment.

The New Ireland Forum

To undermine the threat posed by the militantly nationalist Sinn Féin and IRA, the government in the Republic set up the New Ireland Forum. The role of the Forum was to seize the nationalist initiative from Sinn Féin and direct it down a constitutional road.

The Forum members came from all but one of the major nationalist parties, both North and South: Fine Gael and Labour (the then governing coalition), Fianna Fáil (the then main opposition in the Republic), and the Social Democratic and Labour Party (the nationalist party which still commands the greatest vote amongst Catholics in Northern Ireland). Sinn Féin was specifically excluded.

In his opening speech to the Forum, the Taoiseach (prime minister) Garret FitzGerald said:

All of the political parties in the New Ireland Forum will in effect for a period of months be sacrificing some of their interests and some of their independence . . . By this decision, our parties, which are supported by the votes of well over 90 per cent of the nationalist people on this island, demonstrate on behalf of those we represent a powerful collective rejection of murder, bombing and all the other cruelties that are being inflicted on the population of Northern Ireland in an attempt to secure political change by force. Let the men of violence take note of this unambiguous message from the nationalist people of Ireland: the future of the island will be built by the ballot box, and by the ballot box alone.

The Forum was a huge exercise. It commissioned a number of major research reports and took evidence from a very great range of individuals and organizations. Among those who appeared before the Forum were representatives of the Catholic church. In proceedings that were televised, they were sharply questioned on a range of moral/political questions. John Kelly TD (MP) wanted to know whether the bishops would oppose a removal of the constitutional bar against legislation permitting divorce –

Bishop Cathal Daly of Down and Connor: I am afraid, with very great respect, I would feel that that is a political question which is not appropriate for us to answer.
John Kelly TD: It is not a political question, but I do agree that it is probably the first time since St Patrick arrived that the representatives of the hierarchy were asked to think on their feet.

The Forum also invited submissions from Northern Unionists, and though none of the Unionist political parties responded, a few individuals did.

In May 1984, after a year of deliberations, the Forum reported. It reaffirmed constitutional nationalist commitment to a united Ireland. But it also emphasized that this unity could only be achieved with Protestant consent, and would have to include protection for the interests of the Northern Protestants within a united Ireland. The Forum report contained a range of options for moving towards unity. They were not well received by either the unionists in Northern Ireland, or the militant Nationalists. And the British government's public response was less than enthusiastic too. However, what was important from Britain's point of view was the Forum's blunt rejection of enforced unity, and its willingness to consider very modest and interim measures in the meantime. Though the Forum's specific options and proposals have not been implemented, the exercise did produce a very concrete response.

Following hard on the issue of the Forum's report, there commenced a round of constitutional negotiations between the British and Irish governments, such as had not been seen in the ten years since the Sunningdale experiment collapsed. Eighteen months after the Forum had concluded, these negotiations came to fruition. On 15 November 1985, in the small Northern Ireland town of Hillsborough, the British government and the government of the Republic of Ireland signed the Anglo-Irish Agreement. This agreement, which brings us to the present day, is discussed in chapter 9.

5 Casualties of War

The conflict now in progress in Northern Ireland has brought in its train immense social, economic and political costs. These costs have been felt both within the province and within neighbouring countries.

As we shall see in following chapters, the conflict has done great damage to the industrial base of Northern Ireland. Indeed, it is the most important single factor preventing a sustained economic recovery in the province. Meanwhile the total monetary cost to Britain of running the war and supporting the enfeebled economy of the North is approaching £2,000 million a year. In proportionate terms the burden to the Republic of Ireland is still greater: it now devotes over a quarter of its total budget to policing the border and controlling the activities of Republican paramilitaries.

The cost of the conflict has also been great in terms of life and limb. Since 1969 there have been over 2,500 deaths and 26,000 people injured, many very seriously. Acceptable standards of civil rights and liberties have also fallen victim. Within Northern Ireland civil liberties have been severely curtailed. The police and the army have almost unlimited powers to search, arrest and detain whoever they choose. Thousands of actual or alleged paramilitaries have been imprisoned for long periods of time, some for life, and tens of thousands have been detained for interrogation. No-jury courts, media censorship and mistreatment of suspects have all become commonplace. All of this has left a legacy of bitterness that could last for generations.

In this chapter we present a brief survey of the impact that the conflict has had in human terms on people within Northern Ireland and in mainland Britain. The bulk of investigation into this area has been carried out by the Cobden Trust and the National Council for Civil Liberties, and by a very few determined journalists and researchers.

We draw heavily on their original work, details of which are given in our bibliography. We also include a very brief account of the effect which the conflict has had on civil liberties in the Republic of Ireland.

Emergency legislation

From its birth Northern Ireland has been in a state of more or less continuous emergency. Special laws, harsh policing methods and, on occasion, the British army, have all been used to suppress opposition to the regime. Many civil liberties taken for granted in Britain and other West European countries have always been severely restricted in the province. Nowadays they are virtually absent. Legal constraints on the police and the army are minimal – insofar as these forces are held in check, it is more by political than by any legal considerations.

Alongside its effect on civil liberties within Northern Ireland, the conflict has external ramifications. In Britain, special emergency laws have been enacted giving the police new arbitrary powers of arrest and detention; censorship of television and radio has been extended; and some of the harsh policing methods used in Northern Ireland have been imported for use in mainland trouble spots. An even greater erosion of civil liberties has occurred in the Republic of Ireland, where there is a whole panoply of special courts, special laws and censorship designed to isolate and destroy the IRA.

We begin by considering the situation within Northern Ireland itself, which is governed by two main emergency laws: the Emergency Provisions Act (EPA) and the Prevention of Terrorism Act (PTA). The former was first passed in 1973 and was designed to replace the old Special Powers Act, which had been in continuous operation since the foundation of the Northern Ireland state (see chapter 3). It applies only to Northern Ireland. By contrast, the PTA, which was originally passed following the Birmingham pub bombings in 1974, applies throughout the UK and is frequently used in mainland Britain.

Though stated to be temporary measures (they have to be regularly renewed by vote of Parliament), both Acts have been consistently updated in less-pressured circumstances. The current law is to be found in the 1978 EPA and the 1984 PTA. Effectively they are now here for good. Renewal debates in Parliament are generally brief and ill-attended formalities, and most people have completely forgotten the supposedly temporary and emergency nature of these laws. In 1988 the Government announced that the PTA would be made permanent.

The Prevention of Terrorism Act

The PTA gives the police the power to stop, search and detain, without warrant, anywhere in the UK, anyone suspected of involvement in 'terrorist' activities. It also gives examining officials at ports of entry into the UK extensive powers to detain and interrogate travellers. Included is the power to detain people who are *not* suspected of involvement in 'terrorist' activities, so long as the officials concerned believe it *may* be useful to question them. In effect, this means that officials at UK ports of entry can legally arrest anyone they wish.

Once arrested, a detained person can be held by the police for up to 48 hours, and then for up to five more days with the permission of the secretary of state. During this whole period a detained person need not be charged with any offence or brought before a court.

Another power which is especially important in Britain is that of exclusion. Under the PTA the secretary of state can issue an executive order excluding a person of Northern Ireland origin from mainland Britain. The scope of the secretary of state's discretion here is extraordinary. Anyone who has been ordinarily resident in Great Britain for less than three years can be served with an exclusion order. While there is a notional right to appeal, the actual appeal procedure renders this right almost worthless. A person subject to an exclusion order has no entitlement to legal representation; no right to know the reason for the exclusion; and no right to know or to challenge the evidence on which the decision to exclude is supposedly based. Moreover, the appeal is considered informally by a government adviser whose decision is final and cannot be challenged in the courts.

Over the period 1974-84 some 245 people were removed from mainland Britain to Northern Ireland under the PTA, while a few people were transferred in the opposite direction. The exclusion powers contained within the PTA constitute, in effect, a form of internal banishment. Their existence is an implicit recognition that Northern Ireland really is a separate country from the rest of the United Kingdom.

The Emergency Provisions Act

Whilst the PTA is used mainly for intelligence-gathering and harassment purposes, the EPA is a more serious affair. This Act widens both police and army powers of arrest; it gives the secretary of state power to intern people indefinitely without trial; and it establishes special no-jury 'Diplock' courts which can impose severe punishments, including life imprisonment, for 'terrorist' offences. The power to intern has not been used since 1975, though it is still on the statute book and could be reactivated at any time. In any event, a result similar to internment is already achieved in another way: the majority of accused are remanded in custody, even though the evidence the police produce in bail applications is frequently extremely flimsy. And most of those held in custody wait upwards of a year before sentence is passed or they are released.

Three features of the administration of justice under the EPA are particularly important: no-jury courts, confessions, and accomplice evidence.

In 1973 jury trials for so-called 'Scheduled Offences' (mainly 'terrorist' offences) were abolished, and special 'Diplock' courts were set up to try such offences. These courts have no juries and cases are tried by a single judge sitting alone. The establishment of no-jury courts was recommended by Lord Diplock, on the grounds that juries in Northern Ireland are likely to be heavily biased and their members subject to intimidation by paramilitaries. This argument has been strongly challenged by civil libertarians, but remains the official justification for retaining no-jury trials in Northern Ireland.

A striking feature of the Diplock courts is the degree to which the police rely on confessions and accomplice evidence to obtain convictions, and the amount of intimidation and bribery which accompanies this process. It has been estimated (Dermot Walsh, *The Use and Abuse of Emergency Legislation in Northern Ireland*) that confessions are obtained from 85 per cent of people tried for 'terrorist' offences. The confession often provides the main, or even the only, evidence against the accused, and without it the prosecution case would fall to the ground. This reliance on confessions arises because the police find it hard to obtain reliable corroborative evidence in the case of 'terrorist' offences: potential witnesses are either frightened of or sympathetic to the paramilitaries involved. Under these conditions the police clearly have a strong incentive to extract confessions out of suspects by almost any means at their disposal. Moreover, the legal constraints governing interrogation are relatively lax in Northern Ireland, and permit procedures which would be regarded as quite improper elsewhere in the UK.

In mainland Britain the admissibility of confessions is strictly governed by the Judges Rules. These state in paragraph (e) of their preamble, that it is a fundamental condition of the admissibility in evidence against any person, equally of any oral answer given by that person to a question put by a police officer and of any statement made by that person, that it shall have been voluntary, in the sense that it has not been obtained from him by fear of prejudice, or hope of advantage exercised or held out by a person in authority, or by oppression.

The Judges Rules place severe constraints on police interrogation procedures. Members of the police who overstep the mark may find that any confession they obtain is ruled inadmissible when the case comes to court. Even under the old Special Powers Act the Judges Rules used to apply in Northern Ireland. However, when the new Emergency Provisions Act was introduced in 1973, the Judges Rules were, to all intents and purposes, abolished for the Diplock courts, and replaced by much looser guidelines. For a confession to be ruled inadmissible it must now be established beyond reasonable doubt that it was obtained by 'torture, inhuman or degrading treatment'. These terms are interpreted so narrowly in practice that it is virtually impossible to secure a ruling of inadmissibility in the courts.

The use of physical violence during interrogation in Northern Ireland has gone through several phases. While internment operated there was no need for the police to build a case against suspects, as they could be detained simply by executive order. However, once internment ended in 1975, then the police had to secure evidence which could be presented in court.

Given the difficulty of obtaining independent testimony, the police were forced to rely heavily on confessions and accomplice evidence. To obtain this kind of evidence they set up special interrogation centres where suspects could be questioned intensively until they broke down, incriminating both themselves and others. Over a period of years there was an avalanche of complaints about police brutality in these centres. Amnesty International sent a mission to inquire into these allegations; police surgeons complained and one of them, Dr Elliot, actually resigned in protest over the government's failure to stop the beatings. Eventually, following the report of the Bennett Committee, which effectively vindicated many of the allegations, new guidelines for interrogation were laid down.

Since then the number of complaints about physical brutality has fallen sharply. However, it remains the case that prisoners are often subject to harsh, prolonged and intensive interrogation. And there are still frequent allegations of prisoners being subject to religious and sexual abuse, threats to themselves and their relations, deprivation of sleep and other forms of maltreatment. By their nature such allegations are difficult to prove or disprove. Yet it would be naive simply to reject them out of hand. Given the great difficulty of obtaining independent evidence, confessions and accomplice evidence inevitably play a central role in the securing of convictions. So it would hardly be surprising if the police were tempted to use every device possible to obtain such evidence to put before a court.

The second major form of evidence used in the Diplock courts is provided by alleged accomplices. In Britain when this kind of evidence is utilized, it is normally corroborated by other independent evidence. Indeed, juries in Britain are specifically warned of the dangers of over-reliance on accomplice evidence, and where judges omit such warnings convictions will be quashed. As a result, it is rare for people in Britain to be convicted on accomplice evidence alone. In the Diplock courts, however, such evidence is treated very differently. There are no juries to be warned, and the judges themselves have frequently convicted defendants simply on the word of an alleged accomplice, without any corroborative evidence whatever. Moreover, the sentences which follow are often extremely long - 20 years or more is not uncommon.

This means, in effect, that a judge sitting without a jury can sentence a person to prolonged imprisonment on the word of a single informer. Not only does this put immense power in the hands of a judge; it also gives the police an enormous incentive to engage in precisely those malpractices which the normal requirement for corroborative evidence is supposed to discourage. These include intimidating or bribing prisoners into implicating people whom the authorities would like to see taken out of circulation, and fabricating testimony and coaching witnesses to make their story seem plausible to the judge hearing the case. All of these practices appear to have occurred during the 'super-grass' episode of the early 1980s.

Supergrasses

After interrogation procedures were tightened up following the Bennett Report, it became much more difficult to beat confessions out of prisoners. The RUC, which had been forced to pay compensation to some of the victims of its interrogation methods, then turned to a new device for obtaining convictions. Through a combination of threats and promises, selected prisoners from paramilitary organizations were induced to implicate other paramilitaries.

Prisoners facing heavy sentences, perhaps for the second or third time, were offered complete immunity from prosecution or a greatly reduced sentence in return for their co-operation with the police. Others volunteered on their own initiative to co-operate in the hope of such favours. To ensure the future safety of these people, the government undertook to ship them out of the province and finance a new life for them and their families abroad. In return they were expected to stand up in court and give evidence against their alleged accomplices.

The outcome of this new police strategy was a series of spectacular trials in which anything up to 40 or more people were arraigned on the word of a single informer. Lord Gifford QC, in his study on the subject (*Supergrasses: the Use of Accomplice Evidence in Northern Ireland*), has estimated that in 25 trials over the period 1981–3 a total of 446 people were charged on the basis of supergrass information. They included members of both Catholic and Protestant paramilitary organizations.

From a police point of view, the appeal of the supergrass system was obvious. It allowed them to put away large numbers of people whom they genuinely suspected to be paramilitaries, but against whom firm evidence was difficult or impossible to obtain. However, its dangers were equally obvious. Informers had a strong incentive to please their captors by fabricating evidence, and the police themselves had an equally strong incentive to fabricate evidence so as to obtain convictions. In a word, the system was wide open to corruption. For this reason it was strongly attacked by the legal profession at the time.

In recent years the supergrass system has been largely abandoned. One reason for this development was its failure to produce firm convictions. Many initially co-operative supergrasses subsequently withdrew their statements out of fear or remorse, so causing prosecution cases to collapse. Sometimes these supergrasses had already been granted legal immunity before retracting their evidence – which was a double embarrassment to the authorities. In a number of cases which did proceed, either the trial judge or the appeal judges rejected the supergrass evidence because of its transparent dishonesty or inconsistency. In only a minority of instances did supergrass information result in convictions which were upheld on appeal. However, this does not mean that the whole exercise was a complete waste of effort for the RUC. While in operation it caused demoralization and dissension in paramilitary ranks, and put hundreds of paramilitaries behind bars for several years at a stretch.

Policing methods

The Royal Ulster Constabulary is not simply a police force in the
ordinary sense of the term. Intermittently since the early 1920s, and
consistently since the late 1960s, the RUC has been occupied in trying
to crush guerrilla opposition to the state. This involves both a quasi-
military campaign against the guerrillas themselves and repression of
those sections of the civilian population which support the guerrillas.
Both tasks require the use of methods different in kind and intensity
from those employed in ordinary policing. Except for a brief period in
the early 1970s, the police in Northern Ireland have always been
heavily armed. Their present equipment includes automatic weapons
and armoured land-rovers.

We shall not here attempt a comprehensive analysis of the diverse
strategies and techniques used by the RUC today in their anti-guerrilla
campaign. Rather, we shall focus on two aspects which deserve special
mention. These are: 'shoot to kill' and plastic bullets.

'Shoot to kill'

Through much of the present conflict there have been persistent
allegations that the Crown forces in Northern Ireland have engaged in
'dirty tricks', including the assassination of troublesome opponents.
These allegations have always been denied by police, army and
government, but on occasion, there has been substantial evidence to
support them.

One notorious case occurred towards the end of 1982 when six Catholics were killed by undercover police in three separate incidents. The
police were part of the secret E4A squad which had been especially
created to engage in covert operations against paramilitaries. Of the six
Catholics, two were members of the Irish National Liberation Army
(INLA), three were from the IRA and one was completely uncon-
nected with any paramilitary organization. All were shot dead in
highly controversial circumstances: five were certainly unarmed, and
all could have been captured alive.

A suggestion that there was some unease, even at official levels, was
first indicated when four of the police involved in these killings were
prosecuted in the Diplock courts. However, one was acquitted in early
April 1984 and three more at the beginning of June. In the latter case
the defendants were exonerated by the presiding judge, Lord Justice

Gibson, who said, in his summing-up on 5 June 1984, that the three police officers were 'absolutely blameless' and commended them for 'their courage and determination in bringing the three deceased men to justice, to the final court of justice'. After the immense criticism produced by these comments, Lord Justice Gibson, in a very unusual move, issued the following statement from the Bench:

I would wish most emphatically to repudiate any idea that I would approve or that the law would countenance what has been described as a shoot-to-kill policy on the part of the police.

Nevertheless prosecution had not ended the affair. The mysterious circumstances of the six deaths, plus mounting evidence that the police had falsified or concealed information, produced a continuing uproar. Between the two acquittals, the government set up an inquiry to investigate the alleged police cover up. However, the British police-man, John Stalker, who was appointed to head the inquiry was con-fronted with massive obstruction within the RUC. He was then, himself, the target of corruption allegations and removed from the inquiry. Though subsequently cleared of any malpractice, Stalker was never allowed to return to his Northern Ireland investigations, and shortly after resigned from the police force.

Between 1982 and 1986 more than 30 people, 18 of them unarmed, were shot dead by the police and the army. Though few were left in any doubt that some measure of 'shoot to kill' policy had been followed, it was never established whether such policy was officially sanctioned at top level, or was simply a grass-roots initiative within the police force. Amnesty International called, unsuccessfully, for an independent judicial inquiry, citing as cause for concern, not only the deaths, but the delays of several years before inquests into these deaths were held.

From 1987 onwards the scale of such suspicious killings by the security forces has escalated significantly. Eight IRA members who were surrounded by the army and police in an incident at Loughgall were all shot dead, having apparently been given no opportunity to surrender. In early 1988 an unarmed Sinn Féin sympathizer on his way to work was killed by a soldier at a border checkpoint. The army described the shooting as accidental. A few weeks later, three unarmed IRA members were shot dead by the SAS in Gibraltar. Local civilian eyewitnesses stated categorically that the three were given no chance to give themselves up and were deliberately finished off at close range while lying wounded on the ground. If the testimony of these local people is correct, then, in law, the Gibraltar shootings constitute murder. Killing defenceless victims, even 'known terrorists' is permitted neither by the normal peacetime rules of policing, nor under military rules of engagement.

Plastic bullets

As well as tackling the IRA and other paramilitary forces, the police in Northern Ireland also have the job of controlling the local communities from which these forces come. Hostility to the British government is often widespread in these communities, especially in the Catholic working-class ghettoes. This hostility is expressed through civil disorder and rioting, to which the police response is sometimes very brutal.

A common weapon used by the police for quelling disorder is the plastic bullet, which itself replaces the earlier rubber bullet. Plastic bullets have been used on a staggering scale. For example, in the space of a single month during the hunger strikes - May 1981 - a total of 16,656 plastic bullets were fired in Northern Ireland. And though described as a method of crowd control, plastic and rubber bullets can be lethal.

Since 1972 plastic bullets have killed 16 people in Northern Ireland and seriously injured many more. All except one of those who died were Catholics; six were aged 14 or under; and at least five were expressly declared by inquests not to be involved in rioting. Only once has a police officer been prosecuted for such a killing: when Catholic John Downe was shot at close range by an RUC man during a demonstration in Belfast. Uniquely in that instance, the entire event was shown on television. However, when the police officer, who was charged not with murder but with manslaughter, came before a Diplock court, he was acquitted.

Deaths, injuries and bombings

Detailed statistics on violence in Northern Ireland are given in Appendix 4. The general picture is as follows. Since 1969, in occurrences connected with the present conflict, there have been over 30,000 shooting incidents, 8,000 explosions, 6,000 malicious fires and 12,000 armed robberies inside Northern Ireland.

There have been hundreds of casualties in bombing incidents in

Britain and the Republic of Ireland, while within Northern Ireland itself over 2,500 people have been killed and 26,000 injured. These figures are large in themselves; when viewed as a proportion of the small population of Northern Ireland they are immense. Violence on such a scale in mainland Britain would mean around 90,000 deaths and 900,000 people injured.

Both the nature and scale of violence have fluctuated considerably. The peak was in 1972 when fighting between the IRA and the British Army was at its most intense, and Loyalist groups were at their most active in killing Catholic civilians. In the space of this one year, 467 people were killed, of whom 146 were members of the security forces (mainly British soldiers), 75 were paramilitaries (mainly Provisional IRA) and 246 were civilians (mainly Catholics). Since 1972 the scale of violence has diminished and during the 1980s the death toll has averaged around 76 a year. This total can be broken down roughly as follows: Royal Ulster Constabulary 15, Ulster Defence Regiment 9, regular British Army 8, paramilitaries 10 and civilians 34.

These figures indicate two main things about the current state of the conflict. To begin with, apart from occasional very major incidents such as the Warrenpoint and Droppin' Well explosions in 1979 and 1982 respectively, relatively few British soldiers have been killed in recent years. Most casualties amongst the security forces are accounted for nowadays by the locally recruited RUC and UDR. This is very different from the early 1970s when British Army casualties were heavy.

What has produced the change is Britain's Ulsterization policy. Under this policy British troops have been withdrawn from action wherever possible, and security put into the hands of locally recruited forces, especially the police, who have been rearmed and placed in the front line. The implications of the figures for RUC deaths are startling. If these deaths continue at the rate observed in the mid-1980s, then *the average career policeman in Northern Ireland will have nearly a 1 in 20 chance of being killed by the IRA during his period of service.* (This assumes that there are 10,000 male full-time members of the RUC, 30 years of service for the average career policeman and 15 policemen killed a year.) If serious injuries are also taken into account, the risk is higher still. To be a policeman in Northern Ireland today is clearly to be in a dangerous profession. The decline in regular British Army deaths and injuries may be a gain for the people of mainland Britain, but it means a new burden for Northern Ireland Protestants who provide the personnel for the local security forces. *Relative to popu-*

lation, 50 per cent more Protestants have been killed in the security forces between 1969 and 1988 than the USA lost during the entire Vietnam War.

The second striking feature about the statistics is the small number of paramilitary deaths in recent years. Apart from some exceptions, like the raid on the Loughall Police Barracks in 1987, few paramilitaries are killed in action nowadays. This is mainly because of the lower scale of violence in recent years, and also the greater professionalism of the IRA.

The second feature to note is the reduction in civilian casualties. This is partly due to the decline in purely sectarian killings by Loyalist paramilitaries, and partly to the greater effort the IRA leadership has made in recent years to minimize civilian casualties. These efforts, it must be said, have not prevented some appalling incidents, such as the massacre at Enniskillen, when eleven innocent bystanders were killed by an IRA bomb on Remembrance Sunday in 1987.

The general picture can be summarized as follows. The situation of virtual insurrection of the early 1970s has given way to a prolonged war of attrition between dedicated professionals. The British Army now plays only a supporting role in this conflict and the main protagonists are all local: on one side the IRA, whose members are virtually all drawn from the Catholic community; and on the other side the RUC and UDR, whose personnel are mainly Northern Ireland Protestants in the service of the British Crown. In the shadows stand the Protestant paramilitaries, who launch sporadic forays into Nationalist areas where their victims are mainly Catholic civilians. Compared to the early 1970s, the violence is no longer so dramatic; the number of civilian victims is greatly reduced; and the bulk of the casualties are people from Northern Ireland.

Even so, it is still significant in both human and political terms. Quite apart from the suffering it represents for the people of Northern Ireland, this violence prevents a return to anything like normality in the province and places a permanent question mark over its future.

Imprisonment and detentions

Since 1972 more than 12,000 people have been charged with 'terrorist-type' offences in Northern Ireland. An equivalent figure for a population the size of Britain's would be well over 400,000. The numbers charged each year fluctuate, but at present the annual average is around 600. An equivalent figure in Britain would be around 20,000.

In addition to people formally charged with offences, a vast number are detained and released after questioning.

While statistics regarding numbers detained are not complete, the information that is published does give a fair idea of the scale of the detention process. Over the period 1975-86, 44,273 persons were detained in Northern Ireland under the Emergency Provisions Act, of whom 40,933 were later released without charge. Over the same period, a further 6,968 persons were detained in Northern Ireland under the Prevention of Terrorism Act, of whom approximately 4,700 were not charged with any offence. The number of detentions has fallen in recent years, but even so it remains very high. In 1986 the total number of people held in Northern Ireland under the two Acts was 2,279, of whom the overwhelming majority were later released without charge.

Some of the people who are detained without subsequently being charged are suspected of illegal activities, but many others are held merely for interrogation. It is thought they *may* have information of value to the authorities. Indeed, the enormous disparity between numbers detained and numbers charged suggest that detention is being used for two main purposes: to enable 'fishing expeditions' by the authorities; and as a mechanism for harassing or intimidating people hostile to the regime.

In England and Wales during 1986, 59,481 persons, mostly Irish, were detained at ports of entry under the PTA. This was an increase of more than 4,000 on the previous year. However, a mere handful were actually charged with any offence. In addition, within mainland Britain, a total of 6,246 persons were detained during the period 1974-86 under the PTA in connection with Northern Ireland. Of these only 528 were charged with an offence. In the mid-1980s detentions in mainland Britain under this Act have varied in the range 150-200 a year.

Treatment of prisoners

We have already described some of the interrogation methods used by the police in Northern Ireland. Another practice which has been widely criticized is that of 'strip searching' women prisoners. This kind of search is most frequently applied to remand prisoners before and after court appearances and after visits, though it may also be applied to other prisoners too. During a strip search, the prisoner concerned first takes off all her clothes and then is examined by a prison officer to see if she is carrying any forbidden article. Menstruating women are ordered to remove their tampons or pads, and if they refuse their sanitary protection is forcibly removed and inspected.

There has always been strip searching in Northern Ireland, but its use has been greatly intensified since November 1982 when it was made routine in Armagh gaol. Since that date something like 3,000 strip searches have been carried out at Armagh, where at any one time the prison population is approximately 40. Republican women have also been repeatedly strip searched in other prisons. The most striking case was perhaps that of Martina Anderson and Ella O'Dwyer who were each strip searched almost 200 times between January and May of 1986 while on remand in Brixton Prison.

The intensive use of strip searching is justified by the authorities on security grounds, as a vital safeguard to prevent the importation of such items as weapons, explosives and keys into prisons. Critics, on the other hand, argue that strip searching is deliberately intended to punish and degrade prisoners. Whatever the motive behind it, there is no doubt that the practice of strip searching is extremely humiliating for the prisoners concerned, and has profound psychological effects, especially when it occurs during menstruation, or when it is frequently repeated.

Criminalization

Paramilitaries in gaol in Northern Ireland, whether Loyalist or Republican, see themselves as 'political' prisoners or prisoners of war, who have risked their lives and sacrificed their liberty for their beliefs. This is also a common view in the communities from which they come. Between 1972 and 1976 the same view was also accepted by the British government, which gave such prisoners 'special category' status. This meant that they could wear their own clothing, maintain their paramilitary organization and command structure, and that their officers were recognized by the prison authorities.

However, as we saw in chapter 4, special category status for new prisoners was abolished in 1976. Since that time, paramilitary personnel entering gaol have ceased to be treated as prisoners of war; now they are treated as ordinary criminals. This policy of 'criminalization' struck directly at paramilitary prisoners' sense of dignity, and weakened the mutual support system which their tight paramilitary organization had provided. It was fiercely resisted through a series of hunger strikes in 1980-1, during which ten Republican prisoners starved themselves to death in an effort to gain prisoner-of-war status for their fellow inmates.

Length of sentences

Paramilitary prisoners face extremely long sentences, and have great difficulty in obtaining release. In May 1986 there were 133 Republicans serving life sentences in Northern Ireland, and another 23 'SOSP' prisoners. The latter are prisoners who were under 17 at the time of their alleged offence and hence too young to receive a formal life sentence. Instead they were detained at the 'Secretary of State's Pleasure' - which in practice means a sentence of life. It should be noted that the great majority of life and 'SOSP' prisoners were arrested and/or convicted between 1976 and 1979. This was the time when allegations of police beatings to produce confessions reached a peak. Though investigation practices were subsequently reformed following the recommendations of the Bennett Committee (see p. 55), convictions dependent on confessions which were secured during that period were allowed to stand.

For paramilitary prisoners in Northern Ireland a life sentence is typically much longer than is normal for ordinary criminals. The latter are, on average, released after eight to ten years, in contrast to many Republican prisoners (and a few Loyalists) who have been in gaol for 15 years already, and are likely to remain there for more years to come. The source of this disparity lies in government policy that paramilitary life prisoners should only be released if they completely renounce their political beliefs.

One group of paramilitary prisoners who deserve special mention are those in gaol in mainland Britain. In 1986 there were 37 Republican prisoners in this category. There were also 11 prisoners whom the IRA claims were framed by Britain in connection with events like the Birmingham and Guildford bombings (and over the accuracy of whose convictions there is widespread doubt in establishment circles). There are also a number of Loyalist prisoners on the mainland. Of the Republicans, 23 are serving life sentences and the remainder sentences of 20 to 25 years.

Keeping paramilitary prisoners in Britain when their families still live in Northern Ireland, causes immense hardship. Their relatives, most of whom are very poor, are put to great expense and difficulty when making visits. This burden is increased by the practice of moving prisoners around the country without notice and keeping them for prolonged periods in solitary confinement. The policy towards paramilitary prisoners contrasts strongly with the compassionate treatment received by British soldiers charged with serious offences in Northern Ireland. They are routinely returned to Britain to serve their sentences. Indeed, the only regular soldier to be convicted of murder while on duty in Northern Ireland, was rapidly transferred to a prison in Britain, and though sentenced to life imprisonment was released on parole within 2½ years and returned to his regiment.

Censorship

The record of the British media in covering events in Northern Ireland has been a sorry one. Ranging in their approach from the superficial to the positively misleading, both the newspapers and the broadcasting services have done little to clarify the reasons for the conflict. They have presented the differences between Northern Ireland's two communities as a curious, archaic, tribal struggle between people who cannot live peaceably beside each other as normal people supposedly do. The paramilitaries, especially the Republicans, are shown solely as murdering madmen with no respect for human life or the rule of law. Overall, media coverage has concentrated on violence and 'terror' shorn of any political context - and hence of any rational basis, and of any hope of its ending.

In part the distorted and inadequate media presentation of Northern Ireland is due to the views of journalists and those directly controlling broadcasting and the press. However, it also reflects the degree to which media - in particular television - coverage is shaped by government demands. Over the years both the BBC and the IBA have repeatedly bowed to political pressure to modify programme content.

The best known and most public example of television censorship occurred in 1985 when a film in the BBC series *Real Lives* was withdrawn following representations by the government. In this film, Martin McGuiness, a leading member of Sinn Féin, and Gregory Campbell, a prominent Loyalist, were interviewed at length. The home secretary objected strongly and the BBC's governors withdrew the programme even though it was already complete and advertised in the *Radio Times*. However, following a widely supported protest strike by BBC journalists, the governors backed down and agreed to put on a modified version of the film in which Martin McGuiness was shown in a more unfavourable light.

Yet the *Real Lives* incident is only the most publicized in a long series. Since 1968 some 50 major programmes have been banned, delayed, cut or altered in accordance with government objectives, for the most part without the public knowing that any of these interventions have occurred. Most affected have been news or current-affairs programmes (including *This Week, Tonight, Panorama, World in Action, 24 Hours,* and also a large number of documentaries), but other programmes have also fallen foul of the censorship process. Thus, in 1981, BBC's *Top of the Pops* was forbidden to screen a video which included a collage of street scenes from Northern Ireland (described by *The Times* as 'utterly uncontentious'). Several plays have also been delayed or dropped.

The rules governing the screening of television programmes about Northern Ireland are contained within two documents. BBC programmes must be dealt with according to the Corporation's *News and Current Affairs Index* (see Appendix 6), while those on ITV are subject to the Independent Broadcasting Authority's *Official Guidelines.* Both of these documents specify that all programmes dealing with Northern Ireland must be 'referred upwards' for approval by top-level management. *No other political topic is subject to such rigid oversight.* It amounts in effect to a form of managerial censorship, and ensures the content of programmes is centrally controlled and coverage of Northern Ireland determined in accordance with government priorities.

This does not quite result in Republicans being kept off TV screens altogether. However, their appearances are rare, and when they do appear, the manner in which they and their views are presented is never positive, and generally very unsympathetic. Senior BBC personnel have stated explicitly that it is Corporation policy to give Republican spokespersons a hard time, and to treat them as 'hostile witnesses'. Republican interviewees are subjected to hostile questioning, repeated interruptions and sharp contradiction. In addition they are always balanced by a countervailing view. By contrast, pro-British politicians are frequently interviewed; they are rarely met with hostility; and it is normal practice that no rebuttal is included from the Republican side.

None of this is surprising. No state engaged in military struggle allows genuinely unpartisan coverage of their opponents' viewpoint. However, it does underline how the conflict in Northern Ireland makes nonsense of the supposed independence of the British media.

And it also highlights how little access people in Britain have to any information about Northern Ireland other than that which matches the government's point of view.

The Republic of Ireland

The erosion of civil liberties resulting from the conflict in Northern Ireland extends beyond the United Kingdom. It also affects the Irish Republic, where a whole series of special measures have been used to control the IRA.

In the 1940s hundreds of Republicans were interned and six IRA members were tried by military tribunal and executed. In 1972 a 'Special Criminal Court' was set up in Dublin, in which trials would be conducted by three judges sitting without a jury. Since then around 2,000 Republicans have been tried in this court, of whom three-quarters have been convicted and sentenced to imprisonment.

Alongside this judicial apparatus, there is also a severe system of censorship designed to prevent Republicans obtaining any exposure at all in the official media. Under section 31 of the Broadcasting Act it is illegal to interview on public radio or television any member of Sinn Féin, or of any organization banned in the North by the British government, or to promote the activities of any of these organizations.

This is a more overt form of censorship than exists in either Britain or Northern Ireland. It means that news and current affairs coverage in the Republic is badly distorted. For example, while hard-line Loyalist MP, Ian Paisley, can be broadcast, the Sinn Féin MP for West Belfast, Gerry Adams, can not. Indeed, when Adams retained his seat in the 1987 general election, the Republic's radio and television services carried interviews with his opponents commenting on why they had lost, but nothing from Adams himself. To hear the Sinn Féin MP, southerners had to rely on radio and TV from Northern Ireland, where he *was* interviewed.

In fact, the operation of section 31 is so extreme, it can be quite absurd. If anyone, from a champion dog breeder, to the duly elected chairperson of a local council highways committee, happens to be a member of Sinn Féin, she or he cannot appear on radio or television, even to be interviewed about dogs or holes in the road. Section 31 has been severely criticized by, for example, Irish trade unions and Cardinal O'Fiach, Catholic Primate of All Ireland. A poll carried out in 1986 by the National Institution of Higher Education in Dublin showed that 53 per cent of people disapprove of section 31 and 73 per cent think Sinn Féin should have access to public radio and television. Approval of the ban was concentrated in upper-middle-class people over 50. However, this law remains in force today.

Twenty years into the present Northern Ireland 'troubles' the abuse of civil liberties has now become the norm - in Britain as well as Northern Ireland, and also in the Irish Republic. Internal banishment, detention without cause on entering Britain, no-jury trials - all are sanctioned by law. Arbitrary arrests, shooting dead rioters or suspected 'terrorists', fabricating trial evidence - none of these are legally sanctioned, but all have happened and all have gone unpunished. Deaths and injuries have occurred on a scale whose immensity is only masked by the small size of the Northern Ireland population.

Meanwhile, news in the media is censored and manipulated. As a result, people in Britain are denied the opportunity to arrive at an informed opinion about Irish events, and about policy making in this area.

6 The Northern Ireland Economy since Partition

In this chapter we examine what has happened to Northern Ireland's economy since the state was established. We also investigate the impact of the current armed conflict on investment, employment and the standard of living. We conclude by comparing key aspects of Northern Ireland's economic performance with the performance of the Republic of Ireland.

Early days: part of the Empire

When Ireland was partitioned in 1921 the country was a striking example of highly uneven economic development. As we have already seen, the mainly Catholic south and west was backward, poor and overwhelmingly rural.

By contrast, the north-east around Belfast was more industrialized and, compared with the south, relatively prosperous. It produced linen for the United States and ships and other manufactured goods for Britain and the Empire. British-based companies had a stake in the region, but there was also a strong local employing class with extensive interests in Northern Ireland industry. The vast majority of these local employers were Protestants. Within the working class, Protestants had much greater access to employment, and enormously greater access to skilled jobs, than did Catholics.

When Northern Ireland was established, the British government saw it as a self-supporting part of Britain's Empire. It was expected to generate more wealth than it consumed, with the surplus being used to help finance the military and other expenses of running the rest of the Empire. Thus, each year the province was supposed to pay to the British government an *Imperial Contribution*. However, within only a short time it became obvious that Northern Ireland could not meet its obligations and the amount paid to Britain fell rapidly.

Eventually the weakness of the province was officially recognized and its intended economic relationship with Britain turned on its head. In 1938 Britain agreed that, henceforward, it would subsidize the costs of running Northern Ireland, instead of the province helping to cover the costs of the Empire. The reason for this rapid slide into dependency is to be found in the structure of Northern Ireland's economy.

The 1930s crisis

Massive unemployment hit the whole of the United Kingdom in the early 1930s. However, in Northern Ireland the crisis was deeper and lasted longer than in most of the UK. This was because of its economy's heavy emphasis on agriculture, linen and shipbuilding - all industries which experienced especially severe difficulties between the first and second world war.

On mainland Britain there was an economic recovery from the mid-1930s onwards, based on house building and the expansion of new industries. In Northern Ireland there was no housing boom, little modernization of industry and no economic recovery. In 1939, on the eve of war, unemployment in the province stood at 20 per cent compared with 7.5 per cent in Britain. Income per head of the population was only just over half the UK average. Social services were very backward and the infant mortality rate was 80 per 1,000 live births, compared to 60 per 1,000 in the rest of the UK. (See table 6.1.)

Table 6.1 Deaths of infants under one year per thousand live births, 1900-52

	United Kingdom	Northern Ireland
1900–02	142	113
1920–22	82	86
1930–32	67	75
1940–42	59	80
1950–52	30	40

Source: UK Annual Abstract of Statistics

A short boom

The war finally brought relief to Northern Ireland's economy in the form of a major boom in shipbuilding and other industries providing military supplies. The boom continued for a few years into peacetime as post-war scarcities created a seller's market for Northern Ireland's products. But by the early 1950s the old problems had re-emerged. Ships and linen were again in trouble and long-term employment prospects were bleak.

The fifties and sixties: big changes in the structure of employment

The Northern Ireland Unionist government was initially slow to come to grips with the extent of the unemployment problem. With its Victorian politics, it was very reluctant to intervene on an appropriate scale. However, faced with pressure from working-class Protestants, who began to shift their voting allegiance to the Northern Ireland Labour Party, the Unionist government did eventually start vigorous measures to foster the development of new industry.

Lavish investment grants, tax concessions and other inducements were used to attract British, American and continental-European firms to the province. The effect on output was impressive. During the 1960s manufacturing production rose much faster in Northern Ireland than in the UK as a whole, with growth totalling 60 per cent over the decade. However, the effect on numbers in manufacturing employment was less impressive. New jobs were created, but even more were lost in declining industries and through rationalization of existing enterprises.

Manufacturing, agriculture and services

By the end of the 1960s about 65,000 new jobs had been created with the help of government initiatives. Even so, total *manufacturing* employment was only 180,000, compared with the post-war peak of 185,000. Expansion of employment in synthetic fibres, mechanical engineering, metal goods and other growth industries was more than offset by decline elsewhere, in linen and shipbuilding in particular.

Meanwhile, even more striking changes were taking place in agriculture and services. At the end of the war, about a quarter of the total labour force was employed in agriculture, often on very small farms, using extremely backward methods of production. This situation was transformed during the 1950s and 1960s. Farm holdings were concentrated and production mechanized, with the result that even though many small farms remained, *agricultural* employment had fallen to around 10 per cent of the total workforce by 1970.

By contrast, there was a rapid increase in *service* employment. Under popular pressure, Northern Ireland's Unionist government had reluctantly been compelled to follow Britain and accept the provisions of the Welfare State. With British financial support, a major drive was launched to improve the province's backward public services and bring them into line with those in mainland Britain. This led to a rapid expansion of public-service employment. For example, between 1954 and 1970, the number of secondary school teachers more than trebled and the number of nurses and medical staff in hospitals doubled.

Emigration

Despite the new jobs in manufacturing, construction and services, *total* employment was hardly affected – the gains were virtually cancelled out by the equally large decline in the old manufacturing industries and in agriculture. Given Northern Ireland's traditionally high birth rate, this failure to increase total employment would have led to a huge surplus of labour, were it not for an enormous exodus of people from the province. During the 1950s a third of all school leavers were forced to emigrate in search of work. Many were Protestants, but a majority were Catholics.

The standard of living in the 1950s and 1960s

Wages increased significantly in Northern Ireland during these two decades and by 1970 average earnings had risen to about 90 per cent of those in mainland Britain. Even so much poverty still remained. High unemployment, large families, a lack of jobs for women and low pay in certain sectors meant that incomes were often very low. Indeed, in 1970 consumption per Northern Ireland inhabitant was still only three-quarters of the UK average.

Meanwhile public services were showing a considerable improvement. New hospitals were constructed; others were modernized; and medical services were extended. In education, despite a large increase in the school population, class sizes were reduced and gross overcrowding was virtually eliminated. (Even so, many working-class children continued to receive an inferior education. As late as 1970, two-thirds of all children left school without the minimal qualification of one O level pass.) Housing was another area where gains were made, with many new houses being built. However, the backlog was so great that a survey done in 1974 showed 38 per cent of all dwellings to be either scheduled for demolition or in need of major repair.

The differing experience of Catholics and Protestants

Both communities benefited from the economic progress of the period, but its impact on them was uneven, and the gap between them remained wide.

In education Catholics experienced an enormous rise in standards. Additional government finance allowed Catholic schools to employ far more teachers and led to a major reduction in the size of classes. By the end of the 1960s the facilities offered by Catholic schools were similar to those of their Protestant equivalents. Academically they were still some way behind, but were catching up fast. Catholics also experienced an improvement in their housing, though discrimination in the allocation of public housing continued in some parts of the province and the housing conditions of Catholics remained, on average, worse than those of Protestants.

In the job market, however, the situation was much less positive. Catholics continued to have great difficulty finding work, and throughout the 1950s and 1960s their rate of unemployment was much higher than that of Protestants. According to the 1971 Census of Population, the overall (male and female) rate of unemployment for Catholics was 14 per cent compared with 6 per cent for Protestants. There were two key reasons for this. As we have seen, discrimination by employers in their recruitment and training practices was a major problem which Catholics faced. The other main obstacle was the very location of industry itself.

Location of industry

In the 1950s and 1960s most new investment in the province went to the Protestant areas around Belfast: Antrim, Down and North Armagh. Relatively little went to the city of Belfast itself, or to Catholic areas of the province.

Table 6.2 shows that, with the exception of Belfast, Protestant areas prospered, while Catholic ones stagnated. In the rural, and majority Catholic counties of Fermanagh and Tyrone, total employment fell

Table 6.2 Religion and economic change in Northern Ireland 1961-71, by county

| County | % Catholic 1961 | % Unemployment | | Percentage change 1961-71 | | | | |
		1961	1971	Employees only	Total employment[a]	Population aged 15-64	Net migration 1961-71[b]
Londonderry CB[c]	67.1	17.5	14.3	−5.4	−6.4	−3.0	−17.6
Co. Tyrone	54.8	12.3	12.6	+6.1	−2.8	+3.1	−5.9
Co. Fermanagh	53.2	9.8	9.2	+7.6	−6.7	−1.3	−6.0
Co. Armagh	47.3	12.8	9.6	+17.3	+9.8	+11.0	+0.3
Co. Londonderry	42.6	11.5	8.8	+24.0	+14.5	+13.7	+2.7
Co. Down	28.6	8.3	6.2	+20.2	+17.5	+15.6	+7.4
Co. Antrim	24.4	6.7	5.9	+33.3	+28.1	+26.7	+11.0
Belfast CB[c]	27.5	8.5	9.6	−22.2	−21.7	−13.9	−17.4

[a] Includes employers and self-employed.
[b] As a percentage of total population in 1961. (−) indicates net outflow from the county concerned; (+) indicates net inflow.
[c] CB = County Borough.

Source: NI Census of Population, 1971

and there was a considerable outflow of people seeking work. New jobs were created in these counties, but not on the scale required to compensate for an enormous reduction in the number of self-employed farmers.

In the city of Belfast, economic decline affected both Catholics and Protestants, but Protestants had some important advantages in searching for employment: they had more marketable skills than Catholics did, and could travel out more easily to the new jobs in the immediate vicinity of Belfast. For Catholics many of these jobs would have been too difficult, costly or even dangerous for them to reach.

Some indication of how badly Catholics in Belfast fared can be obtained from the Census of Population. In 1971 the unemployment rates amongst males in the Falls and Dock wards - both predominantly Catholic - were 23.8 per cent and 21.7 per cent respectively; while for Belfast as a whole the rate was 12.1 per cent. In no major Protestant ward was unemployment over 15 per cent.

Northern Ireland government policy

It is not possible to quantify how far, by deliberately steering investment towards Protestant areas, the Northern Ireland Unionist government was directly responsible for this pattern of growth. There are examples of very obvious discrimination. Thus, in 1964 the government chose to site the New University of Ulster in Protestant Coleraine rather than Catholic Derry, even though Derry was much larger and had an established college which could have formed an integral part of the NUU.

However, deliberate discrimination is only part of the story. Prior to 1963 the Northern Ireland government did not have any explicit policy about where companies should be sited. It made no systematic attempts to direct investment towards any particular parts of the province during this period. Rather it played an essentially passive role, supplying finance and support services as and where required by private firms.

Yet this in itself was enough to ensure the bulk of private investment went to Protestant areas, since they were often more conveniently situated and usually possessed larger supplies of suitably skilled labour than Catholic parts of the province. So, merely by allowing firms to invest where they wanted, the government could rely on a pattern of growth favourable to its Protestant supporters.

MAP 3 Catholics as a percentage of population in
Belfast Urban Area in 1971

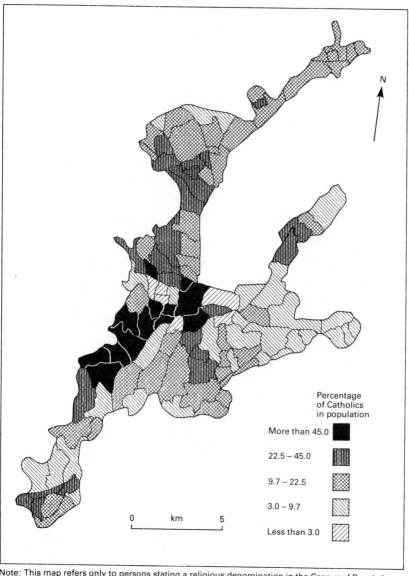

Percentage
of Catholics
in population

More than 45.0

22.5 – 45.0

9.7 – 22.5

3.0 – 9.7

Less than 3.0

0   km   5

N

Note: This map refers only to persons stating a religious denomination in the Census of Population.
The geographical areas shown are electoral wards.

Source: P.A. Compton, *Northern Ireland: A Census Atlas*, Dublin 1978.

MAP 4 Catholics as a percentage of population in Northern Ireland in 1971

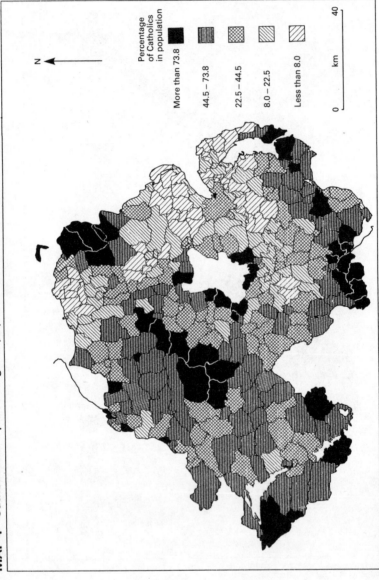

N

Percentage
of Catholics
in population

More than 73.8

44.5 – 73.8

22.5 – 44.5

8.0 – 22.5

Less than 8.0

0   km   40

Note: This map refers only to persons stating a religious denomination in the Census of Population.
The geographical areas shown are electoral wards (except in the case of towns and cities
which combine a number of wards).

Source: P. A. Compton, *Northern Ireland: A Census Atlas*, Dublin 1978

To sum up, many Catholics did benefit from the growth of the 1950s and 1960s. However, overall the location of new jobs was very much to the advantage of Protestants.

The seventies and eighties: crisis and decay

Since the early 1970s the economy of Northern Ireland has experienced a dramatic reversal of fortune. The province has been gripped by a prolonged industrial crisis, the rapid growth of the previous decade has been reversed and industrial output is now well below the historic peak achieved in 1973. Factories have closed, industrial employment has fallen massively and investment is at a low ebb. This crisis is partly a reflection of the more general problems of the UK economy as a whole. However, Northern Ireland has been particularly badly affected.

Manufacturing decline

With the world slump of 1974 Northern Ireland's manufacturing expansion came to a halt. That and the subsequent slump of 1979–80 hit Britain too, but their impact was more severe in Northern Ireland where recovery has also been much weaker.

Manufacturing employment has fallen almost continuously throughout the crisis and by 1985 was more than 40 per cent below its 1974 level. The decline slowed down in the mid-1980s, but has not stopped entirely, and the province is still losing manufacturing jobs.

It is true that if we look at individual industries we find there are marked variations. Some – such as clothing and chemicals – have so far weathered the storm and are showing signs of growth in the mid-1980s. A few have even done well and managed to increase their output considerably despite the recession. Of these the most important are aircraft and motor vehicles and parts.

Much more significant in employment terms, however, are those industries – such as plastics, metal goods and synthetics – which have experienced a major fall in output. The most extreme example has been the synthetic fibre industry which has gone from star performer to almost total collapse within the space of a few years. Synthetic producers have faced a combination of world recession and competition from cheap imports. Most of the fibre plants opened in the 1960s have closed down, and this former growth sector now faces extinction.

Increasing productivity

Alongside the widespread collapse of industry there has, nevertheless, been a striking and rapid growth in labour productivity. Production methods have been rationalized and new labour-saving equipment installed, usually with generous financial aid from the British government. This has certainly helped many firms to survive which would otherwise have not.

But it has not been enough to prevent a fall in total manufacturing output. Between 1973 and 1985 Northern Ireland experienced a 17 per cent fall overall in manufacturing output and a simultaneous 41 per cent rise in output per worker. It should not be forgotten, however, that despite the improvement in recent years, manufacturing productivity in Northern Ireland is still, on average, about 15 per cent below the level in Britain. Compared to more advanced countries of continental Europe and elsewhere, the gap is, of course, much greater.

The Irish Republic

It is instructive to compare the experience of Northern Ireland with that of the Republic during the crisis. In both parts of Ireland there has been a rapid improvement in *labour productivity* in the manufacturing sector. The average worker in manufacturing now produces 50–60 per cent more than in the early 1970s. In this respect the two Irish economies are similar. In most other respects they are very different.

In Northern Ireland the increased productivity in the manufacturing sector has taken place against the background of falling *total output*. As a result, employment in this sector has been cut dramatically and is now only half of its early 1970s level. In effect, in Northern Ireland, a greatly reduced workforce is now producing slightly less total output than it was 15 years ago.

In the Republic, on the other hand, total output has continued to rise strongly, though unevenly. This increase in output has not been enough to prevent a fall in manufacturing employment in recent years but the fall has been much less dramatic than in Northern Ireland (see figure 6.1).

The manufacturing sector of the Republic may not be an unqualified success, but its performance is, in all respects, superior to that of Northern Ireland. The main reason for this difference has been the Republic's continued ability to attract outside investment in modern

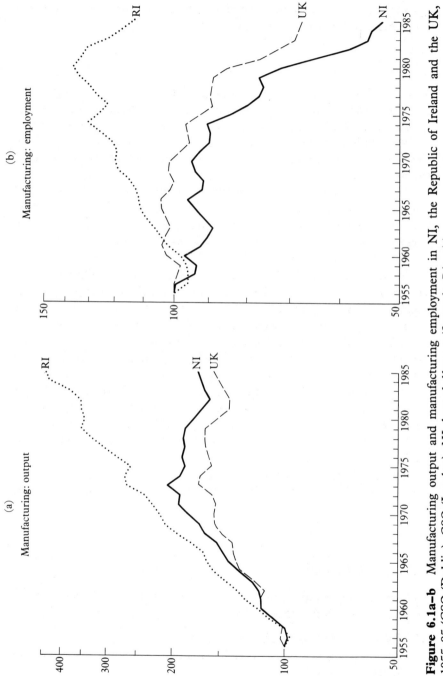

Figure 6.1a–b Manufacturing output and manufacturing employment in NI, the Republic of Ireland and the UK, 1955–85 (CSO (Dublin), CSO (London), *NI Annual Abstract* (formerly *Digest*))
Note: 1956=100

(a) Manufacturing: output

(b) Manufacturing: employment

growth sectors of manufacturing industry. As we shall see, in this area Northern Ireland has conspicuously failed.

The importance of subsidies

The fall in manufacturing output, together with the rise in output per worker, has produced a spectacular fall in manufacturing employment since the early seventies. There are exceptions like aircraft or motor vehicles and parts where employment has increased. But the number of jobs involved is small and does not affect the general picture of almost universal manufacturing decline.

What is far more significant is that even where firms have done well and managed to grow, or at least survive, this has often been at considerable expense to the British government. *Industrial subsidies in Northern Ireland are approximately twice the level in other depressed areas of the United Kingdom.*

In some cases the scale of these subsidies has been immense. For example, during the mid-1980s Harland and Wolff shipbuilders has received financial support averaging around £8,000 per worker per year. This amount has been almost sufficient to pay the entire wage and salary bill of the company. This firm, which now employs less than 5,000 people, has so far received government aid totalling more than £500 million at today's prices. Another case is Shorts, the aircraft manufacturer. This is often regarded as one of Northern Ireland's more successful companies because of its diversified product range and extensive sales in the USA and elsewhere. Even so, it has lost money almost every year since the mid-seventies, and after one profitable year in 1985 went into the red again.

These examples illustrate clearly the fragile nature of Northern Ireland's industrial base. The continued growth or even survival of many companies depends crucially on British government aid, without which they would not be viable in their present form.

Why has it happened?

There are five main reasons why the Northern Ireland economy has performed so badly since 1973:

1   Events in the world economy as a whole.
2   The dependence of the Northern Ireland economy on exports to Britain.

3 The industrial structure of Northern Ireland.
4 The 'branch plant' nature of the Northern Ireland economy and its dependence on outside firms.
5 The armed conflict and political instability in the province.

The first three reasons are closely linked. Northern Ireland's manufacturing industry is strongly export-oriented and therefore very vulnerable to events in the outside world. The slow growth of the world economy since 1973 has undermined the export market for Northern Ireland's products and brought a more hostile competitive environment. Despite the recent boom, the average growth rate of Britain's economy since 1973 has been extremely low. Since Britain is Northern Ireland's main trading partner, this has further reduced the demand for industrial exports from the province. At the start of the crisis in 1973 the economic structure of the province was particularly unfavourable. It had an above average share of problem industries, like artificial fibres and shipbuilding, both of which have suffered grievously throughout Western Europe.

The final two reasons are of especial importance, not only in explaining the past, but in indicating likely future industrial prospects in Northern Ireland.

A 'branch plant' economy   Under the development strategy pursued before the crisis, the province became almost totally dependent on the goodwill of outside firms. Only 8.5 per cent of all industrial jobs promoted during the period 1947-67 were in native Northern Ireland companies. As local companies disappeared, they were replaced by subsidiaries of large outside firms, from the UK, the USA and elsewhere.

The subsidiaries were typically 'branch plants'; that is, they lacked the freedom to take their own major administrative decisions, and had few research, development and marketing facilities of their own. As this type of plant came to dominate the economy, the entrepreneurial, marketing and innovative skills of the local population withered. In this way the province lost its capacity to generate internally its own manufacturing growth.

In addition, as a branch plant economy, it became extremely vulnerable to a general crisis such as we have had over the last decade, which has forced large firms to restructure their global operations.

In the case of synthetic fibres, for example, the big European producers have been severely hit by a combination of world recession and cheap naphtha-based imports from the USA. These firms have responded by closing down many of their branches and concentrating production on a few core plants. Tobacco is another example. In response to falling demand for their products, the large tobacco firms have also closed down many of their Northern Ireland facilities, so as to concentrate production on core plants elsewhere.

The effect on Northern Ireland has been devastating: jobs in these industries have been lost by the thousand, and efforts to compensate by encouraging local industry have had very limited success. At the last count, in February 1984, the total employed on projects sponsored by Northern Ireland's Local Economic Development Unit (LEDU) was 7,896. Although no precise figure is available, about three-quarters of these were in manufacturing industry and the rest in services. Moreover, some of the enterprises fostered by LEDU act as sub-contractors to outside firms operating in the province. Without these outside firms the local subcontractors could not survive.

The armed conflict   In Northern Ireland the ordinary vulnerability associated with a branch plant economy is intensified by the armed conflict. When deciding whether to set up new plants, or to close down existing ones, a large firm will normally choose those locations where the long-term security of its operations is assured.

The IRA's bombing campaign of the early 1970s produced serious problems for industry generally. It caused widespread damage to commercial property and severely harmed the tourist trade. Several hundred factories suffered some form of disruption, though few were completely destroyed. Predictably this created an atmosphere of doubt and uncertainty which has deterred outside firms from investing in the province. There is much evidence to show that many multinational companies have, indeed, decided to locate their activities in safer places, such as the Irish Republic or mainland Britain. (See figure 6.2.)

Over the period 1966–71 multinationals set up 51 new manufacturing units in the province and created 11,600 new jobs. By contrast, between 1972 and 1976 they established a mere 15 units and created only 900 jobs. Although there was then a brief flurry of investment by outside firms – mainly American – this did not last.

Growth in the 1970s: services and security

In spite of the crisis, until 1979 the total number of people in employment actually rose. This is because throughout the 1970s declining

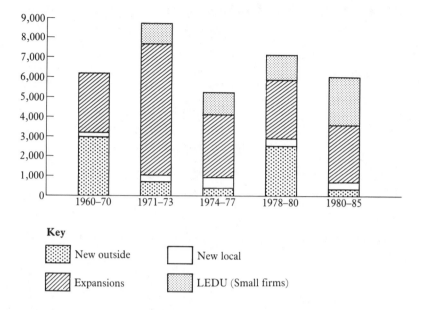

Figure 6.2 Annual job promotions in Northern Ireland, 1945-85 (from *UK Regional Trends*, formerly *Regional Statistics*)

industrial employment was offset by a rapid growth in service-sector jobs.

The main driving force behind the growth of service employment in the 1970s was the massive expansion in government services. This had a direct impact on employment in the 'social services' such as health and education, and also on employment in the security forces. Indirectly it also stimulated employment growth elsewhere in the economy, by creating a demand for non-government services such as distribution, transport and finance (see table 6.3).

In just five years, between 1974 and 1979, employment in government services rose by 25 per cent and in non-government services by 14 per cent. Over the 1970s as a whole, the increase was even larger. Several factors account for this. In the case of 'social services' such as health and education, there was a general expansion throughout the UK at this time. However, the increase in Northern Ireland was much faster than average, mainly because of the 'catching up' effect. Despite big improvements since the war, the 'social services' in Northern Ireland were still inferior to those in the rest of the UK. This was seen

Table 6.3 Northern Ireland working population 1974–85 (thousands)

Employment*a*	1974	1979	1985	% Change 1974–79	% Change 1979–85
Agriculture, etc.	58.2	57.0	54.5	−2	−4
Energy and water supply	9.7	10.2	9.0	+5	−12
Manufacturing	172.1	147.0	103.3	−15	−30
Construction	46.9	45.4	31.2	−3	−31
Non-government services	164.3	187.8	181.5	+14	−3
Wholesale distribution	23.2	24.3	20.2	+5	−17
Retailing and repairing	53.7	57.3	55.7	+7	−3
Hotels and catering	11.4	13.8	14.8	+21	+7
Transport and communications	24.3	22.5	19.3	−8	−14
Finance and business services	23.6	28.1	28.3	+19	+1
Other services	28.0	41.7	43.1	+49	+3
Government services*b*	125.8	157.2	165.4	+25	+5
Public administration*c* and defence*a*	47.3	57.0	59.3	+21	+4
Education	46.6	56.1	57.9	+20	+3
Health	31.8	44.1	48.2	+38	+9
Total employment	577.0	604.6	545.1	+5	−10
Unemployment	25.5	59.6	121.4		
Working population	602.6	664.2	666.5	+10	0

a Includes full-time members of UDR, but excludes other members of HM forces.
b Includes non-government institutions (e.g. church schools, private hospitals).
c Includes sanitary services.
Source: NI Annual Abstract

by the Heath and Wilson governments in Britain as a factor behind the turmoil in the province.

How much extra money would have been available in more peaceful times to bridge the gap between standards in Britain and Northern Ireland is a matter of speculation. It is, however, certain that the conflict brought urgency and encouraged the British government to accelerate the process of bringing Northern Ireland's services into line with their British equivalents. Thus, the spectacular rise in social service employment in Northern Ireland during the 1970s was partly a political response to the state of conflict in the province.

The security forces

The conflict was also responsible for a massive expansion in the security forces during this period. When it began, troops were dispatched to the province from Britain and soon took over the bulk of military operations. However, this was only a temporary phase and the mid-seventies saw a shift of policy towards 'Ulsterization'.

Under this policy, the task of controlling the province was increasingly returned to the local security forces: the Royal Ulster Constabulary (RUC) and the Ulster Defence Regiment (UDR). Thousands of jobs were thereby created for local people – mainly Protestants – who were willing to serve in these forces. In addition, the prison service was greatly expanded to deal with the vastly increased numbers of those gaoled, thus creating still more jobs, chiefly taken by Protestants.

The impact of Thatcher

Since the Thatcher government took office in 1979, there has been a marked change in British policy towards expenditure in Northern Ireland. Spending on the local security forces has continued to increase rapidly. For example, the number of full-time members of the RUC rose by 38 per cent over the period 1979–85. However, the rest of the public sector has been severely restrained. The former growth in 'social services' has largely come to a halt, and in some areas has gone into reverse.

This policy change is motivated by a combination of budgetary and political considerations. The Thatcher government has imposed severe financial restrictions on the social services throughout the UK. However, unlike previous British governments, the Tories now do not regard Northern Ireland as a special case. In part this reflects the Tories' general indifference to the problems of poor regions. But it also indicates their disbelief in the idea that it is cost-effective to try to defuse political opposition in Northern Ireland through spending on social services. Such expenditure does not, in their opinion, have much effect on political attitudes towards Britain in the province. So in this respect it is a waste of money. Finally, they consider that, after the rapid growth of the 1970s, many social services in Northern Ireland have now caught up with those in Britain. Therefore, in the

Tories' view, there is no case for exempting the province from its share of spending cuts.

Because of this modern Tory policy, total employment in government services in Northern Ireland has risen quite slowly during the 1980s. Moreover, employment in non-government services has actually fallen. Combined with the accelerating decline in industrial employment, this has meant that total employment under the Thatcher government has fallen sharply. By 1985 it was 10 per cent below the level achieved in 1979. Between 1979 and 1986 the unemployment rate in Northern Ireland has more than doubled (see figure 6.3).

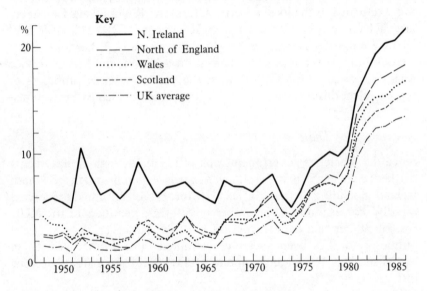

Figure 6.3 Percentage unemployment rate in selected regions of the UK
(*Source*: *British Labour Statistics, Economic Trends Annual Supplement*)

The jobs people do

The changes just described have had a major impact on the kind of jobs people do in Northern Ireland. In 1974 services accounted for just over 50 per cent of total employment. Of this, 22 per cent was in government services, such as health and education. The other 28 per cent was in non-government services, such as distribution, transport and finance. By 1985, these figures had risen to 64 per cent, 30 per cent and 33 per cent respectively. Over the same period, the share of manufacturing employment fell by a third to 19 per cent of all employment. This means that services in Northern Ireland now employ well over three times as many as the manufacturing sector, and almost twice as many as manufacturing, agriculture, construction, energy and water supply combined.

This transformation has had far-reaching implications. It has meant a shift from manual to non-manual labour, and from a male to a female workforce. It has also affected Catholics and Protestants rather differently, because it has influenced the geographical location of jobs, and the type of jobs that they are. The significance of what is happening should not be underestimated. To the world at large, the representative Northern Irish worker has been Protestant, skilled, manual and male, employed in shipbuilding, engineering, and other manufacturing industry in the Belfast area. Workers like this have occupied a strategic position in the economy of Northern Ireland – and have played a central role in its politics.

The last decade has seen the economic position of these workers greatly weaken. Their numbers have been reduced by the decline in manufacturing industry; and their weight in the economy has been lessened by the shift to services. Politically they still matter, but their influence is waning.

Women

The employment of women in Northern Ireland has been affected by two factors: a long-term decline in female-intensive manufacturing industries such as linen; and a long-term expansion in female-intensive service activities such as health and education.

Between 1950 and 1970 women's share in employment held steady, as service expansion matched manufacturing decline. Then in the 1970s the extra jobs in the service sector far outstripped the losses in manufacturing.

By 1985 women held an all-time high of 46 per cent of all jobs. However, almost all the increase in female employment has been in part-time work, most of it very low paid. At the same time, unemployment amongst women has risen sharply over the past decade. Even though there are now more female-dominated jobs than before, the supply of jobs open to women has not kept up with demand. Between 1974 and 1985 unemployment amongst women rose nearly fivefold from 2.7 per cent to 12.9 per cent. For men it went up a little over fourfold from 5.1 per cent to 21.8 per cent.

Northern Ireland today: the standard of living

For the average person in Northern Ireland, the standard of living has improved noticeably over the past 20 years. Between 1966 and 1984 consumption per head went up by over 30 per cent in real terms and the gap between Britain and Northern Ireland narrowed considerably. A similar development can also be observed in real wage rates. (See figure 6.4.)

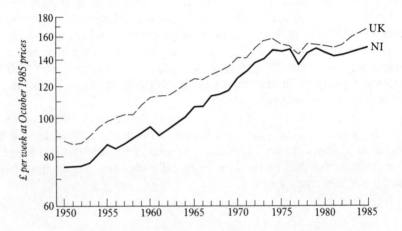

Figure 6.4   Real weekly earnings of male manual workers in manufacturing, 1950–85
Source: *British Labour Statistics, Employment Gazette*

Ownership of consumer durables has increased substantially. Since 1970 the proportion of households with fridges has gone up from 32 per cent to 89 per cent, and of those with washing machines from 40 per cent to 74 per cent. The average *employed* worker now appears to have a level and pattern of consumption similar to that of the average British worker in the late 1970s (see table 6.4).

Public consumption – i.e. social provision – shows a massive gain. In just ten years, from 1974 to 1984, it rose by over 50 per cent in real terms. It is now considerably higher than in the UK as a whole. Even though the figures include items such as the police and prison service, which are much more extensive in Northern Ireland, there is no doubt that social facilities have improved a great deal.

The pupil–teacher ratio in maintained secondary schools has fallen from 19.0 in 1970 to 15.2 in 1984 – lower than the UK average. There

Table 6.4 Living standards in Northern Ireland

		Northern Ireland	*United Kingdom*	*NI as % of UK*
1 Ownership of consumer durables[a]				
Percentage of households with:				
Central heating	1969–70	13.2	27.2	48
(full or partial)	1983–84	56.4	65.3	86
Washing Machine	1969–70	39.8	63.8	62
	1983–84	74.4	79.8	93
Refrigerator	1969–70	32.0	62.8	51
	1983–84	89.9	94.3	94
Television	1969–70	32.0	91.3	35
	1983–84	95.0	97.6	97
Telephone	1969–70	23.1	33.5	69
	1983–84	69.1	77.4	89
2 Social facilities in 1984				
(per 1,000 inhabitants)				
Health service employees		24.8	19.2	129
Hospital beds		10.6	7.6	139
Primary school teachers[b]		42.7	45.5	94
Secondary school teachers[b]		66.2	62.5	106
Percentage of dwellings built since 1944[a]		66	51	129
3 Poverty and unemployment in 1984				
Full-time adult earnings (£ per week)[b]				
male		172.3	192.4	90
female		122.2	126.4	97
Personal disposable income (£ per week)		64.8	75.1	86
Number of dependants per person		2.00	1.37	146
Unemployment (% of working population)		18.5	11.3	163
Average percentage of family income derived from unemployment and supplementary benefits		7.8	3.5	225

Table 6.4 *continued*

	Northern Ireland	United Kingdom	NI as % of UK
Percentage of pupils taking free school meals	28.0	18.1	155
Percentage of households with income less than £75 per week	31.1	22.3	139
Percentage of dwellings lacking inside WC*ad*	8.7	2.7	322
Infant mortality (deaths per 1,000 live births)*e*	10.5	9.6	109
Net civilian migration (per 1,000 of population)*f*	− 3 6	+ 0.8	− 450

a UK Column refers to Britain only
b Public sector and grant aided only
c 1983-84
d 1981
e Deaths of infants under 1 year of age; figures are provisional
f Includes 'other adjustments'; figures refer to mid-1983-mid-1984
Source: UK Regional Trends

are more hospital beds and more doctors per head of the population than in mainland Britain. The infant mortality rate has dropped from 25.5 per 1,000 live births in 1966 to 10.5 per 1,000 in 1984 - about the same as in Britain two years earlier. A lot of houses and flats have been built - proportionately more in Northern Ireland since 1945 than in any other UK region - though some, like the notorious Divis Flats, are already in poor condition and are undergoing demolition.

A widening gap between the 'haves' and the 'have nots'

Though *average* living standards have improved, the gains have been very unevenly distributed. Those who have kept their jobs during the crisis of the 1970s and 1980s have, for the most part, done quite well and enjoyed some increase in their real income. Also, the massive growth in the public sector has created many thousands of comparatively well-paid jobs for people like teachers, administrators, doctors, police and prison warders.

At the other end of the scale, however, there is widespread deprivation. By 1983 almost 22 per cent of the population in Northern Ireland was dependent on supplementary benefit. In the late 1980s the proportion is considerably higher as unemployment has continued to rise. Particularly striking is the gap between the incidence of deprivation in Northern Ireland and that within the rest of the UK. In 1985 the unemployment rate in Northern Ireland was 18.5 per cent compared with 11.3 per cent for the UK as a whole; unemployment and supplementary benefit accounted for 7.8 per cent of average family income (UK 3.5 per cent); 31 per cent of all households had income of less than £75 per week (UK 22 per cent); 28 per cent of children needed free school meals (UK 18 per cent).

So alongside prosperity for some, there exists a large and growing underclass of very poor people. Apart from unemployment, there is another key factor responsible for the province's widespread poverty. This is the high cost of living and the low level of pay in certain occupations. Professional people, and those working in some highly paid sectors such as engineering and vehicles, usually earn much the same as their counterparts in Britain. However, in traditionally low-paid sectors, like agriculture, construction, distribution and personal services, earnings in Northern Ireland are often well below their already meagre level in mainland Britain, sometimes by a margin of 15–20 per cent.

Some key economic effects of the armed conflict

Earlier we discussed the way in which the conflict has created an atmosphere of economic uncertainty, which has deterred outside firms from investing in the province. We also saw how new jobs have been created in the state sector as the local security forces have been enlarged to combat the IRA, while the 'social services' have been increased in an attempt to lessen local opposition to British rule. In addition, the British government has taken a series of measures to safeguard existing jobs and create new employment. It has set up the Local Enterprise Development Unit and the Industrial Development Board to provide money and guidance for would-be investors. It has also given support to firms in difficulty, organized special programmes of urban and rural improvement, and created extensive facilities to train school leavers and retain existing workers.

Despite all this, the Northern Ireland economy is in severe trouble and its industrial base is much weaker than it was fifteen years ago.

In the following section we examine how far some key aspects of the province's current economic state should be specifically attributed to the armed conflict. It is impossible to be absolutely precise about this. However, by comparing the experience of Northern Ireland with that of other depressed regions of the UK, we can produce a rough but adequate indication.

The impact on the type of employment available in Northern Ireland

According to table 6.5, despite all the special measures taken by the government, the conflict has destroyed or prevented the creation of some 46,000 manufacturing jobs in Northern Ireland. This is equivalent to about 25 per cent of the province's manufacturing employment in 1970. At the same time, it has led to the creation of around 36,000 jobs in the public sector (police, prisons, health, education, etc.), plus about 5,000 security-related jobs in the private sector. Taking all these into account, the conflict has caused a net job loss of perhaps 5,000. This is only around 1 per cent of total employment in 1970.

The conflict appears to have had only a minor effect on the overall *level* of employment. However, since different sectors of the economy have been affected very differently, it has altered the *structure* of

Table 6.5 Effects of the conflict on employment, 1970-85

	Change in employment due to the conflict (thousands)	% of 1970 employment
Agriculture	nil	nil
Manufacturing	− 46	− 25
Other industry[a]	0	0
Non-government services	+ 5	+ 3
Government services	+ 36	+ 38
TOTAL	− 5	− 1

[a] Construction, energy and water supply

Sources: Authors' own estimates using methodology employed by Bob Rowthorn in 'Northern Ireland: an economy in crisis', *Cambridge Journal of Economics* 5 (1981); and D. Canning, B. Moore and J. Rhodes in 'Economic growth in Northern Ireland', in *Beyond the Rhetoric*, ed. P. Teague (London, 1987)

employment considerably. Industrial employment is now much smaller and public-service employment much larger than would have been the case had the last decade been peaceful. Of this shift from industry to services, about half can be explained by the conflict, the rest being due to other factors.

Religion and employment

These developments have had major implications for the religious composition of the workforce.

Protestants, who dominated industry, have suffered most from the loss of manufacturing jobs; but on the other hand they have obtained most of the additional jobs in security-related activities (police, prison officers, UDR, civilian searchers, etc.). They have also gained many of the extra jobs in health, education and other public services. All in all, it is unlikely that the conflict has had much effect on the *overall* level of Protestant employment.

Meanwhile, Catholics have lost fewer manufacturing jobs – because they had fewer to begin with. On the other hand, Catholics have received virtually none of the additional security jobs. They have, of course, filled many of the new jobs created in health, education and the like. On balance, the overall effect on Catholic employment is also almost certainly very small.

The conflict has thus led to redistribution of employment *within* each community. But it has probably not had much effect on the share of each community in the total number of jobs available.

Northern Ireland: a workhouse economy

Output

On average, Northern Ireland produces per inhabitant 72 per cent as much output as the United Kingdom. This rises to 76 per cent if North Sea oil is excluded. However, these figures conceal very big differences between the various categories of output. For example, Northern Ireland 'produces' a third more government services per inhabitant than the average for the UK. This is mainly owing to the large numbers of police and soldiers deployed there, though it also reflects the relatively big health and education sectors.

However, the province produces only 52 per cent as much in the way of 'transportable goods' (food, fuel and manufactured goods, etc.)

per inhabitant as the UK average. This is because its fuel output is negligible and its manufacturing sector small. Fuel production will increase when the deposits of brown coal (lignite) around Lough Neagh are developed, which will reduce the province's dependence on imported coal. However, the manufacturing gap between Northern Ireland and the UK will almost certainly continue to widen - as it has done since 1974.

The one relatively successful area is agriculture, where output per inhabitant is almost 80 per cent above the UK average. However, there is little potential for further growth here, and the sector is highly vulnerable to changes in Common Market agricultural policy.

Taking transportable goods as a whole, Northern Ireland is very backward, and, with the exception of brown coal, its future prospects are poor. Figure 6.5 underlines just how far behind the province is, in comparison with the UK as a whole, and with other West European countries, including some of the poorest. In per capita terms the

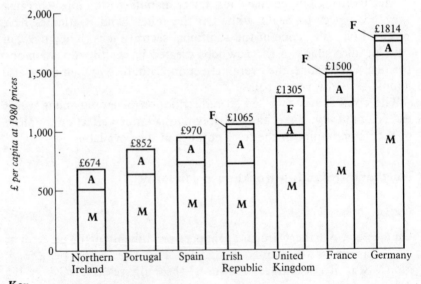

Key
A = Agriculture, forestry and fishing
F = Fuels (includes non-fuel mining
  and quarrying for France,
  Germany and the Republic of Ireland)
M = Manufacturing (includes fuels for
  Portugal and Spain)

Figure 6.5 Output of transportable goods in 1984
Source: *UK Regional Trends*, *OECD National Accounts*, CSO (Dublin)

productive capacity of Northern Ireland is now about equal to that of a Latin American country like Argentina or Mexico.

By contrast, the Irish Republic's performance is relatively good. Its output of transportable goods in 1984 was nearly 60 per cent above the level in Northern Ireland. It is only North Sea oil which gives the rest of the UK an edge over the Republic. Despite its tremendous economic problems - unemployment, a huge national debt etc. - the Republic is no longer a desperately poor country, and the performance of its manufacturing sector has in some ways been quite impressive.

Northern Ireland's economy is also very backward when it comes to private services. In recent years, one of the main exports under this heading has been the revenue earned from day trippers coming over the border from the south on shopping expeditions, to take advantage of the lower prices in the north. However, even this revenue is neither secure nor very large. Also, much of it goes on items which are imported into Northern Ireland from elsewhere, so the net revenue to the province is small. Though Northern Ireland does get some export earnings from tourism, finance, computer software, etc., this is more than cancelled out by the amount its own residents spend on similar imported services such as external travel.

The trade deficit: the gap between output and spending

For many years the province has had a large trade deficit with the rest of the world; its spending is relatively high but it produces relatively little. For example, just taking transportable goods, we find that Northern Ireland's spending currently exceeds output by an estimated 70 per cent. Or, to put it another way, Northern Ireland's output of transportable goods is only just over half of what it consumes. While the gap between Northern Ireland's spending and output is of long standing, what is new is its size, and also the province's method of paying for it.

In 1970, just after the outbreak of the conflict, Northern Ireland was still attracting a great deal of outside investment from private firms. This covered 30-40 per cent of the then trade deficit and helped pay for the importation of goods and services from abroad. In addition, money was sent back to Northern Ireland by emigrants. From these two sources the province was able to cover a substantial part of its deficit without total reliance on government aid.

Since 1970 outside investment has plummeted and money from emigrants has probably gone down. The income/expenditure gap is filled by a dramatically increased amount of aid from Britain and some funding from the EEC. These together make up the 'official subvention'. At the same time, the gap itself has increased in size, with the expansion of public consumption - health, education, police, etc. In recent years it has averaged over £1,200 million at 1980 prices. In 1985 at current prices the subvention stood at £1,700 million, which is about £1,100 per inhabitant of Northern Ireland (see figure 6.6).

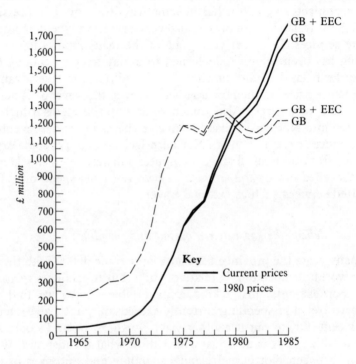

Figure 6.6   Official subvention to Northern Ireland
Source: NI Office and New Ireland Forum

It would be little exaggeration to describe Northern Ireland in the late 1980s as a workhouse economy. A large part of its population is unemployed. Those who are not are chiefly engaged in servicing or controlling each other - through the provision of health, education, retail distribution, construction, security and social services. Relatively few people within the province are engaged in the production of tradable goods and services which can be sold outside. On the other hand, Northern Ireland imports a vast amount of such items. Like a typical workhouse, it is supported by taxes levied on the external community, while providing very little in return.

If forced to live within its means, Northern Ireland would experience a catastrophic fall in living standards. It would drop well below standards in the Irish Republic, and could end up on a par with Latin American countries like Mexico or Argentina.

The Irish Republic: a comparison

Tables 6.6 and 6.7 show that both parts of Ireland are poorer than the UK, with lower levels of output and consumption per inhabitant, plus higher rates of unemployment. Thus, in some ways the two 'Irelands' are quite similar. However, in other ways they are very different indeed.

The standard of living   For the average person this is higher in Northern Ireland. Personal consumption is about 20 per cent greater on average, while more is also spent on public services such as health and education. In one major respect only is the Republic significantly better off: by 1983 infant mortality in the Republic had fallen to 9.8 per 1,000 live births, while in Northern Ireland it was 12.1.

The export sector   In a small open economy the export sector is of key importance. This covers transportable goods (food, fuel and manufactured goods, etc.) and international services (foreign tourism, international finance, etc.). If the export sector is weak, the standard of living will be low, unless the economy is fortunate enough to receive external financial aid.

Comparing the two Irelands, we find that for transportable goods as a whole, the Republic produces about 40 per cent more per inhabitant than Northern Ireland. For international services, no estimate is possible, but it is likely that output per head is considerably greater in the Republic than in Northern Ireland. Particularly significant is the gap in manufacturing output. This gap is of recent origin and is increasing rapidly. It has arisen because the Republic has become a popular location for multinational companies engaged in 'new' industries such as electronics and chemicals. The result has been a spectacular growth in modern, export-oriented manufacturing industry.

This has been accompanied by a prolonged crisis in the Republic's traditional industries - textiles, clothing, footwear, food, drink and tobacco. Here, output has stagnated and employment has fallen

Table 6.6   The two Irelands (and the UK) compared

	Reference Period	Irish Republic	Northern Ireland	United Kingdom
Population (thousands)	1984	3,535	1,579	56,488
Unemployment (% of working population)	Sept. 1986	18.3	19.9	12.1
Consumers expenditure[a] (UK £ per inhabitant)	1985	2380	3040	3710
Infant mortality (per 1000 live births)	1983	9.8	12.1	10.2
Economic Indicators (UK £ per inhabitant)[a][b]				
Gross domestic product[c]	1985	4200	4500	6220
Balance of trade in goods and services	1985	+ 100	− 1070	+ 70
Net property income from abroad (interest, profits and dividends)	1985	− 490	?[d]	+ 60
Net transfers from abroad[e] (aid, migrants' remittances etc.)	1985	+ 250	+ 1060	− 40

[a] At market prices. The figure for the Irish Republic is converted at estimated consumers expenditure purchasing power parity IR £1 = UK £0.87
[b] Converted at estimated GDP purchasing power parity IR £1 = UK £0.86
[c] The figure for Northern Ireland is an estimate
[d] Unknown, but probably fairly small
[e] The figure for Northern Ireland excludes private transfers and refers only to aid from the British government and the EEC (i.e. the official subvention)
Source: CSO (Dublin), *UK Annual Abstract*, *NI Annual Abstract*

sharply. Since most of these traditional industries are dominated by native Irish firms, the change from traditional to modern industry is bringing a shift in control from Irish to foreign capital. Thus, in terms of control, the Republic's economy is becoming increasingly like that of Northern Ireland.

However, when it comes to industrial performance there is a world

Table 6.7 The two Irelands (and the UK) compared: gross domestic product by sector in 1985

| Sector at factor cost | *UK £ per inhabitant at factor cost* | | |
	Irish Republic (estimate)	*Northern Ireland (estimate)*	*United Kingdom*
Agriculture, forestry and fishing	370	170	100
North Sea oil and gas	—	—	320
Manufacturing plus other fuels	1020	800	1480
Total transportable goods[a]	1390	970	1900
Other non-government	1700	1860	2670
General government[b]	670	1090	850
GROSS DOMESTIC PRODUCT[c]	3760	3920	5420

[a] Excludes public utilities, which are included under 'other non-government'
[b] Includes all non-market activities
[c] Note that GDP is measured here at factor cost. Hence these figures differ from those shown in Table 6.6, which are measured at market prices

Sources: Figures for NI and the UK are from *Regional Trends*; those for the Irish Republic are estimates based on information provided by the CSO (Dublin), converted to UK £ using the estimated PPP factor IR £1 = UK £0.86

of difference. Official statistics indicate that the Republic's output of manufactured goods per inhabitant is now around 25–30 per cent greater than that of Northern Ireland.

The trade balance   The Republic is an independent country which, over the long term, must finance public expenditure from its own resources. Its ability to support a large government sector depends on the strength of its economic base – its export industries. Northern Ireland, by contrast, is a dependent economy, whose public expenditure depends not on its economic base but on the willingness of Britain to foot its bills.

The different financial situation of the two Irelands is reflected in their balance of trade with the outside world. By contrast with

Northern Ireland's estimated £1,100 per inhabitant deficit, the Republic now has a modest trade surplus. In 1985 this was approximately £100 sterling per inhabitant. This trade surplus is, however, only recent. And the trouble is, it is nowhere near as much as the country needs. For the Republic has never recovered from the disastrous effects of the 1979 oil crisis.

Hugely dependent on fuel imports, the Republic experienced a dramatic deterioration in its trade balance as a result of the oil crisis. To cover the deficit, the Irish government borrowed heavily from abroad. The result is that it now owes foreigners more than IR £8,000 million (about £7,000 million sterling), equal to £2,000 sterling per inhabitant. The interest repayments on this are, of course, immense.

There is also the problem of the profits of foreign multinationals, whose operations now dominate much of the Republic's economy. To attract investment, the Republic provides very generous tax concessions. These, together with the relatively low wages, enable the multinationals to earn a higher rate of profits in the Republic than anywhere else in Europe. For example, US companies make average profits of 5.6 per cent in Europe as a whole, but 24 per cent in the Republic. The cost to the Republic of interest payments and export of profits by foreign multinationals is now equal to $1/8$ of its total production and $1/5$ of all its export earnings. This is about £500 sterling per inhabitant.

The debt trap   The Republic is thus caught in a debt trap of Third World proportions. To pay for its enormous borrowings and also to finance the outflow of profits to foreign multinationals, the country requires a very large trade surplus. After years in debt it has achieved a small surplus, but not enough to cover the cost of interest and profits owed to foreigners. Thus, like many a Third World country, it is sinking ever deeper into the red because it has to borrow to service its original debt.

Though its economy is otherwise much less healthy than the Republic's, Northern Ireland does not have this terrible debt problem, because it has an external supporter, Britain, which is willing to finance the province's trade deficit with the outside world.

An austerity programme   The Republic is now approaching its overseas borrowing limit. To bring its debt situation under control and stop the country's spending exceeding its internally generated income, the Irish government is currently operating an austerity programme.

This seeks to reduce borrowing needs by raising the level of non-corporate taxes (i.e. VAT and personal income tax) and implementing public expenditure cuts.

Overall the Irish government's main emphasis is on expenditure cuts. This is justified on the grounds that taxes are now so high it is not practical to increase them significantly any further. This view is, however, questionable. There are still many well off people in the Republic – landowners, lawyers, estate agents, etc. – whose productive contribution is minimal and who could certainly be taxed more heavily without harming the national economy. In addition, given the current rate of profit, it might also be feasible to claw back some of the lavish tax concessions foreign multinationals now enjoy. Nevertheless, whichever path is taken, it is undeniable that some kind of austerity programme is required: the Republic is too vulnerable to be able to solve its problems simply by refusing to pay its national debt.

One effect of any austerity programme may be to limit economic growth for a period. However, it is unlikely to have any serious long-term effect on growth. For, provided the armed conflict in Northern Ireland does not spread southwards, relatively low wages, an educated labour force, very generous tax concessions and geographic location should mean the Republic continues to be an attractive location for multinationals. Moreover, the government is now seeking to encourage the multinationals to locate more of their research, development and marketing facilities in Ireland in addition to basic production. If successful, this could give a real boost to the Republic's economy. Finally, greater efforts are being made to stimulate native producers, especially in industries which manufacture for the export market.

The future   The longer term prospects of the Republic's economy are uncertain. Apart from anything else, political considerations have to be taken into account. At present, the political situation is fairly stable, and the country is still seen as a good security risk by foreign companies. However, this might change, should the turmoil in Northern Ireland spread southwards in the wake of the Anglo-Irish Agreement and the decision of Sinn Féin to play a more active role in the politics of the Republic.

Should the conflict move south, multinationals already in the Republic might run down their operations while others might simply go elsewhere. Such a boycott on a large scale would be an economic disaster, because of the Republic's almost complete dependence on the goodwill of foreign multinationals. Indeed, the consequences would be much worse for the Republic than they have already been for Northern Ireland, which is cushioned by Britain.

However, all of this is a doomsday scenario. What the prospects will be if political conditions continue broadly as they are now is probably more relevant. Under these circumstances the long-term economic prospects are mixed. The Republic still faces a serious problem of very high unemployment – around 18 per cent – while its traditionally high birth rate means the labour force continues to increase. Even with moderately fast economic growth, the number of jobs available will be far below that required. One result, which can already be witnessed, will be rising emigration.

So, while long-term economic prospects in the Republic are much better than for Northern Ireland, they are by no means rosy. The Republic, like the North, will continue to suffer from high unemployment for many years to come, and many of its people will remain poor, even though the economy may enjoy quite a fast rate of economic growth over the longer term.

7 The Economic Situation of Catholics and Protestants

In this chapter we examine the economic circumstances of the two communities within Northern Ireland. After a brief consideration of comparative living standards we focus on employment and unemployment patterns. Here we find the hardest statistical evidence, and also the issues with the most far-reaching political and social consequences.

The standard of living

The Continuous Household Survey for 1983–4 provides the most recent information about living standards of Catholics and Protestants. This shows the following:

Housing

1 16 per cent Catholic and 6 per cent Protestant households had one or more bedrooms below standard.
2 16 per cent Catholics and 10 per cent Protestants considered their accommodation was too small.
3 28 per cent Catholics and 21 per cent Protestants complained of persistent problems of damp.

In other respects the average quality of housing seemed much the same in both communities. Overall, 16 per cent Catholics and 10 per cent Protestants considered their housing to be unsatisfactory. Thus, housing is on average worse among Catholics. However, a large majority of people in each community are fairly satisfied with their accommodation, though in each there is a minority whose housing is grossly inadequate.

Expenses

Table 7.1 Reported difficulty by Catholics and
Protestants in paying rent

	Always	*Sometimes or often*	*Never*
Catholics	20%	42%	37%
Protestants	14%	32%	54%

Source: Continuous Household Survey, 1983–4

There is clearly much poverty and insecurity within the working class
of each community, though it is worse amongst Catholics. The survey
tells us nothing, of course, about the middle and upper classes, who
normally own their own houses.

Employment

Religion and employment

We have seen how employment opportunities for Catholics in
Northern Ireland were restricted by discrimination, lack of education
and skills, and the location of industry. In recent years some effort has
been made to remedy some of these problems.

Catholics' education has improved. Some have acquired technical
skills through special training programmes, and the Fair Employment
Agency has been created to combat discrimination. In certain kinds of
public employment discrimination has diminished. Catholics are now
well represented up to the middle ranks in the civil service, though the
top is still Protestant-dominated (much of this for historical reasons;
i.e. because it takes time for newer entrants to secure promotion, etc.).
However, Catholics remain disadvantaged. There are still many with
inadequate skills, and they continue to suffer discrimination in both
manufacturing and private services, particularly in the Belfast area.
Also there are some types of work which few Catholics will accept: less
Catholics are in the security forces now than 15 years ago.

With regard to location of industry, there has been a gradual shift of
emphasis to create jobs in Catholic areas. Initially efforts were concentrated in Derry and other western parts of the province. This
started even before the introduction of Direct Rule: between 1967 and
1971 the Catholic dominated west of the Bann, which contains 27 per

cent of the population, received 36 per cent of the new jobs which were created with help from the Northern Ireland government. This development was partly due to an approaching scarcity of certain types of labour in the east of the province, and partly for political reasons.

In recent years attention has also focused on west Belfast, where Catholic unemployment is enormous. However, this shift has been operating against a background of industrial decline and the reluctance of outside firms to invest in Northern Ireland. LEDU's attempts to stimulate 'home grown' industry in Catholic areas have also had only limited success.

Who do which jobs? Catholics and Protestants

Protestants hold most of the top managerial, professional, scientific and technical jobs. Catholics are massively underrepresented in those positions and also in relatively well-paid areas like the security forces, and the metal and electrical trades. On the other hand, they are over-represented in such notoriously low-paid occupations as construction and personal services (table 7.2). Thus, Catholics are both more prone to unemployment than Protestants, and where they do have jobs, they are generally lower down the occupational scale. There is, however, one important exception.

They have a strong position in 'Professional and related occupations in education, welfare and health'. This is mainly due to the large number of Catholic nurses and teachers in Northern Ireland. Their overrepresentation in nursing is itself partly a reflection of both religious and sexual discrimination elsewhere in the labour market. Nursing is, quite simply, one of the few professions readily open to educated Catholic girls. The numbers in teaching are explained by the religious segregation of the schools. Children in Northern Ireland are normally taught by people from their own community: Catholics teach Catholics and Protestants teach Protestants. As Catholics generally have much larger families, proportionately more Catholic teachers are required.

Who do which jobs? Women and men

Catholic women suffer from higher unemployment than Protestants, but those in jobs are not seriously worse off. They are underrepresented in top managerial, technical and scientific jobs, but this is roughly

Table 7.2 Occupations and unemployment in Northern Ireland (% of economically active population)

Occupational order	Male		Female	
	Catholic	Non-Catholic	Catholic	Non-Catholic
Order 1 Professional and related supporting management, senior national and local government managers	1.9	3.8	0.6	1.2
Order 2 Professional and related in education, welfare and health	5.5	4.6	19.9	14.6
Order 3 Literacy, artistic and sports	0.3	0.4	0.2	0.3
Order 4 Professional and related in science, engineering, technology and similar fields	1.7	3.7	0.4	0.6
Order 5 Managerial (excluding 04: farmers etc.)	5.2	7.7	2.4	3.4
Order 6 Clerical and related	4.7	6.4	19.0	27.1
Order 7 Selling	2.5	4.0	5.2	7.8
Order 8 Security and protective services	2.3	7.2	0.3	1.1
Order 9 Catering, cleaning, hairdressing and other personal services	3.1	2.2	19.3	19.4

Order 10 Farming, fishing and related (including 04: farmers etc.)	6.6	8.0	0.3	0.6
Order 11 Materials processing, making and repairing (excluding metal and electrical)	8.2	7.7	8.7	7.7
Order 12 Processing, making, repairing and related (metal and electrical)	8.4	14.2	0.9	1.1
Order 13 Painting, repetitive assembling, product inspecting, packaging and related	1.9	2.1	1.9	2.8
Order 14 Construction, mining and related	5.6	3.6	0.0	0.0
Order 15 Transport operating, materials moving and storing and related	6.6	7.4	0.2	0.3
Orders 16, 17 Miscellaneous and not stated	5.1	4.5	3.7	2.3
TOTAL EMPLOYED	69.8	87.6	82.9	90.4
UNEMPLOYED	30.2	12.4	17.1	9.6
TOTAL ECONOMICALLY ACTIVE[a]	100.0	100.0	100.0	100.0

[a] Working population

Source: Census of Population, 1971

cancelled out by their enormous overrepresentation in the middle-range public-service jobs, nursing and teaching.

What is more striking than religious differences is the gap between the sexes. In almost every well-paid or high-status job, the order of precedence is: first, Protestant men; then Catholic men; then women. As a rule, Catholic men have more chance of obtaining a 'good' job than women of either religion. The health and education professions are partial exceptions, though even here women are on the lower rungs of the ladder – nurses and class-room teachers: not doctors, consultants or school principals. (See table 7.2.)

Unemployment

The gap between Catholics and Protestants today

It is widely believed that the economic crisis of the 1980s has hit Protestants more than Catholics and eliminated many of the old inequalities. As far as unemployment is concerned, this belief is false. Unemployment has certainly risen amongst Protestants, and for many of them the future is bleak. However, it has risen even faster amongst Catholics and the gap between the two communities is now greater than ever before.

This is shown by the Census of Population (see table 7.3). In 1971 the male unemployment rates were: Catholics 17.3 per cent and Protestants 6.6 per cent; by 1981 these figures had reached 30.2 per cent and 12.4 per cent respectively. Thus, over the decade, the unemployment rate for Catholics had increased by 12.9 percentage points and for Protestants by 5.8 points.

Exact figures are not available for more recent years. However, evidence provided by the Continuous Household Survey suggests that in 1983–4 the male unemployment rate was around 35 per cent for Catholics and 15 per cent for Protestants. This means Protestant unemployment has only just reached the level considered normal for Catholics at the height of the economic prosperity in the early 1970s. Catholic women have also been worse hit by the crisis and have a higher unemployment rate than Protestant women, though the gap is less than for men.

There are two main factors explaining why unemployment has risen faster among Catholics:

1   The low rate of Catholic emigration in recent years. For a long time Catholic numbers in Northern Ireland have only been kept

Table 7.3 Unemployment in Northern Ireland

	1971 %	1981 %	1983–4 %
Male			
Catholic	17.3	30.2	35
Non-Catholic	6.6	12.4	15
AVERAGE	10.3	19.1	24
For comparison:			
GB	5.5	11.3	14
Female			
Catholic	7.0	17.1	17
Non-Catholic	3.6	9.6	11
AVERAGE	4.7	12.6	13
For comparison:			
GB	4.7	7.4	10

Note: Unemployment is expressed as a percentage of all economically active persons, including the self-employed

Sources: Figures for 1971–81 are derived from the relevant Census of Population. NI figures for 1983–4 are derived from the Continuous Household Survey (see *PPRU Monitor*, No. 2, 1985). GB figures for 1983–4 are derived from information given in the *Employment Gazette*

down by high emigration. Under present conditions, however, emigration is no longer necessarily an option. The economic crisis is now international and there are fewer jobs available in Britain and elsewhere for would-be emigrants. So, many Catholics who would otherwise have left, have remained at home to swell the ranks of the unemployed.

2 The collapse of employment opportunities for Catholics within Northern Ireland itself. The spectacular loss of jobs in the mainly Protestant industries, such as engineering and artificial fibres, has been accompanied by massive losses of Catholic jobs in such industries as clothing and construction. However, there is a crucial

further problem for Catholics. Many of the new, non-manufacturing jobs created in recent years have been in sectors of the economy where Catholics find it difficult to obtain employment, or where, for political reasons, they are unwilling to accept it.

Security work   Of the Protestant growth sectors, by far the most important are the local security forces, which have mushroomed over the last 13 years. The combined strength of the RUC and UDR alone now approaches 20,000. If prison officers and other security and protective workers are included, the total employed in the local security services is around 30,000. Most of these are male Protestants. Approaching one in ten of all Protestant men in paid employment now works for the security forces in some capacity. Without this kind of job to fall back on, the unemployment rate amongst Protestant males would be much higher than it is at present, though still well below the rate amongst Catholics.

Table 7.4   Number of workers in NI security forces, 1985

Sector	no. of workers
RUC	12,800
UDR	6,400
Prison service	3,300
Other security and protective services	6,600[a]
Total	29,100[b]

[a] This figure refers to 1981
[b] Approximately 23,000 full time; the remainder part time
Source: *NI Annual Abstract* and authors' estimates based on NI Census of Population

The geography of unemployment   It is often said that unemployment amongst Catholics is especially high because of where they live: Catholics are concentrated west of the Bann where unemployment has always been relatively high, while Protestants are concentrated to the east where unemployment has always been lower. This is certainly true, and it does help to explain why unemployment is *on average* higher among Catholics (see table 7.5).

However, this is only part of the story. It does not explain why there is such inequality between Catholics and Protestants throughout the province. No matter where they live, Catholics have a much higher

Table 7.5   Unemployment and religion in Northern Ireland, 1981

Local government district	Percentage unemployment		Catholics as % of population (estimate)ᵃ
	Male	Female	
Strabane	32.4	18.3	60.8
Newry and Mourne	30.9	18.8	74.1
Londonderry	29.0	15.5	68.1
Cookstown	28.9	20.3	53.1
Moyle	27.4	16.3	50.7
Limavady	26.8	14.5	54.3
Magherafelt	26.1	14.6	56.5
Dungannon	25.9	18.6	53.3
Omagh	22.1	14.2	64.2
Fermanagh	21.6	14.2	54.1
Belfast	21.3	13.5	38.5
Ballymoney	21.1	10.8	29.3
Coleraine	19.7	11.5	23.5
Craigavon	19.0	13.8	41.0
Armagh	18.8	12.9	45.2
Carrickfergus	16.9	10.8	8.1
Larne	16.2	12.1	24.2
Down	15.6	10.7	59.2
Antrim	15.4	11.7	32.7
Banbridge	14.7	12.9	28.4
Ballymena	13.1	10.1	18.9
Newtownabbey	12.5	9.6	13.4
Lisburn	11.9	11.0	21.1
Ards	11.3	10.4	12.8
Castlereagh	9.1	7.1	7.7
North Down	7.7	7.7	9.0

ᵃ The original census figures for Roman Catholics have been adjusted to allow for the
fact that many people refused to state their religion when completing the census
return. The estimates shown here are taken from Compton and Power, 1986.

Sources: Census of Population, 1981; P. A. Compton and J. P. Power, 'Estimates of
the religious composition of the population of Northern Ireland' (unpublished
paper, 1986)

unemployment rate than Protestants (see table 7.6). In almost every
local government district unemployment amongst Catholics is much
higher than amongst Protestants, sometimes by a gigantic margin.

Table 7.6   Percentage unemployment, 1981

Local government district	Male		Female	
	Catholic	Non-Catholic	Catholic	Non-Catholic
Antrim	24.5	10.5	15.5	9.6
Ards	21.2	9.8	12.0	9.8
Armagh	28.8	10.2	15.9	9.5
Ballymena	22.1	11.1	14.0	9.0
Ballymoney	30.0	16.4	13.7	9.1
Banbridge	23.1	11.0	18.9	9.8
Belfast	31.4	15.6	18.3	10.6
Carrickfergus	20.5	16.5	8.9	10.6
Castlereagh	8.6	9.2	6.9	6.8
Coleraine	27.5	16.4	13.9	10.1
Cookstown	43.3	14.4	26.6	12.6
Craigavon	30.4	11.0	19.5	9.6
Down	19.7	8.9	11.6	9.0
Dungannon	36.7	12.7	24.1	11.6
Fermanagh	30.1	11.1	17.1	10.4
Larne	24.4	13.1	13.7	10.9
Limavady	36.7	14.3	16.2	10.5
Lisburn	22.1	8.8	15.8	9.6
Londonderry	35.8	14.4	17.6	10.1
Magherafelt	31.9	16.5	17.5	11.0
Moyle	31.1	21.0	16.2	15.1
Newry and Mourne	35.5	14.8	20.1	12.0
Newtownabbey	18.1	11.8	11.5	8.9
North Down	11.1	7.1	9.2	7.0
Omagh	27.2	10.9	15.6	9.4
Strabane	39.0	21.9	20.4	13.6
NORTHERN IRELAND	30.2	12.4	17.1	9.6

Source: Unpublished data from the Northern Ireland Census of Population, 1981

The greatest gulf is in Cookstown where the male unemployment rate for Catholics in 1981 was 43.3 per cent as against 14.4 per cent for Protestants. Similar differences exist in Armagh, Craigavon, Dungannon, Fermanagh, Limavady, Lisburn, Derry and Omagh. In each case the male unemployment rate for Catholics is 2½ to 3 times greater than for Protestants. Among women the gap is less dramatic, though still considerable, and throughout the province female unemployment is much higher for Catholics than Protestants.

Unemployment in Britain and Northern Ireland

It is also often said that Northern Ireland, along with Merseyside, has the highest unemployment rate of any region in the UK. Though correct, this statement is misleading, because it ignores the large differences that exist within Northern Ireland itself.

Table 7.7 Unemployment, 1981: NI compared to GB regions

	Male %	*Female* %
Northern Ireland (Catholics)	30.2	17.1
Merseyside	19.5	11.0
Northern Ireland (Average)	19.1	12.6
Central Clydeside conurbation	19.1	11.6
Tyne and Wear	18.1	9.3
West Midlands Metropolitan	16.7	9.6
Wales	14.8	9.7
Remainder of north	14.4	8.8
Greater Manchester	13.9	8.8
South Yorkshire	13.4	7.8
Northern Ireland (Non-Catholics)	**12.4**	**9.6**
West Yorkshire	12.4	7.4
Remainder of Scotland	11.6	8.4
Remainder of Yorkshire and Humberside	11.4	6.7
Britain (Average)	**11.3**	**7.4**
Remainder of north-west	11.2	7.8
Remainder of West Midlands	10.4	7.2
Greater London	10.1	6.6
East Midlands	9.7	6.5
South-west	8.9	6.6
East Anglia	8.5	5.7
Outer south-east	8.1	5.8
Outer metropolitan area (London)	6.6	4.6

Note: The figures give per cent of economically active population, ranked according to the male unemployment rate

Source: Census of Population, 1981

Although it has risen a great deal in recent years, unemployment amongst Northern Ireland Protestants is not especially high by UK standards. At the time of the 1981 Census of Population, for example, male unemployment amongst NI Protestants was 12.4 per cent, while in Britain average unemployment stood at 11.3 per cent. Moreover, there were eight British regions where male unemployment was higher than for NI Protestants, sometimes by a large margin. Indeed, in Merseyside, central Clydeside and Tyne and Wear the male unemployment rate was 1½ times the rate amongst NI Protestants (see table 7.7).

For Catholics the picture is very different. Their male unemployment rate is nearly three times the UK average, and is much higher than for any region in Britain. For example, in 1981, Northern Ireland male Catholic unemployment was 30.2 per cent, while in the worst region on the mainland, Merseyside, the figure was 19.1 per cent.

Belfast   Table 7.8 compares Belfast with some other UK cities where there has been a similar decline in manufacturing. Unemployment amongst Belfast Catholics is much higher than in any of the areas

Table 7.8   Unemployment, 1981: comparison of Belfast with some British cities

	Male %	Female %
Cities in Britain		
Hartlepool	22.1	12.0
Middlesbrough	24.0	12.1
South Tyneside	20.7	10.4
Sunderland	19.9	11.3
Liverpool	24.0	13.3
Clydebank	20.8	12.2
Glasgow	23.8	12.6
Belfast		
Catholics	31.4	18.3
Non-Catholics	15.6	10.6
Belfast Average	21.3	13.5

Source: Census of Population, 1981

shown. Amongst Protestants, however, it is considerably lower than in these areas. The contrast is greater in the case of men. In the cities shown, the male unemployment rate in 1981 ranged from 19.9 per cent to 24 per cent. In the same year, Belfast male Protestant unemployment was 15.6 per cent, while for Catholics the figure was 31.4 per cent.

Table 7.9 Male unemployment and religion in Belfast, 1981

Ward[a]	Male unemployment		Catholics as % of population (estimate)[b]
	number	%	
Whiterock	1,023	56.4	99.4
Falls	357	52.6	99.5
Grosvenor	270	50.2	92.3
New Lodge	575	45.7	94.9
Central	267	42.1	86.6
Ardoyne	614	40.8	79.3
Cromac	250	39.4	61.5
Court	314	37.6	3.0
Suffolk	887	35.3	99.3
Milltown	687	25.1	99.3
Clonard	507	34.7	97.5
Crumlin	278	34.3	60.2
St. James	651	33.4	95.5
Ballymacarrett	391	33.1	44.0
Shankill	447	27.6	0.0
Duncairn	309	27.3	27.0
University	328	26.9	61.2
Island	306	26.3	0.1
The Mount	317	25.3	1.2
Total of above	8,778	36.3	67.5
Other Wards	8,066	14.7	23.1
Belfast	16,844	21.3	36.9

[a] Named Wards are those with above 25 per cent male unemployment. These Wards contain 57 per cent of the city's Catholic population and 16 per cent of its Protestants. The Wards listed are arranged in order of decreasing male unemployment rate.

[b] See note to table 6.12. The estimates used in the present table refer to the enumerated population only; non-enumerated persons are ignored. The method of estimation used is described in Appendix 7.

Source: Census of Population, 1981

Unemployment amongst Belfast men is analysed on a ward-by-ward basis in table 7.9. Detailed information is given for wards in which the male unemployment rate was more than 25 per cent in 1981. Out of the 19 wards in this category, ten were overwhelmingly Catholic, four were mixed, and only five were predominantly Protestant.

The most interesting case is the Shankill ward, whose population is entirely Protestant. The Shankill is often cited as an area of extreme Protestant deprivation, and in 1981 its male unemployment rate was 27.6 per cent. This is an appalling figure. However, it is only half the level recorded in Catholic wards such as Whiterock, Falls and Grosvenor. It is also less than the average rate of unemployment amongst Catholic males in Northern Ireland as a whole. Thus, as far as male unemployment is concerned, the *average* Catholic rate is even worse than that for the most deprived Protestants of the Shankill.

Ethnic minority unemployment in Britain   Table 7.10 compares Northern Ireland Catholics with disadvantaged ethnic minorities in Britain. In 1983–4 unemployment amongst Northern Ireland male Catholics was 35 per cent, compared to 28 per cent for West Indian

Table 7.10   Unemployment in 1983/4: comparison with ethnic minorities

	Males %	Females %
Northern Ireland: by religion, 1983/4		
Catholic	35	17
Non-Catholic	15	11
Average NI	24	13
Britain: by ethnic origin, 1983		
White	11.6	10.1
West Indian or Guyanese	27.6	18.0
Indian/Pakistani/Bangladeshi	21.5	21.6
Other	16.4	14.6
Average GB	12.1	10.4

Note: Figures give per cent of economically active population

Sources: NI: Continuous Household Survey (see *PPRU Monitor*, No. 2, 1985); GB: Social Trends, 1985 edition

men and 22 per cent for men from the Indian subcontinent. The Northern Ireland male Protestant unemployment rate of 15 per cent was less than for any ethnic minority group in Britain. For women the picture is more complex, though even here it is clear that Northern Ireland Catholics are as badly off as most ethnic minorities in Britain.

Summary

Our survey of living standards and of employment and unemployment patterns in Northern Ireland can be summarized as follows:

1 While poverty and insecurity is widespread among the working class of each community, the situation of Catholics is considerably worse.
2 Unemployment amongst Catholics in Northern Ireland has risen faster and is several times greater than amongst Protestants. This inequality can be clearly seen right across the province – it is not confined to any particular district.
3 Unemployment amongst Northern Ireland Catholics is several times greater than the average in Britain. It is well above the level observed in the worst-hit regions in mainland Britain.
4 Male unemployment amongst Catholics in Northern Ireland is considerably higher than amongst any disadvantaged ethnic minority in mainland Britain.
5 Catholics who do have jobs are crowded into low-paid, insecure forms of employment. Most of the better paid jobs in the province are held by Protestants. This inequality is most striking amongst men. Amongst women the situation is more complex and there is no clear pattern of religious inferiority. Catholic women are under-represented in some well paid occupations. However, this is compensated for by their overrepresentation in middle-range public-sector jobs such as nursing and teaching.
6 Unemployment amongst Northern Ireland Protestants is only slightly greater than the average in Britain. It has risen in line with this average over the last 15 years. It is well below the levels observed in the depressed areas of Scotland, Wales and the North of England.
7 Unemployment amongst Northern Ireland Protestants, especially men, has been kept artificially low during the crisis by the provision of thousands of jobs in the RUC, UDR and other security-related occupations.

8   What Future for the Economy?

We consider below the key factors which will influence the economic future of Northern Ireland.

External aid

Central to Northern Ireland's future will be the maintenance of a substantial amount of external aid for a considerable time to come. We have seen how the standard of living would drop should British financial support diminish or cease. Were aid to fall drastically or end abruptly, the economic and social consequences would be severe. The standard of living would go down sharply. Many thousands would be thrown out of work. Social welfare benefits would be heavily cut or abolished altogether, and large numbers of people would be forced to leave the province. Managerial and skilled workers able to get jobs abroad would be among the first to emigrate, and the economy would decline still further.

However, while Northern Ireland remains within the UK, aid on a large scale is effectively guaranteed. For as a part of the UK, Northern Ireland, just like Merseyside, Wales or other depressed areas, is automatically *entitled* to British government support. Of course, outside the UK such automatic entitlement would cease. This means that if Northern Ireland were to depart from the UK, any further aid arrangements would have to be specifically negotiated. This point is well understood throughout both communities in the province, and is a powerful deterrent to anyone contemplating political options which could put the continued receipt of aid at risk.

Peace

The second major factor which will shape Northern Ireland's economic future is the degree of continuing conflict and instability. The present conflict has done enormous damage to the industrial base of Northern Ireland. It is one of the greatest obstacles to a sustained economic recovery. To establish a stable peace would not, in itself, guarantee economic recovery, but it would be a major step in that direction.

Northern Ireland is, in fact, quite an attractive location for multinational firms. It has an educated professional class and a large pool of skilled workers. Wages are relatively low and land is fairly cheap. It covers a small territory and its communications are reasonably good. All of these are important economic advantages. In addition, the province has beautiful and accessible countryside, good leisure facilities and a very hospitable population, which makes it a pleasant place for incoming staff to live. There is the disadvantage of being located on the fringe of Europe, but in this it is no different from the Republic, which continues to attract substantial foreign investment.

With a stable peace, Northern Ireland would start to draw in a significant amount of outside investment. This in turn would stimulate home-grown firms by providing a demand for locally produced goods and services. Peace would also stimulate local production by generating an atmosphere of optimism and hope. This would mean that many creative and skilled people who under present circumstances want to leave the province would remain. It would also give a big boost to the tourist industry.

However, peace might have some negative economic effects as well. Many types of expenditure in Northern Ireland are related to the conflict. The British government spends approximately £600 million a year on security, much of which goes to the local RUC and UDR. If the conflict ended, these forces would be either severely reduced or transferred out of the province. Moreover, many of the mainland troops now stationed in Northern Ireland would be brought home. This would all mean some reduction in income and employment for Northern Ireland.

Protestants, who make up nearly the entire membership of the local security forces and the bulk of those who service these forces, would take the brunt of the losses. (This would not be the first time. In 1926, following the defeat of the IRA, the all-Protestant A and C sections of the Special Constabulary were disbanded within the space of a few months.) On the other hand, Protestants would gain some of the new civilian jobs created by the economic recovery following the establishment of peace. For Catholics the situation would be more straightforward. The number of Catholics currently employed in the police and other security services is relatively small. In the event of peace, this number would be likely to increase substantially. Moreover, Catholics would also gain some of the new civilian jobs arising from economic recovery.

Thus, in the short term, Catholics would benefit unambiguously from peace, while for Protestants it would, at first, be a mixed blessing. Over the long term, gains would far outweigh the losses for both communities.

These remarks apply to a situation where peace was achieved with Northern Ireland remaining within the UK. *However, the general principles would remain the same under a different framework such as an independent Northern Ireland or a United Ireland. Regardless of constitutional arrangements, peace would greatly help economic recovery, though in the short term some people would lose.*

Is peace essential?

Peace is clearly important, but is economic recovery conceivable without it? Here we investigate whether there are any measures which could generate economic recovery even under present conditions of conflict. We also consider whether there are economic policies which, in themselves, might end the conflict and establish peace.

It is not difficult to identify some theoretical possibilities. But we then have to ask two questions: are they politically feasible; and, assuming they are, how effective would they be at promoting growth in Northern Ireland under present conflict conditions? Three major policy approaches need to be examined here: the direction of investment; increasing government financial aid; expanding the British economy.

Direction of investment   If Britain were a centrally planned socialist economy it could promote economic recovery in Northern Ireland simply by directing investment into the province. State enterprises would have to obey, no matter how unhappy their managements were about operating in such a conflict situation. However, Britain is a capitalist country where the state has only limited powers over private industry, especially over the multinational firms which now dominate the UK economy. Under these conditions, compulsory direction of investment into Northern Ireland is impractical.

Increasing government financial aid Another possibility would be to increase the incentives for new investment and subsidies for existing firms in Northern Ireland. However, there are some serious difficulties with this approach.

To begin with, the investment incentives and subsidies available for Northern Ireland are already very generous. Improvements would probably not make that much difference. Furthermore, unduly generous financial support has drawbacks: it removes the stimulus of competition; discourages innovation; and encourages incompetence and complacency – all of which may hinder the long-term capacity of the economy to recover. In any event, further incentives might simply attract more of the 'cowboy' operations like that of De Lorean, which are so desperate for funds they will go anywhere. Such firms would, at best, make a marginal contribution to Northern Ireland's long-term recovery.

There is also a major political obstacle to raising Northern Ireland's subsidy – the rivalry between the various regions of the UK. In 1986 the government decided to award Harland and Wolff in Belfast the contract to build an Auxiliary Oil Replenishment (AOR) vessel for the Royal Navy. Swan Hunter on Tyneside, which failed to get the order, was forced to lay off nearly a thousand workers. Tynesiders were naturally very angry at what they saw as a political choice. They are not alone. Other depressed regions are also already resentful at the preferential treatment given to Northern Ireland industry.

Any attempt by the British government to increase the degree of preference for Northern Ireland significantly would run into strong political opposition at home. This would be true even under a Labour government. Indeed a Labour government which sought to increase preferential treatment for Northern Ireland would face even more severe political problems than the Tories. The depressed regions of mainland Britain are Labour's heartlands and they would strongly oppose greater help for Northern Ireland which was provided at their expense.

Expanding the British economy Northern Ireland would certainly benefit from measures taken to stimulate the UK economy generally. Faster British growth would increase potential demand for the province's exports, 80 per cent of which come here already. However, the weakness of Northern Ireland's economy would limit its ability to profit from such demand. This can be seen from the experience of the last few years, when output in Northern Ireland has stagnated despite sustained growth in mainland Britain.

The 'real issues' approach

These three approaches therefore are incapable of achieving the desired results. Compulsory direction of investment into Northern Ireland is impractical. There are both political and economic limits to the effectiveness of government aid as a stimulus to private investment in the province. And, while somewhat faster economic growth in mainland Britain may be feasible, such growth would only have a minor impact on the economy of Northern Ireland under present conditions of conflict.

Nevertheless, many in the Northern Irish and the British labour movements including the British Labour Party, hold strongly to the belief that economic recovery is the key to peace in Northern Ireland. The roots of the conflict, they claim, are to be found in poverty and unemployment. These are the 'real issues' which concern people in Northern Ireland from whichever community they come. To end the conflict these problems must be tackled directly. This means adopting vigorous measures to revive the local economy and generate investment and jobs. Such measures would, it is said, reduce intercommunal conflict, undermine support for the paramilitaries, and open the way to a durable peace.

We have already argued that this approach would not have the economic results which are sought. But it also suffers from two other limitations.

First, even if major economic improvements were a practical possibility, they might have the reverse effect of that intended. Since partition, discrimination has helped to preserve the Protestant majority in Northern Ireland by keeping the number of Catholics artificially low. Denied housing and jobs, Catholics have been forced to emigrate on a much larger scale than Protestants. This has partially offset Catholics' higher birth rate. To reduce the level of Catholic alienation – and indeed to ensure adequate benefit to the most disadvantaged section of Northern Ireland's population – would require a sustained economic recovery and the allocation to Catholics of a disproportionate number of the resulting jobs. Of itself, this would cause considerable discontent within the Protestant community. In addition, providing Catholics with jobs would mean that fewer of them would emigrate. With their continuing higher birth rate, Catholics' share of the population would increase quite rapidly. While this might not overturn the Protestant majority, it would certainly threaten it (see Appendix 7). As the proportion of Catholics in the population increased, the political situation might become even more unstable, and the result could well be greater strife rather than less.

Second, this approach ignores the impact of 20 years of conflict on the Catholic community. Had the British government, at the start of the present troubles, targeted immediate and substantial economic reform towards Catholics, while firmly resisting any consequent Unionist hostility, it may be that the conflict would never have developed in the way it has. But this is something we will never know, and, in any event, is water under the bridge. What we do know is that the questions of political control and national identity have been high on the political agenda of Catholics for two decades. This is too long for them simply to go away. They now have a life of their own. Too many people have been gaoled and have died, and Sinn Féin and the IRA have built up too much popular Catholic support for the Catholic community as a whole to be prepared to put aside constitutional concerns in return for economic benefits alone.

In this, of course, the Catholics of Northern Ireland are just like people in Britain. As well as being greatly concerned about their economic circumstances, they also care deeply about who has political control over the place where they live and to which nation-state they belong. Though the 'real issues' approach is presented as an even-handed way of solving Northern Ireland's problems, in fact it has a built-in bias. Involving as it does the indefinite maintenance of British rule, its appeal for Protestants is evident. Meanwhile it simply ignores Nationalist aspirations and desires; as such it is completely unacceptable to many in the Catholic community.

Clearly it is possible under present conditions to do *something* for Northern Ireland. However, both political and economic concerns impose severe constraints on how much can be achieved. To be fully effective, any measures intended to stimulate the province's economy must be accompanied by political initiatives to end the conflict. Moreover, even in the unlikely event that significant economic advance could be made in Northern Ireland while the conflict continues, this would not eliminate the need to tackle the underlying political problems.

9 The Way Forward

The previous chapters demonstrated the immense depth of Northern Ireland's economic problems. They underlined the extent to which achieving a sustained economic recovery is dependent on the conflict ceasing. We now examine various ways of trying to end the conflict and secure peace within the province.

Since the present 'troubles' began, there have been innumerable proposals for bringing them to an end. All the permutations come down to four main recurring categories. These are:

1 *Variations on the present theme.* The solution to Northern Ireland's problems which is most commonly proposed is continued *Direct Rule* from Westminster, allied to a programme aimed at moving back to *devolved government.* The most recent and, to date, by far the most sophisticated version of this approach, is the *Anglo-Irish Agreement* of 1985.

2 *Cutting loose. Independence* for Northern Ireland is an idea that surfaces from time to time from the Unionist side of the divide. It comes up in one of two forms: either that independence should be *negotiated* and agreed with the British government; or that there should be a *unilateral declaration* of independence.

3 *Using geography to solve the problem.* A solution more favoured by people outside than inside the province is shifting the border to produce a *repartition* of Ireland, with a smaller and overwhelmingly Protestant North.

4 *Unity.* Nationalists seek the removal of the border altogether to produce a *united Ireland.*

The Anglo-Irish Agreement

This is the latest attempt by Britain to find a way of ending the conflict in Northern Ireland by constitutional means. It is ambitious and complex and demands close scrutiny.

The contents

The agreement has six main planks. These are:

1 The right of the majority of the people of Northern Ireland to determine the future constitutional status of the province
The agreement starts out by underpinning the status quo, reaffirming the security of Northern Ireland's position within the United Kingdom. At the same time it provides that if a majority of the people in the province wish to see a united Ireland established, then the British and Irish governments will legislate for this.

Article 1 of the agreement states:

The two governments

(a) affirm that any change in the status of Northern Ireland would only come about with the consent of a majority of the people of Northern Ireland
(b) recognise that the present wish of a majority of the people of Northern Ireland is for no change in the status of Northern Ireland
(c) declare that if in the future a majority of the people of Northern Ireland clearly wish for and formally consent to the establishment of a united Ireland they will introduce and support in their respective Parliaments legislation to give effect to that wish

2 A permanent intergovernmental conference
The agreement provides for regular meetings at both civil servant and ministerial level to consider relations between the two parts of Ireland. These meetings are to deal with:

(a) Political matters.
(b) Security.
(c) Legal issues, including the administration of justice.
(d) Promotion of cross-border co-operation.

3 A consultative role for the Irish government in the administration of Northern Ireland
While ultimate decision-making power over Northern Ireland's affairs

remains with the British government, the Irish government has the right to be consulted and to put forward its views on any matters.

4 Support for attempts to establish a devolved (i.e. Northern Ireland-based) government acceptable to both Catholics and Protestants

If such attempts are successful, it is intended that a new Northern Ireland government take over some of the powers of the British government. Northern Catholics will then have their own elected representatives in the devolved government, so that the advisory role of the Southern government will gradually diminish.

5 Examination of a range of human rights reforms

Among areas which the agreement specifically identifies are:

(a) Measures to foster cultural heritage.
(b) Changes in electoral arrangements.
(c) Use of flags and emblems.
(d) Avoidance of economic and social discrimination.
(e) A Bill of Rights.

The agreement also recognizes the hostility many Catholics feel towards the security forces, when it accepts the need for special measures to

improve relations between the security forces and the community, with the object in particular of making the security forces more readily accepted by the nationalist community.

In addition the agreement envisages possible changes in the administration of justice, such as 'mixed' courts – i.e. courts made up of judges from Northern Ireland and the Republic – which could try certain types of offence, both north and south of the border.

6 The strengthening of security

The agreement provides for closer co-operation between the British and Irish security forces, especially the police. It also implies that the possibility of the Republic relaxing its extradition laws will be considered (so that Republican suspects who take refuge in the South can more easily be returned to the North for trial). It says that the intergovernmental conference

shall also be concerned with policy aspects of extradition and extra territorial jurisdiction as between North and South.

To help monitor the operation of the agreement and organize inter-governmental relations, a small group of civil servants from the Republic is now permanently based in Maryfield, near Belfast.

Two aspects of the agreement are particularly important:

1 Concession by Britain of consultation rights to the Republic.
2 Acceptance by the Republic of the 'unity by consent' principle.

Traditionally the British government has denied the Republic any right to be consulted about Northern Ireland. It has said that the province is no different from any other part of the United Kingdom and, as such, no foreign power should interfere in its affairs. Now, under the Anglo-Irish Agreement, Britain has conceded to the government of the Irish Republic the *right* to express its opinion about the way Northern Ireland's affairs are managed.

For its part the Irish government has, effectively, abandoned its claim that Northern Ireland belongs to the Republic. While not turning its back on its aim of eventual Irish unity, the Republic's government has signed a treaty accepting that unity will only happen with majority consent in the North.

Both governments were prepared to make similar concessions under the Sunningdale experiment over a decade ago. However, the Sunningdale initiative never had the opportunity to be of any lasting importance or impact: it was destroyed by Loyalist direct action almost as soon as it had begun, with the British government of the time making very little effort to save it. This time, things have been different. Though many within Northern Ireland have been fiercely opposed to the agreement, at no stage has its survival ever been under serious threat.

Militant Republicans have strongly attacked the agreement for strengthening the partition of Ireland and making unity even harder to achieve. For their part and, of course, for very different reasons, Northern Unionists generally have been greatly angered. They have described the agreement as 'selling their birthright', and have held a number of demonstrations to protest against it. What is important, however, is that while some of these demonstrations have been violent, Protestant hostility – even amongst the most militant Loyalists – has, for the most part, taken the form of words rather than deeds. *Practical* Unionist opposition to the agreement has been very limited. At the same time, Britain has shown itself far less willing to be bullied into abandoning its political course than it was at the time of Sunningdale.

Meanwhile, in the Republic there has been a change of government since the agreement was signed. The Fine Gael/Labour coalition has been replaced by Republican Fianna Fáil. Yet significantly, though initially grudging in its acceptance, the new Fianna Fáil government led by Charles Haughey has observed the agreement almost to the letter.

Implementation and achievement

Predictably, the Social Democratic and Labour Party (SDLP), which was one of the main architects of the agreement, is its most enthusiastic supporter. John Hume, SDLP MP, has listed 11 areas where the agreement has produced 'advance'. The most important of these are:

1   A Department of Economic Development (DED) policy document on tackling job discrimination.
2   A commitment to pull down the Divis and Rossville flats.
3   A prospect of a more independent RUC complaints procedure.
4   New public order legislation to deal with marches and flags and emblems.
5   Collapse of the supergrass system.
6   A suggestion for an All-Ireland Declaration of Rights.

This is a fairly impressive list. However, on closer examination it turns out to be less so. Some of the items on it are of minor significance only, while others have nothing to do with the agreement at all – they were in the reform pipeline anyway. To take them in order.

First, the DED proposals had been initiated in mid-1985, as a direct result of pressure from the United States. Second, the decision to demolish the crumbling and hated Divis flats is the result of years of struggle by the tenants themselves, who had cross-party support in Belfast, and such allies as NUPE, the Town and Country Planning Association in London and the British Labour Party's then official spokesperson on Northern Ireland, Peter Archer. Third, the proposed police complaints procedure reform is simply an extension of the change which is taking place in mainland Britain, and which predated the agreement anyway. Fourth, the new public order legislation is also partly an extension of British changes, though it does have some special Northern Ireland features, e.g. the repeal of the Flags and Emblems Act. (This Act, passed in 1954, gave the RUC the power to take down any flag or emblem, whether displayed on public or private property, if they thought its display might lead to a breach of the peace. In practice, the Act has almost always been used to justify removal of the Irish tricolour. However, since the 1960s it has rarely been employed. Nowadays, if the police wish to prevent the flying of the Irish tricolour, they use ordinary British public order law to prevent 'an anticipated breach of the peace'.) Fifth, the supergrass system has collapsed because it has been generally discredited. By the end of 1983 the supply of informers had largely dried up anyway, and the judges have become increasingly sceptical of the evidence these informers have provided. Sixth, the All-Ireland Declaration of Rights is just that – a declaration only, without any legal force.

Even though it is specifically mentioned in the agreement, there is one *really* important change which has so far been firmly ruled out of consideration by Britain. This is replacement of the single judge Diplock courts by mixed courts with judges from the Republic as well as Northern Ireland. Powerful opposition within the Tory government is simply refusing to countenance a reform which would give the Republic not just an advisory position, but a judicial role and status within Northern Ireland.

The political significance of the agreement

A central purpose of the agreement was to strengthen the position of the constitutional Nationalists, the SDLP, at the expense of Sinn Féin and the IRA. To do this, the British government had to make a more vigorous show of tackling the problem of Protestant privilege, and improving the relative position of Catholics.

Challenging Protestant privilege

Even before the agreement was signed, there were growing indications that the Tory government was prepared to toughen its approach towards undermining Protestant privilege in Northern Ireland. Apart from the government's awareness that continued discrimination against Catholics fuels Catholic support for Sinn Féin and the IRA, there was another reason for this shift in official policy. The government has been under constant pressure from the United States, with its large and powerful Irish lobby, to take more effective action to reduce discrimination.

These pressures make it more likely that the process of tackling discrimination will be stepped up; though to assume this will definitely happen is premature: there is still considerable resistance, both from

Unionists and their sympathizers in the British establishment, to the introduction of more effective measures in this direction. Even if such measures are taken, they will most certainly be against the background of mass unemployment. At best, therefore, they will be extremely slow to produce noticeable practical benefits for Catholics.

Symbolic change

Catholics have, as yet, seen little concrete from the agreement. Nevertheless, it has had a certain symbolic impact. The very process of making the treaty has itself done a considerable amount for Catholics' sense of identity and self-respect. As we have seen, the history of Northern Ireland has been one of exclusion: treating the Catholics as the enemy within. Now, for the first time, the tables have been turned. The moderate Nationalist party, the SDLP, was not only kept fully informed of all developments during negotiations over the agreement, its opinions were clearly sought and reflected in the final document. By contrast, the Unionist parties were ignored and left completely in the dark.

Unionist MP Harold McCusker's speech to the House of Commons encapsulates the Protestant community's sense of bewilderment and betrayal:

The agreement deals with my most cherished ideals and aspirations. On three occasions in the week prior to the signing of the agreement . . . it was denied to me that an agreement existed, or had even been reached.

I went to Hillsborough on the Friday morning . . . I stood outside Hillsborough, not waving a Union flag – I doubt whether I will ever wave one again – not singing hymns, saying prayers or protesting, but like a dog and asked the Government to put in my hand the document that sold my birthright. They told me that they would give it to me as soon as possible. Having never consulted me, never sought my opinion or asked my advice, they told the rest of the world what was in store for me.

I stood in the cold outside the gates of Hillsborough castle and waited for them to come out and give me the agreement second hand . . . I had been told three hours before that it would be brought out to me. At 2.45 p.m., 15 minutes after the press conference had begun, I asked a policeman whether he would bring me the declaration that betrayed everything that I had ever stood for. A senior police officer went into Hillsborough castle, asked for the document and brought it out to me.

I felt desolate because as I stood in the cold outside Hillsborough castle, everything that I held dear turned to ashes in my mouth.

Protestant street protest against the agreement has led to numerous clashes with the RUC. While it is unlikely that the Catholic community as a whole has become significantly more 'pro' the police than it was, doubtless many Catholics will have been pleased to see the RUC deal more firmly with Protestant violence and disorder than it has done before.

For the Protestant community, the symbolic importance of the agreement has probably been more profound. It spells out officially that Northern Ireland is not, 'like Finchley', just another part of the UK. For there is no way in which a British government would accept the right of a foreign power to express its views on internal political affairs in Finchley. So the agreement is a way of saying both to Protestants and to people in Britain that Northern Ireland is really a foreign country. Indeed, Protestants are now caught in a cleft stick. The more furiously and violently they oppose the agreement, the more people in Britain see them as foreigners, and ungrateful ones at that.

The future

There is considerable sophistication in the Anglo-Irish Agreement and it has posed both communities with a bigger challenge than any other constitutional initiative that has been tried to date. Nevertheless, the agreement still does not provide the basis for a lasting peace in Northern Ireland. There are three reasons why it does not. To begin with, the economic logic of the agreement is circular. Secondly, the agreement does little to narrow the political gulf between the Province's two communities. Lastly, it will not significantly weaken the IRA.

The circular problem It is clear that the agreement's so-far overwhelmingly symbolic achievements will not satisfy the Catholic community. For it to succeed in bringing peace, the agreement must win Catholics' long term commitment, and to do this it must deliver to them substantial material benefits. Most important of these benefits would be the creation of considerably more and better jobs for Catholics within the province. Theoretically this could be done by the wholesale dismissal of Protestants and their replacement by Catholics. However, such a step would be politically unthinkable. The only other way to produce a major advance in the lot of Catholics would be greatly to increase the *total* number of jobs available. This in turn would require a vast improvement to Northern Ireland's economy. But as we have argued in the chapters on the economy, such an improvement cannot be achieved as long as the present conflict continues.

Thus in order to succeed, i.e. to bring peace, the agreement pre-supposes a dramatic improvement in the economy of Northern Ireland. But an improvement on this scale is itself only feasible *after* the conflict has been brought to an end and a stable peace has been established.

The political gulf   The only really far-reaching and serious attempt previously made to reform the constitution of Northern Ireland – the 1974 power sharing initiative – ended in abject failure after only five months. The 1974 experiment commenced with the establishment of a purely internal body, a power sharing Executive made up entirely of local Catholic and Protestant politicians. This step was to be followed up by the formation of an all-Ireland consultative body – the Council of Ireland – with members drawn from North and South. However, the power-sharing Executive collapsed before the all-Ireland dimension had even got off the drawing board.

Under the present Anglo-Irish Agreement the order of events has been reversed. This time priority has been given to the all-Ireland aspect, with the cross border Intergovernmental Conference being established in advance of any potential internal power-sharing arrangement.

This approach avoids the major weakness to which the 1974 Executive so rapidly succumbed. As a Northern Ireland based institution, with a membership of local politicians who needed local support to stay in office, the 1974 Executive was extremely vulnerable to internal pressure. It could only survive with goodwill from both communities, and so fell apart when faced with widespread Protestant hostility. The new Anglo-Irish Agreement avoids this pitfall. Its survival depends on the cooperation of two externally based governments and does not require local support at all. This means it can continue indefinitely no matter what people 'on the ground' in Northern Ireland think of it.

Such a strategy presents Protestants in particular with a serious problem. The agreement's survival does not depend on their support, and it will continue to operate even if they oppose it. At the same time, the main effect of any serious Protestant show of force against the agreement is to put a question mark over Britain's willingness to remain in Northern Ireland. Thus, the external character of the Anglo-Irish Agreement makes it more secure than the 1974 initiative was. However, this very strength is simultaneously its fundamental weakness.

The current arrangement, whereby Britain rules the North directly but in consultation with the Republic, is intended to be temporary. Supposedly, this arrangement will be supplemented, and eventually replaced, by a local institution, in which the SDLP as the party of constitutional nationalism will share power with the various Unionist parties. It must be recognized that such an institution would have some attractions for constitutional politicians from both communities in the North. It would give them status, incomes and, not least, something to do. Whereas the paramilitaries, with their mixture of community politics and violence, often find themselves overstretched in the present situation, the constitutional political parties have a crisis of identity and purpose. Establishing some form of local administration would help to resolve this crisis.

For the SDLP the power sharing aspect of any future administration presents no problem. Indeed, power sharing has long had their active support and advocacy. Unionists, by contrast, are not happy with the idea. However, faced with the *fait accompli* of the Anglo-Irish Agreement, some Unionists are now contemplating power sharing as the price for achieving devolved government. So it is conceivable, though by no means certain, that a power sharing administration of some kind will be set up one day.

However, if such an administration were to be set up, it would probably turn out to have more form than substance. Its operation would be permanently overshadowed by the presence of the Southern government, which would still have the right to be consulted about the North's affairs. Though the Anglo-Irish Agreement envisages the phasing out of the Southern government's involvement, it is clear that this will never happen. Having once got its foot in the door, the Southern government will never willingly remove it. Moreover, the southern presence is an achievement which the SDLP simply cannot surrender: it is the only thing which gives the SDLP real status, and any potential for matching the numerical superiority of the Unionists. Yet at the same time, as long as they have this external support to fall back on, the SDLP's commitment to power sharing will always be suspect. What the SDLP cannot achieve in direct negotiations with the Unionists, they will, naturally enough, seek to secure indirectly through the Irish Government. For their part, faced with this asymmetry, the Unionist parties do not, and cannot, be expected to trust the SDLP. Any future power sharing administration would thus be inherently unstable.

We see, therefore, that the very feature of the Anglo-Irish Agreement which cushions it against local opposition also helps to perpetuate intercommunal divisions. The fact that Northern Catholics can appeal to the Southern government to represent their interests under the agreement, seriously reduces their incentive to engage in genuine dialogue with Northern Protestants. Under these conditions, any future power sharing administration might have quite an impressive appearance, but it would not be the arena in which the crucial decision making would be done. Thus, in the end, the Anglo-Irish Agreement may succeed in having quite the reverse effect from that which was intended. By rendering key political decision making even more remote from local people, instead of breaking down the divisions between the two communities, it could actually cement them.

The IRA   The existence of the Anglo-Irish Agreement has clearly achieved some reduction in political support for Sinn Féin and the Irish Republican Army (IRA). This is not surprising, as many Catholics do see the agreement as representing a considerable – if symbolic – slap in the face for the Protestant community. Nevertheless, it is also quite unrealistic to believe final victory over the IRA is remotely on the horizon.

For many years now the IRA's political wing, Sinn Féin, has had strong support among working class Catholics in the ghetto areas of Northern Ireland. In all the elections which have taken place in the last decade, Sinn Fein has never secured less than 30 per cent of the Northern Catholic vote and has commanded as much as 40 per cent (see Appendix 3). In the 1987 General Election, Sinn Féin still received about a third of the Catholic vote, and Gerry Adams, the party's MP for West Belfast, was returned with a clear majority. At the same time, the IRA has successfully stepped up its military campaign once again, so underlining its continuing power to destabilize Northern Ireland politically and economically.

Even were Sinn Féin's present voting levels to fall off substantially, it would be very hard for Britain to capitalize on this through a major offensive against the IRA. For to stand any real chance of successfully breaking the IRA by military means, Britain would have to engage in a ferocious clampdown on the Catholic population.

In previous colonial wars, in Asia and Africa, Britain has employed very severe repressive tactics – executing prisoners, killing suspects without trial, destroying villages which have sheltered guerrilla fighters, resettling dissident sections of the population, etc. Britain has certainly employed repressive methods in Northern Ireland, including illegal killings. However, they have clearly not been anything like so severe as in these more distant conflicts. This is because the conflict in Ireland is too close to home. Unrestrained use of such ruthless tactics against English speaking Europeans, under the full glare of publicity, would generate too much opposition. It might even prove counter-productive and start to create sympathy for the nationalist cause in Britain and other countries. And since it would inevitably demand a major attack on the Catholic population, any really serious offensive against the IRA would, within Northern Ireland itself, be far more likely to boost Catholic support for Sinn Féin and its military wing than to undermine it.

All of these factors would be serious disincentives to a major British assault on the IRA, whether the Anglo-Irish Agreement existed or not. However, they pose particular problems under present conditions. The Anglo-Irish Agreement cannot succeed without first drastically weakening the IRA, but the power-sharing aspirations of this agreement make it even more difficult for the government to implement the kind of methods which would be needed to marginalize the organization.

Thus the British government is in a double bind. It cannot deliver a death blow to the IRA that would enable the Anglo-Irish Agreement to succeed. But it must, at least, keep the IRA at bay. To do this, it must maintain extensive security operations and suspend civil liberties which are regarded as fundamental in Britain. Yet these government actions themselves perpetuate a situation in which the agreement's objectives cannot be achieved.

The continued strength of the IRA is likely to have a further significant effect. Though at some point in the future the Catholic SDLP may enter a power-sharing devolved government, this would cause the SDLP new difficulties. For were it to join such a government, it would then share responsibility for state policies designed to crush the IRA. And as history shows, such policies are inevitably very repressive. In the end they would be likely to undermine support for the SDLP and lead to a shift in Catholic political sympathy back to the IRA. Such a development would create immense internal strains within the SDLP, and could well force it to withdraw from power sharing.

Over the medium term, therefore, the most likely outcome of the Anglo-Irish Agreement would appear to be threefold: significant Catholic alienation; anger, confusion and divisions within the Protestant community; and rising British impatience with Northern Ireland as a whole.

Cutting loose

Negotiated independence

The idea of a negotiated independence was promoted most significantly by the Protestant paramilitary Ulster Defence Association in
a pamphlet called 'Beyond the Religious Divide'.

The pamphlet envisaged Catholics and Protestants sinking their
differences and agreeing to form an independent state. The new Ulster
would be non-sectarian, with constitutional protection for the rights of
the Catholic minority. It would, of course, face immense economic
problems. The pamphlet anticipated a long transition period, during
which the industrial base would be rebuilt so that the province would
eventually become strong enough to support itself. Over this period
Britain would continue to provide economic assistance.

The idea has obvious economic advantages. For Britain, in the long
term at least, it would lead to the end of a heavy financial burden. For
Northern Ireland it would mean no more conflict, and the creation of
political conditions for economic recovery. In addition, independence
would bring greater wage and salary flexibility – as now exists in the
Republic. Wages would be set more in line with what the local economy could afford, rather than by reference to Britain, a far wealthier
country. This would make Northern Ireland more competitive,
though it would also mean a generally lower standard of living within
the province.

The flaw is that, politically, the idea is a non-starter. Negotiated
independence as proposed by the UDA would only succeed if it could
secure the overwhelming support of the Catholic minority. Quite
bluntly, such support would just not be forthcoming – no matter how
genuinely it were sought. After 50 years of Protestant-dominated
government, Catholics would not voluntarily accept a constitutional
arrangement which would leave them permanently reliant on the
goodwill of the Protestant majority. Furthermore, without Catholic
agreement, it is not possible to imagine Britain consenting to a negotiated independence. As the proposal depends on Britain continuing
to provide financial aid during the long transition period, British
refusal of consent would be an insurmountable obstacle.

A unilateral declaration of independence (UDI)

In the early days of the Anglo-Irish Agreement, some Protestants who
were opposed to the agreement advocated withdrawal of Northern

Ireland from the United Kingdom and the establishment of an independent state. In other words, taking a leaf out of the book of the Southern Rhodesians and going for a modern day UDI. However, genuine enthusiasm for this idea did not last long, which when we examine it in any depth turns out not to be at all surprising.

It is hard to see how such an enterprise would be anything other than doomed from the outset. The British government has both the military power to block it immediately and the economic strength to render an independent state completely unworkable. Quite simply, if Britain so chose, it could defeat a Northern Ireland UDI by a trade embargo and other economic sanctions.

It is true that Britain was not able to cut Rhodesia off economically from the rest of the world by imposing sanctions. But Rhodesia was a large country, rich in natural resources. It possessed many commodities for which other countries were willing to break sanctions. It was also right next door to a friendly neighbour, South Africa. Northern Ireland is not Rhodesia. Its only close neighbours would be hostile and its few exports would be of no great importance to anyone. No country in the world would be likely – or able – to help Northern Protestants by breaking a blockade, or supplying financial aid on a significant scale.

Even if the British government, on humanitarian grounds, decided against a comprehensive blockade following UDI, it could operate selective sanctions designed specifically to hurt the basic sectors of industry and commerce. These are, as we have seen, of more direct importance to Protestants. For example, subsidies could be withdrawn from certain industrial firms and an embargo placed on their exports. This would put many of them out of business and their mainly Protestant workforces out of jobs. The government could still continue to pay welfare benefits to anyone who became unemployed in this way, so as to ensure that no one need starve. But many people, the majority of them Protestant, would be greatly impoverished.

Britain clearly has the economic power to crush any attempt at UDI. Thus the idea of setting up an independent state in the North, in the face of British hostility, is completely impractical.

Repartition

Repartition would involve redrawing the border, so as to give to the South some of the more troublesome and predominantly Catholic fringe areas of Northern Ireland – Fermanagh, Tyrone, parts of South Armagh, South Down, parts of the city of Derry. That a British government would be prepared to adopt repartition as a planned solution to the Northern Ireland conflict is hard to imagine. It is really only conceivable as the *de facto* outcome of civil war.

Whatever the circumstances, repartition would undoubtedly involve large-scale movements of population. Protestants would crowd into the shrunken area which remained of Northern Ireland, while many Catholics would be driven out altogether. Theoretically, if the population transfer were total, as it has been in Cyprus, repartition would bring an unhappy but definitive end to the conflict in Northern Ireland.

However, a total transfer could only be achieved if Britain was prepared cold-bloodedly to enforce it, for it is extremely unlikely that a civil war of itself would lead to such a clear-cut result. In fact, the most likely outcome of any repartition would be a reduced Catholic population overall, but with substantial and embattled Catholic communities remaining in areas such as West Belfast.

This would ensure that repartition would be of minor significance. Disruption and conflict would continue. The diminished region would remain in severe economic difficulties and would continue to require immense economic support from Britain. As a credible strategy for permanently bringing 'the troubles' to an end, repartition is clearly a non-starter.

A united Ireland

Thus, virtually all of the main options usually suggested for Northern Ireland's future would appear to be unworkable. One only remains: that Britain accepts the need for a united Ireland, negotiates with the parties concerned and then withdraws from the province. Yet this solution is usually regarded as impractical too. Even many of those who are generally in favour of a united Ireland are unwilling to call for British withdrawal because they fear it could lead to civil war and a 'blood-bath'.

It has to be recognized that civil war is not an impossibility. Were Britain to leave, there might be bitter strife. Instead of unity the outcome might be repartition, with the Protestants occupying an area somewhat smaller than the present Northern Ireland. Yet it is significant how little detailed attention the 'blood-bath' scenario has received. Often without any discussion it is simply assumed that a united Ireland could not be achieved because it would be impossible to secure Protestant consent, and that without such consent the threat to human life would be too immense to contemplate.

But how great really is the risk of serious bloodshed? Are there ways in which it could be prevented? And could these ways include securing some form of consent from the Protestant community? We examine four key issues which would arise if Britain did decide to leave Northern Ireland:

1   What would happen once Britain's intentions to withdraw became known.
2   What measures Britain could adopt in order to minimize the chances of a violent response.
3   If violence were to occur, whether it could be swiftly overcome.
4   Whether it would be possible to persuade the Protestant community to accept a united Ireland.

The first response

Even before any official announcement, once it became known that withdrawal was a serious possibility, it is likely there would be a spate of violence from the unionist side. How bad this would be we can only guess. In any event, whatever violence were to occur, most or all of the immediate *victims* would be Catholics. However, the real *target* would be the British government. Those unionists who committed violent acts against Catholics would be aiming to raise the fear of civil war and so force Britain to remain in Northern Ireland in order to prevent a bloodbath. Meanwhile, other, less violent unionists could be expected to pursue the same aim by more peaceful methods: strikes, demonstrations, rallies and the like.

At this stage there would be differences amongst unionists about methods and tactics, but overall unity about aim: to keep Britain in Northern Ireland. However, provided the British government kept its nerve, the situation would change rapidly. Once it became obvious that Britain really was going to leave and that *nothing* they could do would prevent it, there would be a tremendous crisis in the Protestant community.

For the first time in their history, Protestants would have to contemplate seriously the prospect of life without Britain. Despite occasional verbal threats to withdraw from the United Kingdom, it is clear – from their actual behaviour; from the demands they make and the expectations they have – that most Protestants have always thought entirely in terms of the link with Britain. Their political life has always been dominated by just two questions: how to ensure Britain remains in Northern Ireland; and how to ensure Britain's policies are favourable to the Protestant community.

The certain knowledge of British withdrawal would be utterly traumatic. Protestants would have to confront a completely new situation. Until now, they have always had Britain to fall back on – and Britain has nearly always obliged. Now, however, established ways of thinking would be overturned and splits would appear as Protestants began to contemplate their future. Some Protestants would take the Rhodesian white settlers' UDI approach as their inspiration and argue for the creation of an independent Protestant state in the north-east. Others would reject such a solution as impractical or too costly. They would advocate making the best of a bad job and accepting a united Ireland under the most favourable terms available. Their example would be Kenya where the settlers did eventually agree to decolonization. A few would positively embrace a united Ireland. Some would make plans to leave.

This disunity amongst the Protestants would strengthen the British government's hand immensely. In such a fluid situation, the government's behaviour would be decisive. With the right approach, it could ensure a relatively smooth and bloodless transition to a United Ireland. But the wrong policy might well provoke a fierce civil war.

We now examine the tactics and strategy Britain would need to follow, so as to maximize the likelihood of a peaceful withdrawal from Northern Ireland.

Withdrawal: the nuts and bolts

If Britain took the decision to withdraw, any further wavering or uncertainty would be dangerous. Above all else, Britain's actions would have to be firm and decisive. These fundamental principles translate into two simple conditions:

1 *Short notice.* If the gap between the decision to withdraw and its implementation were fairly short, this would minimize the time available for resistance to be organized.
2 *Irreversibility.* The decision would need to be public and irreversible: it would have to be made clear to all concerned that, no matter

what happened, the British government would stick to its decision to go. This would, of itself, help to divide and therefore weaken opposition and resistance.

To implement these general principles Britain would have to adopt the following measures: a named date for withdrawal; an enabling bill; a constitutional conference.

A definite date would need to be set by which the withdrawal of British troops would be completed. This date would be absolute and observed no matter what the situation at the time. This may seem harsh, but it would be the only possible workable approach. Most crucially, it would concentrate the minds of all parties in Ireland and encourage them to negotiate seriously about the future. Ideally, the programme for withdrawal should be completed within the lifetime of a single Parliament, thereby avoiding the uncertainties associated with the electoral process. To achieve such an objective, the terms of the programme would have to be announced as early as possible in the government's term of office, so as to ensure sufficient time to complete the exercise before the next general election. This would give a period of up to four years, which should be more than adequate to organize withdrawal and negotiate the transfer of power. It would also be short enough to underline the seriousness of government intentions.

The next stage would be for the government to present an enabling bill to Parliament. This would state that henceforward Northern Ireland was no longer a part of the United Kingdom. However, British troops would remain in the province during the transitional period, as laid down in the programme for withdrawal.

Meanwhile the government would have to convene a constitutional conference to which delegates from all the established political parties, plus representatives from those paramilitary organizations without a political wing (i.e. the Protestant paramilitaries) would be invited. The participants would therefore include the following:

N. Ireland	*The Republic*	*All-Ireland*
Official Unionist Party	Fianna Fáil	Sinn Féin
Democratic Unionist Party	Fine Gael	(who could
Alliance Party	Labour Party	speak for
Social Democratic and	Progressive	the IRA)
Labour Party	Democratic	Workers Party
Ulster Defence Association	Party	
Ulster Volunteer Force		

It would have to be made clear that, regardless of whether any of these walked out or refused to attend, the conference and the transfer of power would go ahead.

To encourage moderation and speed things along, the functions of the conference would be strictly defined from the outset. These would be:

1 To establish a new constitution for a united Ireland.
2 To set up an administrative body to oversee withdrawal.
3 To organize transition to a new system of government.

This would all have to be achieved within a fixed time period, and, failing agreement, Britain would still withdraw on schedule. Thus, delaying tactics on the part of those opposed to withdrawal would be pointless.

The risk of violence: can it be overcome?

So much for the constitutional measures and the principles for implementing them. We are still left with the widely held conviction that there are a million heavily armed Protestants in Northern Ireland, willing to fight to the death to prevent unity with the South. It is this which is the reason most frequently given for the Labour Party's 'unity by consent' policy – concern that any attempt to 'bounce' an unwilling Protestant community into a united Ireland would lead to massive bloodshed.

We take this concern very seriously. But is it well founded? Are Protestants very heavily armed? And would they fight to the bitter end if Britain withdrew? Indeed, would they fight at all?

Here we shall try to remove some of the emotion that generally surrounds this issue and subject it to a very careful analysis. We find that the likelihood of violence resulting from British withdrawal, its extent, duration, and eventual outcome, would depend on the following factors:

1 What military means there are available to those Protestants who might wish to resist a united Ireland by force.
2 What means there are available for overcoming such military resistance.
3 How vulnerable Catholic areas in the North are to attack, and what means there are available for defending them.
  But over and above all of these, the very core of the matter is:

4 When it finally comes down to it, what proportion of the Protestant community are actually prepared to resist reunification by
   force.

We shall look at all of these factors in turn.

How heavily armed are the Protestants? Protestants in Northern
Ireland do hold a great many weapons. There are around 6,000
members of the Ulster Defence Regiment (UDR) and a further 13,000
in the Royal Ulster Constabulary (RUC), including reservists and
part-timers. Most of these carry personal arms for self-defence. Some
also have access to official arsenals containing more destructive
weapons such as high-velocity rifles and sub-machine guns, etc. In
addition, Protestants own most of the 100,000 or so guns which are
legally held by civilians in Northern Ireland. These are mainly shot-
guns used for hunting. There is also an unknown quantity of revolvers,
rifles, machine-guns and the like held illegally by Protestant paramilitaries (unknown, that is, publicly; it is reasonable to assume that
military intelligence has estimates). Finally, if Britain declared an
intention to withdraw, there might be a last ditch attempt to import
weapons.

Thus, the Protestants have a substantial number of light weapons at
their disposal and could possibly acquire more. However, they lack the
heavier weapons required to fight a conventional war against a regular
army. This would put them at a severe disadvantage in a direct con-
frontation with the Republic's army, which is equipped with howitzers, mortars, recoilless rifles, field guns, armoured cars, and some
tanks (see figure 9.1). If necessary, the Republic could easily acquire
more heavy weaponry. With their present arms, therefore, Northern
Protestants would be hard pressed to withstand a really determined
assault by the Republic's armed forces. Moreover, even if Protestants
could upgrade their weapons, they would probably be overwhelmed
by sheer weight of numbers: in Ireland as a whole there are four times
as many Catholics as Protestants.

Clearly, conventional warfare is not really at issue. The key question
is far more likely to be whether the Protestants could engage in an
endless guerrilla campaign such as the IRA has done.

Could Protestant armed resistance be overcome? To prevent a prolonged guerrilla campaign the Protestants would have to be disarmed
or neutralized.

Army Battle Order

Manpower: 12,203
Reserves: 22,100
Conscripts service period: voluntary; 3-year
enlistment
Organization:
11 infantry battalions
1 armoured squadron
1 tank squadron
4 reconnaissance squadrons
3 field artillery regiments
1 anti-aircraft regiment
1 ranger company

Equipment

Tanks: 12 *Scorpion* light tanks
AFVs: 28 AML-90s, 32 AML-60s
APCs: 60 Panhard VTT/M3, 17 *Unimog*, 10 Timoney BDX,
some *Landsverk*
Artillery: 48 25 pounder guns/howitzers, 12 105 mm howitzers
Mortars: 92 120 mm, 250 81 mm, 199 60 mm
(81 mm and 120 mm mortars on order)
RCLs: 477 *Carl Gustav* 84 mm, 96 IIIO 90 mm
AA guns: 26 *Bofors* 40 mm, 2 L/70
ATGWs: *Milan*
SAM: RBS-70

Naval Battle Order

Manpower: 896 (to be increased to 1,500)
Conscripts service period: voluntary; 4-year
enlistment
Fleet:
2 ex-British Ton class coastal minesweepers
3 Emer-class patrol craft
1 Dierdre-class patrol craft
1 P-31-class patrol craft
6 other auxiliaries, training, survey and
stores craft
(NB: Construction of an additional P31-class
patrol craft delayed due to cost; 3 French
Dauphin helicopters planned for use on
the P31-class craft)

Base: Cork

Air Force Battle Order

Manpower: 842
Conscripts service period: voluntary; 4-year
enlistment
Organization:
Based at Casement Aerodrome, Baldonnel
and Gormanston, Meath
1 COIN unit with 6 *Super Magisters*
1 training unit with 9 SIAI-Marchetti
SF-260WU (also used for COIN)
1 liaison unit with 8 Cessna FR 172s (also
used for training)
Transports: 3 Beech *King Air 200*s,
1 HS-125-700
Helicopters: 8 Aérospatiale *Alouette 11*s,
2 *Gazelles*

Key

AFV	= armoured car
APC	= armoured personnel carrier
RCL	= recoilless rifle
ATGW	= anti-tank guided weapon
SAM	= surface-to-air missile

Figure 9.1 Armed forces of the Irish Republic, 1986
Source: Defence and Foreign Affairs Handbook (1986)

The first step would be to disband the UDR. This is an almost totally Protestant and highly sectarian force. During the disarming process a lot of weapons could be recovered, though some would obviously 'disappear'. However, more important, with the UDR disbanded, Protestants' access to official arsenals would be greatly reduced, so that the theft of weaponry would be much easier to prevent.

The RUC presents a more complex problem. Although largely Protestant it is conceivable that this body would remain loyal and co-operate in the transition to a united Ireland. If it did so, this would make the task of controlling the Protestant areas much easier, and greatly reduce the danger of attacks on Catholics during the transition period. Under these conditions it would be unnecessary to disarm the RUC, although restrictions on where the force could operate might be required. On the other hand the RUC might try to obstruct the transition process, or start disintegrating under the strain of controlling the Protestants. In this situation, disarming the force *would* become necessary. Thus the question of what to do about the RUC would depend crucially on how loyal and disciplined it turned out to be. This in turn would be determined by several factors.

If the transition process were accompanied by a virtual civil war involving most of the population, the discipline of the RUC would be so stretched that it might break altogether. In this event, there would be no alternative but to disarm, and possibly disband, the force. But if the transition were to be relatively smooth, and actual resistance were confined to a minority of militant Protestants, the RUC would probably remain loyal and continue to obey orders. In such a situation any individuals or small groups of RUC members who mutinied could be speedily disarmed.

The possibility of ensuring the loyalty of the RUC would be greatly increased if the British and Irish governments were to offer generous financial guarantees concerning the future employment and pension rights to those who obeyed orders. For example, some could be offered permanent jobs in the North, while others could be promised a transfer to the South or to mainland Britain, once the transition to a united Ireland was complete and the situation had quietened down. It should also be made clear that insubordinate police would be dismissed without compensation.

Provided the extent of Protestant resistance is limited, and generous financial guarantees were offered to those who obeyed, loyalty and discipline in the force would probably hold firm. The idea that resistance would be limited might seem optimistic, but it is given credibility by events since the Anglo-Irish Agreement was signed in 1985. The RUC has come into repeated, and sometimes very violent conflict with militant Protestants opposed to the agreement. For the most part, the discipline of the force has held up remarkably well. This is partly because the active opposition to the agreement, though sometimes fierce, has overall been quite limited. Partly, too, it is because few members of the RUC are willing to jeopardize their secure and well-paid jobs by disobeying orders. What might happen during a transition to a united Ireland is uncertain, but there is a fair chance the police would continue to obey orders just as they have done in the last couple of years.

The civilian population   With regard to weapons held by civilians, it is likely that the scope for action would be fairly limited – the location of illegally held weapons is probably unknown, while many legally held ones would simply 'disappear'.

The main way of disarming the Protestant community would be to disband the UDR. The treatment of the RUC would depend on whether it remained loyal. In any event, it would also be essential to close off any possible routes for the illegal importation of arms. However, it has to be recognized that all of this would still leave Protestants with sufficient light arms to cause trouble by using guerrilla tactics should they so wish.

Defending the Catholics   The Catholic population of Northern Ireland is less vulnerable to Protestant attack than it used to be. Right up to the early 1970s quite a lot of areas in the towns were fairly 'mixed' in religious composition. But with people being bombed and burned out of their homes, there were large-scale population movements, especially in Belfast. As a result, most working-class Catholics now live in well-defined urban ghettoes.

In rural areas, however, Catholics and Protestants continue to live side by side. If they wanted, the Protestants could kill literally hundreds of Catholics overnight. The same is true, of course, in the opposite direction, provided the Catholics had sufficient weapons. Indeed, in the countryside, the best protection for everyone would be to ensure that the Catholics were adequately armed. Then both communities would know that any use of force by the other could bring swift and equal retaliation. However, it is important to remember that during the 1970s (and in the early 1920s, when the province was also swept by serious violence), though there were some very nasty incidents in the rural areas, trouble was mainly confined to the towns.

There are four possible ways in which the Catholics in the urban areas could be defended in the period during and immediately after British withdrawal:

1 By an international peace-keeping force supplied by a body like the UN or the EEC.
2 By armed forces from the Republic of Ireland.
3 By the police (RUC and/or Gárda Síochána as appropriate).
4 By the local population.

An international peace-keeping force has been proposed by a number of people. However, history has shown that such forces are only ever effective if the people on both sides of a conflict are disciplined and accept the peace-keeper's role as mediator. Even then, the main task of such forces is to patrol agreed demarcation lines between one sector and another, and to resolve disputes as they arise.

This means that no international peace-keeping force can provide a complete defence for otherwise defenceless areas, without jeopardizing its neutrality as a mediator. Nor can it mediate effectively where there are large, uncontrollable elements determined to make trouble. In such circumstances, the role of a peace-keeping force is, at best, marginal and, at worst, positively harmful. It is obvious that were Britain to leave Northern Ireland, the conditions required for an international peace-keeping force to work successfully would not be met.

The danger to the Catholic areas would not come from a well-disciplined Protestant army or militia, but from smaller groups answerable only to themselves. An international peace-keeping force would not be able either to negotiate effectively with such groups to resolve disputes, or provide adequate defence against attack for Catholic areas. Even if there were some limited role for an international peace-keeping force during the transition to a united Ireland, it would not reduce the need for an effective defence of Catholic areas during that period.

In most cases, however, adequate defence could be provided by the Southern armed forces, the police, or the local population, or some combination of these. The choice would depend both on political and on military factors. Of the former, one important consideration would be that of political control within these areas. Whoever were to organize the defence of the Catholic areas during the transition period would gain a considerable political advantage for the future. For example, if defence of the Catholic areas were in the hands of the local people, Sinn Féin and the IRA would be greatly strengthened. By contrast, if the Southern army took responsibility for defence, it would probably use the opportunity to undermine these organizations.

Would the Protestants actually fight? Though this is obviously the most important question of all, it is one which is rarely, if ever, asked. It is well known that when even minor proposals for constitutional change are floated, threats of violent Loyalist resistance follow immediately. These inevitably help bolster fears that British withdrawal would lead to civil war. However, so far, such threats have been succeeded by only occasional acts of terror. These have sometimes been dreadful, but when all is said and done, they have fallen far short of a serious military challenge.

While recognizing that a move towards a united Ireland would evoke far greater Protestant hostility, this does not mean we should simply believe all threats that are made about civil war. *Most Protestants are opposed to British withdrawal, and they recognize that their best bargaining counter to prevent it is the threat of massive bloodshed. But to threaten is one thing, to deliver may be quite another.* Clearly, the greater the military strength of the Protestants, the more likely they would be to fight. But two other factors are likely to prove even more crucial: war-weariness and economic self-interest.

It is important to stress that many Protestants are heartily sick of the violence and would be opposed to a full-scale civil war. If they were genuinely convinced that British withdrawal was inevitable, it is likely that most Protestants would take one of two paths. Some would emigrate to Britain or elsewhere, while the bulk would probably accept a united Ireland as a *fait accompli* and make the best of it. Should this happen, those Protestants who did wish to fight would find themselves greatly outnumbered on their own side; they would also discover that they lacked the necessary support and lines of retreat within their own community. Without these no guerrilla campaign could survive for long.

Even more crucial, however, than the Protestants' war-weariness are economic considerations. Let us suppose the Protestants are militarily much stronger than we have estimated, and have the weaponry, manpower and organization actually to prevent a united Ireland. It is still highly doubtful whether what they would achieve would be worth the struggle. At most, once the fighting was over, they would control a small corner of north-eastern Ireland around Belfast, together with a few isolated pockets elsewhere in the province. But Northern Ireland's economy is already massively dependent on external aid. Any new and smaller state remaining in Protestant hands after a civil war would be equally dependent. Such a state would also be extremely dependent on access to external markets and would suffer grievously if these markets were cut off.

It is clear, therefore, that although in purely military terms the Protestants might, perhaps, be able to carve out a new state for themselves in the north-east, this state would be highly vulnerable to outside pressure. To destroy it would require no military campaign; it would require merely a concerted programme of economic sanctions. Britain acting alone has the power to wreck the economy of such a new north-eastern state, and could do so at no cost to itself – simply by cutting off financial aid and imposing a trade boycott of the area. This would make the new state completely unviable and its leaders would be forced to sue for peace within a matter of weeks. Thus the Protestants would find that though they had won the war, they had lost the peace.

Northern Protestants are quite aware how dependent the local economy is on external aid and markets, and how vulnerable it is to economic pressure from Britain. The only question is whether Britain would actually apply this pressure should the Protestants attempt to block Irish reunification and set up their own independent state. For obvious reasons, uncertainty on this question could be fatal. Any sign of weakness on Britain's part would merely encourage resistance. The British government would, therefore, have to make its intentions absolutely clear in advance. It would have to announce quite explicitly that any attempt to set up an independent state would be followed by severe economic sanctions. Such a threat, if believed, would be a powerful deterrent. It would both discourage militants hoping to block reunification and undermine their support in the Protestant community at large. As always, in this context, the importance of credibility is obvious. Not only would Protestants have to be convinced that Britain's decision to withdraw was inevitable; they would also need to be persuaded that the final goal was a united Ireland, and that resistance to the achievement of this goal would be both costly and pointless.

Convincing the Protestants: winning hearts and minds

Our discussion so far has been almost entirely negative in tone. We have been concerned with the military and economic means available for limiting and suppressing Protestant resistance. However, this is only one aspect of the problem. There is, equally important, a positive aspect too. Not only would Protestants have to be convinced that resistance to reunification was futile; they would also need reassurance about the kind of future they could expect if they co-operated.

Everything would have to be done to make a united Ireland attractive, or at least acceptable, to Northern Protestants. They must be actually *welcomed* into the new state, and not made to feel at all that they were merely there on sufferance. This would require a vigorous propaganda campaign to win Protestants' 'hearts and minds'. It would also mean specific guarantees being given over such matters as civil and religious liberties, employment policy and the future of the Northern economy. These guarantees would need to be sufficient to safeguard both the liberties of Protestants and their future material well-being.

The virtues of such a positive approach are manifold. It would accord to Protestants the respect they deserve as full citizens of a united Ireland. It would also help to overcome the bitterness and divisions which would inevitably accompany enforced reunification. Finally, by addressing some of the fears surrounding reunification, it would reduce the likelihood of serious Protestant resistance. These are some of the advantages of taking a positive approach to Northern Protestants. However, it would be naive to believe that promises alone would be sufficient. They would have to be backed up by the threat of sanctions if required. Only then would the promises be taken seriously and the virtues of the positive approach fully appreciated.

The guarantees which Britain would need to offer to the Protestants can be considered under three headings: economic prospects; employment; civil and religious liberties.

Economic prospects

Protestants have always been worried that reunification would wreck the economy of the north and greatly impoverish them. One answer to such fears is to point to the potential economic advantages of reunification. Let us examine these briefly.

A united Ireland would mean a single administrative unit for the whole of Ireland, North and South combined. This would eliminate wasteful duplication of government effort. It would mean greater co-ordination in economic policy between North and South and facilitate a more balanced, phased development of the island economy as a whole. It would permit the complete elimination of trade barriers between North and South, thus fostering the integration of the two economies. Finally it would allow a more co-ordinated policy towards multinational firms.

At present the separate administrations of the Republic and Northern Ireland have to compete for multinational investment, thereby forcing up the amount of financial inducements they must offer to the firms concerned. In a united Ireland multinational firms could no longer play North and South off against each other, so their investment would be available on cheaper terms. Grants, tax concessions and the like for firms investing in Ireland would be less than at present.

These are all real benefits and would be useful to the economy and the people of Northern Ireland. However, they should not be exaggerated. The amount of administrative duplication between North and South is limited. There is already a fair degree of policy co-ordination which is likely to increase following the Anglo-Irish Agreement. Trade barriers between North and South have already been largely dismantled since entry into the EEC. Finally, though reunification would certainly strengthen Ireland's bargaining power *vis-à-vis* multinational firms, the country would still face severe competition from other countries seeking to attract multinational investment. Ireland would, therefore, still have to offer quite generous financial inducements to foreign investors.

Although the benefits listed are genuine, they are all fairly limited. In addition to these, however, reunification would have another implication whose potential economic benefit would be considerable. We have explained in previous chapters how the present conflict in the North has damaged the local economy and how sustained economic recovery is virtually impossible while this conflict continues. If a stable peace could be established in the North, it would, of itself, be a major contribution to economic recovery. And this is just where reunification *would* produce results.

If Protestants co-operated with the reunification process, then peace would come rapidly, and with it the benefits of economic recovery. If Protestants were to fight a rearguard action, the benefits of peace would clearly take longer to materialize. However, no matter how difficult the transition to a united Ireland, peace would eventually come. For once Britain decisively set in train a programme for Irish reunification, any Northern Protestant resistance could have but a limited life span. Sooner or later, faced with the reality of British withdrawal and British economic hostility, the opponents of reunification would have to give up or leave the country. Quite simply, no other option would be available to them. Thus, reunification itself would end the present conflict, and eliminate the instability and uncertainty which has plagued the Northern economy. Under these circumstances, prospects for growth in the Northern economy would be good, and the area would be able to achieve the economic recovery which is impossible under present conditions.

So, in a variety of ways reunification would have advantages for the Northern economy and thus for Protestant living standards. However, it would take a number of years for these advantages to be felt. They would not be of prime importance during the actual period of transition to a united Ireland. During this period economic prospects for the North would depend chiefly on two factors:

1   The degree and duration of conflict accompanying reunification.
2   The economic terms of the settlement negotiated with Britain at the time of withdrawal.

Having already examined the first factor we shall turn our attention to the likely settlement terms. We shall begin by looking at what might happen were Britain to leave on the harshest possible terms – by cutting off Northern Ireland's subsidy altogether.

Abandonment   Abandoned by Britain and with no outside subsidy, overall consumers' expenditure in a newly united Ireland would be at least 40 per cent below that of the UK at present. Even under optimistic assumptions, ignoring the disruption caused by reunification itself, the per capita output of transportable goods (food, fuels, manufacturing, etc.) would be around 10 per cent below the present level in the Republic and 34 per cent below the UK level. This is partly because the extremely low output in the North would pull down the all-Ireland average. Thus, the *average* standard of living would be very low by European standards (see table 9.1). What this would mean in practice, North and South, would depend on how the two areas shared out the reduction in consumption. Table 9.2 illustrates some possible options.

Table 9.1 Effects of reunification (£ sterling per inhabitant) using figures for 1985

	Actual 1985				Hypothetical	
	United Kingdom	Northern Ireland	Republic of Ireland	All-Ireland average	United Ireland	
					(with aid)	*(without aid)*
Output of transportable goods[a]						
Agriculture	100	170	370	308	308	308
Manufactures, fuels, etc.	1,800	800	1,020	952	952	952
TOTAL	1,900	970	1,390	1,260	1,260	1,260
Consumers expenditure at market prices[b]	3,710	3,040	2,380	2,580	2,580	2,230

[a] Gross value added at factor cost. The figures for a united Ireland assume that the output of transportable goods in both parts of Ireland is the same immediately after reunification as before

[b] The figures for a united Ireland are estimates which assume that production in the North and South continues unchanged. For consumption two cases are shown. One assumes that external aid continues at the present level, and the other that British aid is cut off completely and no additional aid is provided from elsewhere. The former assumption underlies scenario D in table 9.2; the latter underlies scenarios A–C

Source: Actual – various official publications. Hypothetical – authors' own estimates

Table 9.2   Consumers' expenditure in a united Ireland

	Actual situation in 1985	Hypothetical scenarios			
		A	B	C	D
£ sterling per inhabitant					
North	3,040	3,040	2,230	1,890	3,040
South	2,380	1,870	2,230	2,380	2,380
As per cent of actual figure					
North	100	100	73	62	100
South	100	78	94	100	100

Note: See table 9.1 for some of the main assumptions which underlie this table

The first option – shown as scenario (A) – would be for the South to take over the British role completely and provide sufficient subsidy to maintain living standards in the North at their present level. This would require a huge sacrifice by the population of the South: Southern consumers' expenditure would have to fall by over 20 per cent. The second possibility – shown as scenario (B) – would be for living standards North and South to be equalized. This would involve much less of a sacrifice for Southerners, but would have an immense impact in the North. It would mean a reduction of about 6 per cent in consumers' expenditure in the South, and about 30 per cent in the North. The final way – shown as scenario (C) – would be what would happen if the South refused to make any sacrifice at all. Then consumers' expenditure in the North would have to fall by about 40 per cent.

It is obvious that all of the above options have major drawbacks. It is unthinkable that the people in the South would accept the first option; while the second and third would produce enormous dissension and strife in the North, and stiffen Protestant resistance to reunification.

British aid   This all underlines the fact that Britain could not simply abandon Northern Ireland. Such a decision would impose enormous suffering on Irish people both North and South and would be morally quite indefensible. It would also be extremely foolish, since Britain's interests would obviously best be served by having a prosperous, stable and friendly neighbour on its frontiers. Therefore, regardless of which party was in power at the time, if it were to leave Northern Ireland, it is reasonable to assume that Britain would pursue a more constructive approach.

This would require a two-pronged strategy: actively using the threat of its economic power as a weapon to undermine resistance to reunification, while simultaneously offering to deploy its economic resources to help shore up the new state. Thus Britain would have to make absolutely clear its willingness to use selective economic sanctions against anyone seeking to resist reunification. Such a firm and un-equivocal approach would itself be enough to deter resistance from all but a handful of Protestants. At the same time, Britain would have to emphasize that there was an alternative path it was willing to pursue. As an incentive to Northern Protestants to accept a united Ireland, Britain could promise that, following reunification, external aid would continue for a prolonged period, until the North's economy had been rebuilt. Accordingly, Britain would offer substantial aid to the new state, so long as it received guarantees that the money would be spent on the North, and that satisfactory arrangements would be made for the future employment of Protestants. Such a policy would allow living standards in the North, including those of most Protestants, to be broadly maintained, without imposing an unacceptable burden on the Southern population. This is the assumption underlying scenario (D) in table 9.2.

Since it could take some 15 or 20 years for the economy of the North to be strong enough to stand on its own feet, continuing aid would involve a significant commitment from Britain. Even so, there would be immediate savings following withdrawal. Moreover, these savings could be achieved without damage to the economic or social fabric of Northern Ireland.

The annual British subvention to Northern Ireland is now £1,700 million. Following withdrawal, savings on this sum would be of two kinds. The repatriation of British troops would itself cut Britain's costs by perhaps £200 million with virtually no effect on the local economy. Moreover, other sources, such as the EEC and the USA might be willing to share the burden of aid, as the price of a durable peace in such a strategically important area as Northern Ireland. Together these would represent a significant and almost immediate reduction in Britain's outgoings to the North.

Over the longer term, of course, the savings to Britain could be much greater. As long as Britain remains in Northern Ireland, the conflict is likely to continue and the burden of the province will remain enormous – and constitutionally unavoidable. Following reunification 15 or 20 years of peace should be sufficient to allow for the rebuilding of the Northern Ireland economy and for British aid to be eventually phased out.

Employment

Many Protestants are afraid of losing their jobs, or of a dramatic reduction in their living standards should Britain leave. For most of them, such fears are unnecessary. In the event of withdrawal, Britain would almost certainly continue to provide substantial aid for some years to come, and other countries would probably join in. This would make it perfectly possible to limit the economic effect of reunification on Protestant living standards.

In certain sensitive areas, such as the police and the higher levels of public administration, which are very closely identified with Unionism, changes would be required for reasons of both fairness and politics. The most sectarian and repressive elements in the government machine would have to be dismissed, assuming the people concerned had not already left voluntarily. In the case of the RUC, redundancies would be inevitable amongst the largely Protestant membership. Fewer police would be required under peacetime conditions. It would also be important to create vacancies to facilitate Catholic recruitment, so that some religious balance could be introduced. However, there would be scope for offering RUC members jobs in the South or in Britain, or instead generous severance arrangements. The vast bulk of public employees would keep their jobs – and their right to do so could be explicitly guaranteed. The fair employment legislation would have to be enforced much more strictly, both in the public and private sectors. But this should not have any damaging effects on the continued employment of those Protestants already in work, and the great majority in the private sector too should keep their jobs.

Except in respect of the security forces, where some change in religious composition would be essential, following reunification employment policy in the North would not set out to remove Protestants and replace them by Catholics. Rather, it would aim to create additional jobs for both communities. Because there are proportionately far more unemployed Catholics in the North than Protestants, in the first years of the new state, Northern Catholics could expect to get a higher percentage of any new jobs created. However, the bulk of

Protestants would be no worse off than they currently are. Indeed, given the improved economic performance which peace would bring, the Protestant community as a whole would eventually become better off.

Civil and religious liberties

Since the first Home Rule Bill of 1886, Northern Protestants have opposed any weakening of the link with Britain with such slogans as 'Home Rule is Rome Rule'. Today Protestants still fear that unity with the South would undermine their religion and liberties. It is also widely believed in Britain that this fear is justified – that a united Ireland would mean, for Protestants, subjection to an oppressive Catholic state with many of their most prized civil liberties abolished.

Here we will look closely at the reasons the Protestants themselves give for this fear. They point to the very powerful and influential position of the Catholic church in the Republic. In particular, they give the following examples of Catholic domination:

1　The decline of the Protestant population in the Republic from 10 per cent in 1911, a few years before partition, to 3.5 per cent by 1981.
2　Article 44 of the 1937 Irish Constitution giving a special position to the Catholic church.
3　The Republic's laws on divorce, contraception and abortion, all reflecting the Catholic moral code.

Protestant population decline　Northern Protestants often claim that the fall in the Southern Protestant population is due to discrimination, in particular, to the Vatican's *Ne Temere* decree. This requires that the children of 'mixed' (i.e. Catholic and non-Catholic) marriages must be raised as Catholics. In fact, the reasons for the decline in Protestant numbers in the South are very complex, and there are several factors which are much more significant than the operation of the decree.

To begin with, Protestant numbers were considerably reduced in the early days of the state because of all the young men who had been killed in the first world war. In addition, after partition many strongly Unionist Protestants emigrated. Then Protestant numbers fell again through the combination of a low birth rate and emigration. Though the *Ne Temere* decree *was* an element in the decline of the Southern Protestant community, it was only one of many.

Moreover, in recent years, the decree has been interpreted more liberally by the Catholic church and many children of mixed marriages are now raised as Protestants. Indeed, in their evidence to the New Ireland Forum, the Catholic bishops implied they would like to drop the decree altogether but have been prevented from doing so by the Vatican. This marks an enormous change in attitude compared with even 30 years ago. It is perhaps most important of all to note that the decline in Southern Protestant numbers has slowed considerably in recent years. While once the community appeared to be in danger of imminent extinction, this is no longer the case.

The Constitution   Article 44 is now a complete irrelevance: it was repealed after a popular referendum in 1972. Legally, at least, the Catholic church no longer has a 'special position'. However, it is still a powerful political force in the South, and Protestants do have some cause for concern when it comes to the laws governing personal morality.

Personal morality   The Republic's Constitution expressly prohibits *divorce*, and the Catholic church has been a passionate opponent of change in this area. Furthermore, in 1986 a referendum in the Republic rejected a proposal for legalization. By contrast, in Northern Ireland the divorce laws are similar to those in Britain.

In regard to *contraception*, the situation is somewhat more complex. The North again parallels Britain. In the Republic contraception is legal and widely used, but it is not always easy to obtain, especially outside the main towns. The problem here is not absolute prohibition, but a law which allows people to be denied access by those doctors and chemists who still have a lingering hostility to contraception.

Comparisons become still more complicated when we examine the laws North and South governing *abortion*. In the Republic an old British law – the Offences Against the Person Act, 1861 – made abortion illegal for well over a century. In 1983 the Republic's Constitution was amended by referendum, so that abortion became unconstitutional too. The amendment did not render the actual performance of an abortion within the Republic any more illegal than it already was. However, after it was passed, the Irish High Court ruled that its effect was to prohibit pregnancy counselling services giving information or assistance to Irish women to help them obtain an abortion in Britain. (It may be noted that in spite of the problems this ruling has caused women, there is no evidence of any decrease in the numbers coming to Britain for abortions: several thousand are known to arrive annually.)

Most Southern Protestants supported the existing 1861 law, but were opposed to the constitutional change as being unnecessary and as giving in to fanaticism. However, though it generated great passion, the abortion referendum did not demonstrate any fundamental difference in attitudes between the Catholic and Protestant churches in the Republic towards the issue of abortion itself.

In Northern Ireland the situation is different, but not dramatically different. When abortion law was liberalized in Britain, fundamentalist Protestants and the Catholic church lined up together to resist its introduction in the province. This strong opposition from both communities was successful in preventing the reform being extended to Northern Ireland. Consequently the North's abortion law is the same as it was in Britain before the 1967 Abortion Act. This means abortion is only legal in very restricted circumstances: when the pregnancy puts the mother's life at risk or seriously endangers her physical or mental health.

In practice, abortion is virtually unobtainable within the province. Women from Northern Ireland, unlike those in the Republic, are not barred by law from obtaining advice and assistance about how to get an abortion in Britain. However, just like women from the Republic, in order to have an abortion, women from Northern Ireland have to come to Britain.

The gap between North and South concerning contraception should not prove unbridgeable. For example, one simple way of circumventing any continuing obstructiveness by doctors and chemists in the South would be to permit the sale of condoms through non-medical outlets. State health centres in the South could also be required to extend their provision of contraceptive advice and information.

Even without legal reform, any remaining differences in practice between North and South are likely to diminish, maybe even to vanish, in a world in which adherence to old attitudes is simply impracticable. Thus, since the advent of the AIDS crisis, there are far fewer chemists in the Republic still refusing to stock condoms. Clearly certain moral qualms are already being overtaken by the realities of modern existence. Most people on both sides of the border probably already agree in their opposition to the legalization of abortion. If there is a distinction here, it is that Protestants are probably less equivocal in their acceptance of abortion where a woman's life would otherwise be endangered. While many Catholics would privately agree that abortion should be permissible in such circumstances, the Catholic church would be less accommodating.

Of the three issues, only attitudes towards divorce would appear to differ significantly. But even here all is not always what it seems. Clearly, most Protestants (and many Catholics) in the North are in favour of the right to divorce, as are most Protestants in the South. However, attitudes of Southern Catholics are more complex; while in the 1986 divorce referendum only a minority voted in favour of reform, opinion polls in the Republic continue to show (as they did before the referendum) that a majority of the electorate believe divorce should be legalized.

(This conundrum is probably explicable as the product of a deep moral/economic divide in thinking. Significantly, during the campaign around the divorce referendum, the Catholic church did *not* focus its opposition to reform around moral issues; rather, it concentrated on the predicted economic consequences of divorce, in particular, the (self-evident) impossibility of most men being able to provide adequately for two families. In a society where the majority of women with children do not go out to work, and so are wholly dependent on their husband's income, the argument that divorce would lead to abandonment and impoverishment carried a great deal of weight. That the Catholic church chose to pursue such an opportunist tack is an indication that it lacked confidence in its ability to sway the population through a campaign of moral opposition alone.)

In any event, the *practical effects* of any remaining differences in attitude towards divorce could turn out to be quite limited. The Irish government is supporting major legislative reform regarding marital property and judicial separation. If this reform goes through, which at the time of going to press looks pretty certain, the Republic's marriage laws will end up providing all the legal entitlements associated with divorce, except for the right to remarry.

On other moral issues, such as opposition to homosexual law reform, the views of many Northern Protestants and of the Catholic church are very similar. In fact, while Unionists often refer to the Catholic and anti-liberal attitudes of the Southern state, their own beliefs are frequently not very different. The idea that unification would involve the imposition of reactionary Catholic views on progressive Protestants, is, it should be clear, quite without foundation.

Guarantees We turn here to the question of guarantees. All the nationalist parties now accept the need for constitutional reform as the price of Irish unity. Even Fianna Fáil, the most Catholic and traditional of the Southern parties, agrees. Its leader, Charles Haughey, who is now the Taoiseach (Prime Minister of the Republic) has suggested a 'Scottish solution' to the question of civil liberties. Within a united Ireland, the North would be given the kind of autonomy enjoyed by Scotland within the UK. In his statement to the New Ireland Forum Mr Haughey has said:

I believe that a new constitution will be required for a new Ireland. A united Ireland would represent a constitutional change of such magnitude as to demand a new constitution. That constitution, in our view, can only be formulated at an all-round conference in which all sections of the Irish people, North and South, would participate. It is only in this way that we can provide all the appropriate safeguards and guarantees required for the security and protection of every section of the Irish community. The divergent practice which has been followed in many matters, not just matters of a conscientious or moral nature, North and South, means that complete harmonisation of laws, administrative practices and social structures may only be possible if carried out over a gradual and perhaps extended period. We may have to consider some degree of autonomy for Northern Ireland, be it on the basis of the same area, or a smaller one. We have the example, in the state of Great Britain for instance, of Scotland with its own legal system and its own educational system, an administration in Edinburgh, a Cabinet Minister and a grand committee of Scottish MPs in Westminster who legislate on Scottish affairs.

Other nationalist parties differ in their formulation of the issues, but they too accept the need for guarantees. For example, Gerry Adams, in his speech to the 1984 Ard Fheis (conference) of Sinn Féin, had this to say on the subject:

Sinn Féin's view is that the British government needs to be met with a firm, united and unambiguous demand from all Irish 'nationalist' parties for an end to the unionist veto and for a declaration of a date for withdrawal.

Within the new situation created by these measures, it is then a matter of business-like negotiations between representatives of all the Irish parties, and this includes those who represent today's loyalist voters, to set the constitutional, economic, social and political arrangements for a new Irish state.

We assert that the loyalist people must be given, in common with all other citizens, firm guarantees of their religious and civil liberties, and we believe that, faced with British withdrawal and the removal of partition, a considerable body of loyalist opinion would accept the wisdom of negotiating for the type of society which would reflect their needs as well as the needs of all the other people in Ireland.

The establishment of a society free from British interference, with the union at an end, will see sectarianism shrivel and will see the emergence of class politics proper with a re-alignment of forces along left and right lines.

Later in the same speech he went on to say:

In another equally important and related dimension of life in Ireland there is an absolutely hypocritical attitude on the right to family planning and contraception, the question of divorce and marital breakdown, the invidious social distinctions which surround the question of illegitimacy, one-parent families and so on.

These are questions which we as a people are mature enough to decide and settle for ourselves without fear of croziers or duplicity by salaried politicians.

The question of civil and religious liberties need not be such an obstacle to Irish unity as opponents have often suggested. It would be the task of the constitutional conference, established to mastermind the withdrawal process, to work out the precise form of any civil liberties guarantees. In this context, it should also be remembered that the political balance in a united Ireland would be very different from that in the south today. The addition of a million and a half northerners, mostly Protestant, would alter the balance of opinion on a number of key issues. Over divorce, for example, the combined votes of northerners, and those southerners who supported its legalization, might well outweigh those who were still opposed.

It is clear that Protestant fears about unity with the Republic are often genuine, but are equally often misplaced. In any event, they have been shamelessly exploited. In those areas where there is real cause for concern, Northern Protestants are entitled to, and should and could be given, explicit legal guarantees. Indeed, as a price of economic aid to a united Ireland, Britain might demand such guarantees. As all the nationalist parties have already recognized the need for legal protection, they would have a clear responsibility to translate their words into deeds.

It is also clear that British withdrawal from Northern Ireland need not automatically be followed by a bloody civil war. On the contrary, if Britain acts decisively, it has the power to ensure a relatively orderly and peaceful transition to a united Ireland. Using its considerable economic resources, Britain could make the Protestants a generous offer that they would be extremely unwise to spurn. Should they accept, Protestants would be able to enjoy a secure future in a united Ireland, though many would find the adjustment painful. Should they reject the offer, and seek to create an independent state, the result would be disaster for them. Faced with this choice, there can be no doubt how the vast majority of Protestants would respond. *However, it is important to stress that Britain would have to be firm and decisive. Should Britain waver, this would only encourage resistance, with very serious results. It is very unlikely that there would be a full-scale war, but many would suffer, and reconciliation would be made even more difficult to achieve.*

Conclusions

In this book we have described the historical origins of the present armed conflict in Northern Ireland and explored its economic, social and political background. We have also examined in detail what can be done to end the conflict and establish a durable peace in the region. This chapter provides a summary of our conclusions.

The origins of the conflict: an imperial relic

Northern Ireland is one of the last remaining relics from Britain's once mighty empire. Its Protestant community, descendants of the original settlers sent to colonize Ireland more than three hundred years ago, still behaves as a settler community surrounded by hostile natives. To defend the privileges of this community the state of Northern Ireland was created, at a time when Britain was forced to concede independence to native Catholics in the rest of Ireland.

When the new state was created, its boundaries were deliberately drawn so as to give the Protestants a majority. Yet at the same time, trapped within these boundaries was a large and growing Catholic population. With British acquiescence, the Protestant community kept the government of Northern Ireland almost entirely in its own hands, excluding Catholics from political influence and maintaining widespread economic discrimination against them. However, the Catholic community never really accepted its separation from the rest of Ireland, and there have been spasmodic attempts to reunite the country by force. In the 1960s Catholic discontent reached new heights and the situation erupted into large-scale violence. Continuing into the late 1980s the violence shows no sign of ending.

Britain's response has been a mixture of repression and reform. Basic civil liberties have been suspended, many have been killed and many more imprisoned. On the positive side, some measures have been taken to address Catholic grievances and reduce discrimination against Catholics in fields such as housing and employment. In addition, the autonomous Protestant government in Northern Ireland has been ended and the province is now directly ruled by Britain. Finally, the Republic of Ireland has, under the terms of the Anglo-Irish Agreement, been given a formal advisory role in Northern Ireland affairs, where it can supposedly act as spokesperson for local Catholics.

These changes are often cited as evidence of Britain's goodwill towards the Catholic population. This is a misleading interpretation. Every single reform that Britain has introduced has been, in fact, a grudging response to Catholic agitation and violence. At no stage has Britain itself taken a reforming initiative. Instead its approach has always been to concede as little as possible as late as possible. Britain has only ever brought in reforms at the last moment, and what it has done has normally been inadequate. Indeed, the combined benefit to Northern Catholics of all the changes in the past 20 years has been quite limited.

War without end?

So far Britain's policies have failed to achieve their objectives. Catholic hostility to British rule remains widespread. The IRA has not been defeated, nor, in spite of fluctuations in its level of support, is it likely to be. Even the most optimistic government ministers rarely speak about victory nowadays.

The direct human cost of the conflict to Britain is, at the present time, small. Its Ulsterization policy has transferred most military responsibility to local Protestants in the RUC and the UDR. This has ensured that there are now few British casualties, and that most of the victims on either side are people from Northern Ireland. Of course, while this policy minimizes the human cost to Britain, it simultaneously intensifies the bitterness and hostility between the two communities within the province itself.

However, though few British troops are now killed in Northern Ireland, other costs remain which bear heavily and directly on Britain. The economic burden is considerable. Britain must both finance the military effort and provide a huge subsidy to the shattered economy of the North. The conflict has been accompanied by an erosion of civil liberties within Britain itself as well as within Northern Ireland.

Finally there is the moral dimension to consider. Britain is widely presented by politicians and the media as an honest broker desperately trying to hold two warring groups of Irish apart. In fact, its involvement is highly partisan. Its role in Northern Ireland is to preserve a state whose very existence represents a victory for one community in maintaining its privilege over the other. Thus, under the mantle of preserving 'law and order', Britain is in the morally dubious position of using its military power to crush the victims of a historic injustice, while defending its beneficiaries.

Time to withdraw?

In this situation the obvious question is: should Britain withdraw? Should not Britain pull out, reunite Ireland and thereby reverse the historic mistake of partition? That would be, in our view, both the obvious and the correct solution. Yet many people disagree. The reasons most frequently given for disagreeing are as follows:

1 Majority rule Since democracy is normally equated with majority rule, many people in Britain feel it would be undemocratic to force the Protestants, who are a majority in Northern Ireland, into a united Ireland against their will.

This argument ignores the artificial nature of the Protestant majority. Prior to partition, Protestants constituted a fairly small minority within the whole Irish population. The very existence of Northern Ireland is due to the Protestant community's refusal at the time of independence to accept the results of majority rule in Ireland as a whole. To legitimize that refusal, the Protestants had to be transformed into a majority. This was achieved by carving out a new state in the north of Ireland, whose borders were deliberately chosen to exclude counties which were predominantly Catholic. In this new state, the Protestant community enjoyed a clear majority.

The fact that within Northern Ireland Northern Protestants can outvote Northern Catholics on the question of reunification tells us nothing whatsoever about the justice or democracy of their case. This result is simply an outcome of the way in which the boundary of Northern Ireland was fixed at the time of partition.

2 Minority rights It is often said that in a united Ireland Protestants would be oppressed by the Catholic majority, with their civil liberties severely curtailed.

While many Protestants clearly do fear such oppression, this fear is grossly exaggerated. To begin with, leading nationalist politicians of all kinds have frequently recognized that Protestant political and religious freedoms would have to be guaranteed within a united Ireland. In addition, as we have shown, the gap between Catholic and Protestant moral views is nowhere near as great as is generally made out, and within a united Ireland should by no means be unbridgeable.

Finally, even after reunification, Ireland would still be subject to the ongoing impact of British power and influence. Since Britain's continued financial support of the North would be essential to the stability of the newly united state, Britain would be in a strong position to ensure, should it wish to do so, that the Protestant community was protected against any religious or other form of discrimination.

3 A general blood-bath An even more widespread fear is that British withdrawal from Northern Ireland would lead to a general blood-bath, with very large numbers from both Catholic and Protestant communities being killed. This is a deep and widespread concern, even amongst people who otherwise support a united Ireland.

If Britain were simply to pull out and dump the North, cutting off all aid and abandoning all responsibility for what followed, the result could be a full-scale civil war with all that that would entail. However, we have made it very clear that this is most certainly *not* what we are proposing at all. In fact, we consider such behaviour would be a gross abdication of Britain's obligation both to Catholics and to Protestants within Northern Ireland.

We have argued, by contrast, that Britain should withdraw in a planned and orderly fashion, using its considerable economic power simultaneously to undermine any Protestant resistance and to smooth the transition to a united Ireland. Were Britain to act in this responsible manner, then the risk of a widespread bloodbath would be reduced to become almost negligible. During the actual transition process, there would almost certainly be some sectarian killings, but, it must be stressed, these already occur in Northern Ireland under present conditions. The risk of a short spate of such killings would have to be weighed against the absolute certainty that hundreds, or even thousands will die if Britain remains in Northern Ireland, and countless more will suffer in other ways.

4   Guerrilla warfare in a united Ireland   Catholics have refused to accept Northern Ireland for nearly seven decades. It is sometimes argued that Protestants forced into a united Ireland are likely to be equally disaffected. Enforced unity, it is claimed, would not bring the violence to an end. Rather it would simply mean replacing Catholic guerrillas by Protestant guerrillas.

This argument poses a specious comparison. Many Northern Catholics are prepared to support armed struggle because they have a clear objective to aim for and some prospect of success. They want to unite with a state which already exists alongside them, which will continue to exist, and which will continue therefore to provide a goal to which to aspire. With some justification, they can reason that if they keep up the struggle long enough, Britain will eventually lose heart and leave.

The situation of Protestants in a united Ireland would be radically different. It must be asked: what would they fight for? Having withdrawn from the North, there is no way that Britain would ever return and every Protestant would be quite aware of this fact. The most Protestants could do in such a situation would be to break away and attempt to establish a new and smaller independent statelet in the most north-easterly corner of Ireland. However, this new state would be massively dependent on British economic support. Denied this support, as it doubtless would be once Britain had set out on the road to withdrawal, a new state would have no chance of survival. If established, it would collapse within weeks. Again, the certainty of this outcome would be perfectly clear to all Protestants.

The logical basis for prolonged Protestant guerrilla struggle simply would not exist. A few Protestants might seek to promote guerrilla warfare, but given the obvious futility of their enterprise, they would enjoy very little popular support in their own community and their activities would soon fizzle out. Unlike Catholics in Northern Ireland today, Protestants within a united Ireland would have no credible alternative to fight for. Their options would be obvious: either to accept the *fait accompli* of unity, or to leave Ireland altogether.

The future

When all the various arguments are considered, it is evident that Britain should withdraw from Northern Ireland. Britain is fighting a war it cannot win, to preserve a state which should never have been created and which cannot be saved. The costs are economically burdensome and morally unacceptable.

To bring peace to Northern Ireland, Britain should announce a clear, public timetable for withdrawal and stick to it. For once in its long and sorry relationship with Ireland, Britain should do the right thing at the right time. And that time is now.

Appendix 1
Some Key Events

c.200 BC	Celtic settlement of Ireland
c.800 AD	Viking invasion of Ireland
1169	Norman invasion of Ireland
1609	Plantation of English and Scottish Protestants in Ireland
1641	The Great Catholic Rebellion
1649–50	Cromwell restores Protestant control in Ireland
1689	Siege of Derry
1690	Battle of the Boyne
1695	Penal Laws passed to crush Catholic religion
1791	Wolfe Tone forms Society of United Irishmen
1795	Protestant Orange Order formed
1798	Uprising of the United Irishmen
1800	ACT OF UNION
1840s	The Great Famine
1858	Irish Republican Brotherhood – the 'Fenians' – formed
1867	The Fenian Uprising
1870	Irish Home Rule Party formed
1879	Irish Land League formed
1886	Gladstone's first Home Rule Bill defeated
1893	Gladstone's second Home Rule Bill defeated
1905	Sinn Féin established
1912	Third Home Rule Bill passed by House of Commons
	Ulster Covenant signed
1913	Loyalist Ulster Volunteer Force and Nationalist Irish Volunteers formed
	Dublin Lock Out and formation of Irish Citizen Army
1916	Easter Rising
1918	Dáil Éireann established

1919-21 War of Independence
1921   PARTITION. Establishment of Northern Ireland
1922-3   Civil war and the establishment of the Irish Free State

Appendix 2
The Constitutional Status of
Northern Ireland

We reproduce here various statements, legal and political – from Britain, the Republic of Ireland, and from the two states jointly – indicating their perception of the constitutional status of Northern Ireland.

The British Position

The Ireland Act, 1949:

It is hereby declared that Northern Ireland remains part of His Majesty's dominions and of the United Kingdom and it is hereby affirmed that in no event will Northern Ireland or any part thereof cease to be part of His Majesty's dominions and of the United Kingdom without the consent of the Parliament of Northern Ireland.

The Northern Ireland Constitution Act, 1973:

In no event will Northern Ireland or any part of it cease to be part of Her Majesty's dominions and of the United Kingdom without the consent of the majority of the people of Northern Ireland voting in a poll.

British Declaration at Sunningdale, 1973:

The British Government solemnly declared that it was, and would remain, their policy to support the wishes of the majority of the people of Northern Ireland. The present status of Ireland is that it is part of United Kingdom. If in the future the majority of the people of Northern Ireland should indicate a wish to become part of a united Ireland, the British Government would support that wish.

The Irish Position

The Irish Constitution, 1937:

Articles 2 and 3 of the Irish Constitution remain legally in force in 1988.

Article 2. The national territory consists of the whole island of Ireland, its islands and territorial seas.

Article 3. Pending the re-integration of the national territory, and without prejudice to the right of the Parliament and Government established by this Constitution to exercise jurisdiction over the whole of that territory, the laws enacted by that Parliament shall have the like area and extent of application as the laws of Saorstat Eireann (i.e. the twenty-six-county Free State) and the like extra-territorial effect.

Irish Declaration at Sunningdale 1973:

There could be no change in the status of Northern Ireland until a majority of the people of Northern Ireland desired a change in that status.

Joint Anglo-Irish declarations

The Anglo-Irish Summit Communiqué, 1981:

The Prime Minister affirmed, and the Taoiseach agreed, that any change in the constitutional status of Northern Ireland would require the consent of a majority of the people of Northern Ireland. The Prime Minister said that if that consent were to be expressed as a result of a poll conducted in accordance with the Northern Ireland Constitution Act 1973 the British Government would of course accept their decision, and would support legislation in the British Parliament to give effect to it.

The Hillsborough (Anglo-Irish) Agreement, 1985:

The two governments
(a) affirm that any change in the status of Northern Ireland would only come about with the consent of a majority of the people of Northern Ireland;
(b) recognise that the present wish of a majority of the people of Northern Ireland is for no change in the status of Northern Ireland;
(c) declare that, if in the future a majority of Northern Ireland clearly wish for and formally consent to the establishment of a united Ireland, they will introduce and support in the respective Parliaments legislation to give effect to that wish.

Appendix 3
Election Results in Northern Ireland 1975–87

The electoral performance of political parties in Northern Ireland

(Percentage of valid votes cast)

	OUP	DUP	Other Unionist	Alliance	SDLP	Sinn Féin	Other Nationalist	WP	NILP	CP	Other
1975 Convention election	25.8	14.8	21.9	9.8	23.7	–	–	2.2	1.4	0.1	0.3
1979 General election	36.6	10.2	12.3	11.9	19.7	–	6.5	1.7	0.6	–	0.5
1979 European election	21.9	29.8	7.3	6.8	24.6	–	5.9	0.8	–	–	2.9
1982 Assembly election	29.7	23.0	5.7	9.3	18.8	10.1	–	2.7	–	–	0.7
1983 General election	34.0	20.0	3.1	8.0	17.9	13.4	–	2.0	–	–	1.6
1984 European election	21.5	33.6	2.9	5.0	22.1	13.3	–	1.3	–	–	0.3
1987 General election	37.9	11.7	5.3	10.0	21.1	11.4	–	2.6	–	–	–

Source: Irish Times

Key
OUP = Official Unionist Party
DUP = Democratic Unionist Party
SDLP = Social Democratic and Labour Party (includes independent SDLP in 1979 general election)
WP = Workers Party (formerly Republican Clubs)
NILP = Northern Ireland Labour Party
CP = Communist Party

Appendix 4
Statistics on the Conflict in Northern Ireland

Table A4.1 Political violence in Northern Ireland, 1970–86

| | Type of activity | | | | | | Armed robberies | |
| | | | | Estimated weight of explosives (lbs) | | | | |
	Shooting incidents	Explosions	Bombs neutralized	Explosions	Neutralized	Malicious fires	Number of robberies	Total stolen (£ thousand)
1970	213	153	17	746	59			304
1971	1,756	1,022	493	10,972	3,001		437	791
1972	10,628	1,382	471	47,462	19,978		1,931	612
1973	5,018	978	542	47,472	32,450	587	1,215	573
1974	3,206	685	428	46,435	27,094	636	1,231	
1975	1,803	399	236	13,753	11,159	248	1,201	572
1976	1,908	766	426	17,596	16,252	453	813	545
1977	1,081	366	169	2,839	2,188	432	591	447
1978	755	455	178	5,343	5,860	269	442	233
1979	728	422	142	11,180	4,530	315	434	855

Table A4.1 (*continued*)

	Type of activity						Armed robberies	
				Estimated weight of explosives (lbs)				
	Shooting incidents	Explosions	Bombs neutralized	Explosions	Neutralized	Malicious fires	Number of robberies	Total stolen (£ thousand)
1980	642	280	120	9,059	6,405	275	412	497
1981	1,142	398	131	9,621	9,168	536(a)	587	555
1982	547	219	113	11,199	7,300	499	580	1,392
1983	424	266	101	6,923	7,503	528	622	830
1984	334	193	55	8,545	6,114	840	627	702
1985	237	148	67	11,711	7,715	740	459	656
TOTAL 1970–1985	30,422	8,132	3,689	260,856	166,776	6,358(b)	11,582	9,564
1986	392		254					

(a) Period excludes April to June 1981
(b) Total = 1973 to 1985 inclusive

Sources: NI Annual Abstract of Statistics; Royal Ulster Constabulary Chief Constable's Report

Table A4.2 Loss of life from political violence in Northern Ireland, 1969–85

	1969	1970	1971	1972	1973	1974	1975	1976	1977	1978	1979	1980	1981	1982	1983	1984	1985	1986	Total 1969–85
Regular British Army	0	0	43	103	58	28	14	14	15	14	38	8	10	21	5	9	2	4	386
Ulster Defence Regiment	0	0	5	26	8	7	6	15	14	7	10	8	13	7	10	10	4	8	158
Royal Ulster Constabulary	1	2	11	17	13	15	11	23	14	10	14	9	21	12	18	9	23	12	235
Republican paramilitaries[a]	1	5	17	65	32	17	17	14	6	7	5	4	16	9	3	11	4	5	238
Loyalist paramilitaries	–	–	–	10	8	4	18	5	6	–	–	1	3	4 }					
Civilians[b]	11	18	98	246	131	145	181	226	57	43	46	45	38	44 }	41	25	21	32	1,507
TOTAL	13	25	174	467	250	216	247	297	112	81	113	75	101	97	77	64	54	61	2,524

[a] Mainly Provisional IRA; figures for 1983–86 cover Provisional IRA only
[b] Includes unclassified

Sources: New Ireland Forum; NI Annual Abstract of Statistics; *An Phoblacht*

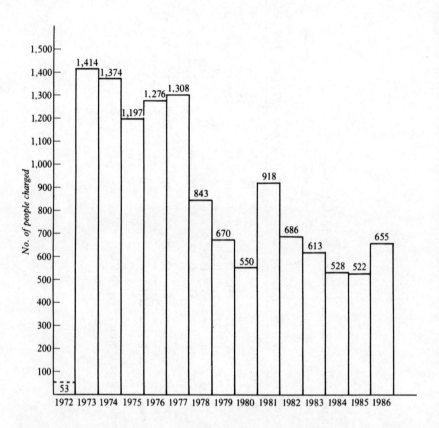

Figure A4.1   Number of people charged with offences connected with political violence in Northern Ireland, 1972–86 (the 1972 figure is for 1 July to 31 December only)

(*Sources*: Northern Ireland Office; Royal Ulster Constabulary)

Table A4.3 Persons detained under the Prevention of Terrorism (Temporary Provisions) Act in Britain, 1974–86

	Total detained	Charged with an offence	Exclusion order made	Not charged or excluded
Dec. 1974–80	4,524	302	195	4,027
1980	537	42	45	450
1981	274	39	10	225
1982	220	22	11	187
1983	191	31	13	147
1984	159	23	1	135
1985	194	38	2	154
1986	147	31	7	109
TOTAL	6,246	528 (8.5%)	284 (4.5%)	5,434 (87.0%)

Source: *Home Office Statistical Bulletin*, issue 11/87

Table A4.4 Detentions under the Prevention of Terrorism Act in Northern Ireland, 1975–87

(a) *Persons detained*

1974 (from Dec.)	—
1975	8
1976	246
1977	162
1978	155
1979	162
1980	222
1981	495
1982	828
1983	1,175
1984	908
1985	938
1986	1,309
1987 (to July)	659
TOTAL	7,627

(b) *Classification by outcome*

Total detentions	Charged with an offence	Exclusion order made	Not charged or excluded
7,627	2,462	31	5,134

Source: NCCL

Table A4.5 Detentions under the Emergency Provisions Act in Northern Ireland, 1975–86

	Section 14	Sections 11 and 13	Total	Number charged
1975	4,141		4,141	
1976	8,321		8,321	
1977	5,878		5,878	
1978	3,692	1,186	4,878	384 (7.9%)
1979	2,572	2,035	4,607	588 (12.8%)
1980	1,629	1,719	3,348	435 (13.0%)
1981	1,993	2,555	4,548	780 (17.2%)
1982	1,288	1,901	3,189	361 (11.3%)
1983	476	1,222	1,698	197 (11.6%)
1984	241	1,326	1,576	223 (14.1%)
1985	142	986	1,128	202 (17.9%)
1986	71	899	970	170 (17.5%)
TOTAL	30,444	13,829	44,273	3,340

Source: Northern Ireland Office

Note: Figures on sections 11 and 13 are only available from 1 June 1978

Appendix 5
Paramilitary documents

This appendix consists of two paramilitary documents. From the UDA's pamphlet, *Common Sense*, we reprint the preface and introduction which contain a useful statement of the philosophy underlying the document. We omit the body of the text as this is simply a detailed and technical discussion about voting arrangements. We have reprinted the whole Sinn Féin discussion document, *A Scenario for Peace*, as its scope is more wide ranging.

Common Sense

J. McMichael, Ulster Political Research Group
(*Ulster Defence Association*)

Preface

At the time of writing we are suffering yet another Ulster constitutional crisis, this time provoked by the Anglo-Irish Agreement.
Violence, intercommunity strife, polarization and uncertainty are all at
a higher level than at any time for almost a decade. The 'accord' will
not bring peace, stability or reconciliation to Northern Ireland because
it is a contract between two governments and not an agreement
between those in the cockpit of the conflict – Ulster Protestants and
Ulster Catholics.

This whole document could be used to expound the faults and
failures of the Anglo-Irish approach to the Ulster problem, but that is
not the purpose of this paper. It is enough to say that after more than a
year in existence the 'accord' has not won over the support of even one
small Loyalist group, opposition to the agreement remains absolute.
Any scheme which is opposed to such a degree has little or no chance
of developing into a solution.

Yet the Anglo-Irish Agreement has at least done two things which
may speed movement towards a real internal agreement in Ulster. The
increased exposure and examination of Southern Irish society has
further increased disillusionment for Ulster Catholics in the prospect
of a united Ireland. At the same time Ulster Protestants are increasingly heard to say that whilst they are totally resolved to defeat the
Anglo-Irish Treaty they recognize the need for a reasonable and
acceptable alternative to the agreement. They recognize that it is not
enough to simply say *no*. With this in mind the Ulster Political
Research Group presents this paper for discussion as one possible
alternative.

We are all part of the problem, but how many are prepared to be part of the settlement? It costs nothing to think about it.

Introduction

Who (in 1969) would have thought that after nearly 20 years the 'troubles' would still rage unabated with the Ulster Protestant-Loyalist-Unionist community and the Ulster Catholic-Irish-Nationalist-Republican community still locked in stalemate? Yet here we are in 1987 with nothing to show for it all but the prospect of looking forward to an ever polarizing society brutalized by violence, ravaged by fear and demoralized by economic depression.

How long can this go on?

The stubborn determination of each community not to 'give in' to, nor be beaten by, the other ensures that the conflict could continue indefinitely unless we can produce a settlement which removes the main sources of antagonism to each side. In the quest for proposals which may lead to a social and political solution to the Ulster conflict we must first identify the parameters within which such proposals are realistic. Surely by now we recognize that there are limits beyond which each community will not (under any circumstances) retreat or indeed be forced. It is not always that which is true which is important, but that which is believed to be true. Each community tends to form its impression of the other from the rhetoric and posturing of the most zealous and vocal sections of that group. The trouble with the silent majority is that it is indeed silent, and therefore makes little impression.

What impression then does each community have of the other?

Ulster 'Protestants' do not fear or mistrust Ulster 'Catholics' because they are Catholics but because they believe them to be Irish Nationalists – fifth columnists – uncommitted citizens, intent on the destruction of Northern Ireland in pursuit of a united Catholic-Gaelic-Irish-Nationalist-Republic. Loyalists fear that if these Irish Nationalists are allowed any authority or position of 'power' within the political framework of Northern Ireland then they will use that 'power' and authority to undermine, or even overthrow the state to achieve their Nationalist ambitions. For this reason Loyalists have opposed, and will continue to oppose, any proposal or scheme which contains an 'Irish dimension' or which Loyalists believe is contrived by Irish Nationalists to either undermine the 'Union' with Great Britain or bring a United Ireland one step nearer.

The Unionists are a majority in Northern Ireland, but their political behaviour there can only be understood if they are seen, as they feel themselves to be, as a threatened minority on the island of Ireland. Theirs are the politics of the besieged. Hence their stubborn refusal to share power with the minority in Northern Ireland, whom they fear as the Trojan horse of the real majority in Ireland, the Catholics. (John Hume, SDLP)

Ulster Loyalists live in a state of eternal siege; a people instinctively driven by the overpowering need to defend the frontiers against the enemy without, and to suppress the enemy within. Ulster 'Catholics' generally believe that Ulster 'Protestants' wish to preserve an ascendancy society – a religious and political hierarchy from which they are excluded, or 'alienated' – for no apparent reason other than that they are Catholics (the symptoms of mistrust and uncertainty are mistaken for bigotry and intransigence). A situation which 'Catholics' resent bitterly, and they have increasingly demonstrated that resentment.

Catch 22

The more Loyalists suspect 'Catholics' of being Irish Nationalists, the more defensive they become and close ranks. The more defensive 'Protestants' become, the more 'Catholics' believe themselves to be excluded and display disaffection and agitation usually through the medium of Irish Nationalism. In turn 'Protestants' interpret the display of agitation as further evidence that the minority is nothing more than a bunch of 'rebels' and become even more defensive. And so it goes on.

The consequence is a stalemate situation where Protestants feel threatened, and Catholics feel alienated and dominated by a Protestant majority. It creates a society that can not move forward, so it does not move. If we are to break this deadlock or if any proposed solution is to stand any serious chance of success then it must attempt to ensure two things:

1 That Ulster 'Protestants' no longer feel compelled to defend the frontier.
2 That Ulster 'Catholics' support, and play a full role, in society.

Whilst we have no doubt that compromise and accommodation can be reached between Catholics and Protestants in Northern Ireland, it is impossible to compromise on the existence of Northern Ireland itself – it either exists or it doesn't. At present it exists and is a part of the United Kingdom. This situation may not be the whole-hearted wish of everyone in the province but must be recognized to be the wish of most. Surely then this is the logical place to make a beginning.

It is our firm conviction that the vast majority of both religious communities long for peace, reconciliation and the chance to create a better future for their children. But longing is not enough; there must be a mechanism created to harness the love, generosity, courage and integrity of Ulster people in both religious communities and direct its great power towards the light of a new beginning.

In an attempt to create such a mechanism we propose the following:

(a) Devolved legislative government for Northern Ireland and a written constitution. A set of constitutional laws, agreed by Ulster Catholics and Protestants together which would lay the foundations on which to build a new progressive democracy. An agreement instituted by Ulster people at referendum which can only be changed by Ulster people at referendum.
(b) A modern democratic political structure based on consensus government, proportional representation and shared responsibility.
(c) A Bill of Rights.
(d) A Supreme Court charged with the responsibility to uphold constitutional law and safeguard the rights of the individual as represented in the Bill of Rights.

There is no section of this divided Ulster community which is totally innocent or indeed totally guilty, totally right or totally wrong. We all share the responsibility for creating the situation, either by deed or by acquiescence. Therefore we must share the responsibility for finding a settlement and then share the responsibility of maintaining good government.

A Scenario for Peace

Sinn Fein

National self-determination

The island of Ireland, throughout history, has been universally regarded as one unit.

The historical and contemporary existence of the Irish nation has never been in dispute.

The Irish people have never relinquished their claim to the right to self-determination.

What has been in contest is the right of the Irish people, as a whole, to self-determination and their freedom to exercise that right.

For centuries, the relationship between the British government and the Irish people has been the relationship between the conqueror and the conquered, the oppressor and the oppressed.

The perennial cycle of oppression/domination/resistance/oppression has been a constant feature of the British government's involvement in Ireland and the Irish people's rejection of that government's usurpation of the right to exercise control over their political, social, economic and cultural destiny.

From the late seventeenth century onwards, that usurpation provoked both revolutionary resistance and – within the narrowest confines of British constitutional legality – constitutional opposition. In the course of the nineteenth century, British oppression and famine caused the population of Ireland to be halved.

The last occasion when the Irish people nationally exercised their franchise was in the 1918 general election. Sinn Fein, with a political programme demanding complete independence for the unitary state of Ireland, won the election with 69.5 per cent of the vote. Those democratically elected representatives of the Irish people formed

Dail Eireann and, on 21 January 1919, enacted the Declaration of Independence.

The Anglo-Irish Treaty of 1922, the partition of Ireland and the Constitution of the Irish Free State were imposed on the Irish people under the threat of *'immediate and terrible war'*. They were not submitted to the Irish people for ratification and their imposition represents a denial to the Irish people of the freedom to exercise their right to self-determination.

The pretext for partition – the wishes of a national minority to maintain British rule – holds no validity against the express wishes of the vast majority of the Irish people.

Secession is not the same as self-determination.

Partition perpetuates the British government's denial of the Irish people's right to self-determination. It perpetuates the cycle of oppression/domination/resistance/oppression.

In the words of Sean MacBride, winner of the Nobel and Lenin Peace Prizes:

Ireland's right to sovereignty, independence and unity are inalienable and indefeasible. It is for the Irish people as a whole to determine the future status of Ireland. Neither Britain nor a small minority selected by Britain has any right to partition the ancient island of Ireland, nor to determine its future as a sovereign nation.

Law

Ireland's right to sovereignty, independence and unity – the right of the Irish people, as a whole, to self-determination – is supported by universally recognized principles of international law.

The right to self-determination is enshrined in the two United Nations' Covenants of 1966 – the *International Covenant on Civil and Political Rights* and the *International Covenant on Economic Social and Cultural Rights*. Article 1 of each covenant states:

1. All peoples have the right to self-determination. By virtue of that right they determine their economic, social and cultural development.

The landmark *Declaration on Principles of International Law Concerning Friendly Relations and Co-operation Among States in Accordance with the Charter of the United Nations* declares:

all people have the right freely to determine, without external influence, their political status and to pursue their economic, social and cultural development and every state has the duty to respect this right in accordance with provisions of the Charter.

Partition is in contravention of the *United Nations' Declaration on the Granting of Independence to Colonial Countries and Peoples*. Article 6 of which states:

Any attempt aimed at the partial or total disruption of the national unity and the territorial integrity of a country is incompatible with the purposes and principles of the Charter of the United Nations.

Loyalists

The major stumbling block to independence is British colonial inter- ference. The creation of the Six-County state around an artificial majority, the Loyalists, was meant to give a veneer of democracy to the foothold which Britain maintains in Ireland. The loyalist demand for the continuation of the union not only provides Britain with its pretext for remaining in the North, but allows Britain to falsely claim that it is not the obstacle to Irish independence, and allows Westminster off the hook, projecting itself as the 'honest broker'.

While we in no way wish to ignore the economic challenge which reunification presents, or minimize the extent of the problem, or the great trauma that will be experienced by the Unionist population, we believe that Loyalism derives an artificial psychological strength from the British presence, from the Union. Indeed, the relationship between Unionist intransigence and past *unconditional* British support is recognized (though unacknowledged) by Thatcher's government, part of whose present strategy via the Hillsborough Treaty, is to rock the morale of Loyalists, split the Unionists and force the emergence of a pragmatic leadership which will do an internal deal with the SDLP.

The Loyalists are a national minority in Ireland. According to most opinion polls, the majority of people in Britain want to wash their hands of Ireland. Increasingly, Loyalists are finding themselves in an untenable position. Their protest campaign against the Hillsborough Treaty has cost them dearly in PR terms and to the British public it has only emphasized the differences between the Six Counties and Britain. Their refusal to enter into dialogue (with anyone) and their disillusion- ment with the British government is producing a momentum towards disaster where civil war, or a unilateral declaration of independence, or repartition are among the irrational proposals put forward by some of the paramilitaries and politicians.

Sinn Féin seeks a new constitution for Ireland which would include written guarantees for those presently constituted as 'Loyalists'. This would recognize present-day social reality and would include, for example, the provisions for family planning and the right to civil divorce.

The resolution of the conflict would free Unionists from their historic laager mentality and would grant them real security instead of tenure based on repression and triumphalism. We do not intend to turn back the pages of history, or to dispossess the Loyalists and foolishly attempt to reverse the Plantation. We offer them a settlement based on their throwing in their lot with the rest of the Irish people and ending sectarianism. We offer them peace. We offer them equality.

It is only through the process of decolonization and dialogue that a peaceful, stable Ireland will emerge. Only when independence is restored can Ireland hope to prosper and take its place among the nations of the world. Britain must take the initiative and declare its intention to withdraw. That is the first step on the road to peace. Republicans will respond quickly and positively.

A scenario for peace

The ending of partition, a British disengagement from Ireland and the restoration to the Irish people of the right to exercise self-sovereignty, independence and national self-determination remain the only solution to the British colonial conflict in Ireland.

The Hillsborough Treaty and the processes it involves seek merely to camouflage the fact that the Six-County state is a failed entity, socially, economically, and politically. The Treaty does not challenge the constitutional status of the Union but actually reinforces it.

Sinn Fein seeks to create conditions which will lead to a permanent cessation of hostilities, an end to our long war and the development of a peaceful, united and independent Irish society. Such objectives will only be achieved when a British government adopts a strategy for decolonization.

It must begin by repealing the 'Government of Ireland Act' and publicly declaring that the 'Northern Ireland' statelet is no longer part of the United Kingdom.

Furthermore, it must declare that its military forces and its system of political administration will remain only for as long as it takes to arrange their permanent withdrawal.

This would need to be accomplished within the shortest practical period. A definite date within the lifetime of a British government would need to be set for the completion of this withdrawal.

Such an irreversible declaration of intent would minimize any Loyalist backlash and would go a long way towards bringing round to reality most Loyalists and those of their representatives genuinely interested in peace and negotiation. It would be the business of such negotiations to set the constitutional, economic, social and political arrangements for a new Irish state through a Constitutional Conference.

Constitutional Conference

Free elections to an all-Ireland Constitutional Conference would be arranged. The conference would consist of the elected representatives of the Irish people and would be open to submissions from all significant organizations in Ireland (e.g. the trade union movement, the women's movement, the churches) and would draw up a new constitution and organize a national system of government.

While this conference could have no influence on the decision by Britain to withdraw, it would play an important role in organizing the transition to a new governmental system. Should it fail to find agreement on a new constitution, or any other matter, a British withdrawal would proceed anyway within the fixed time period.

Republicans have consistently asserted that the Loyalist people, in common with all other citizens, must be given firm guarantees of their religious and civil liberties and we repeat our belief that, faced with a British withdrawal and the removal of partition, a considerable body of Loyalist opinion would accept the wisdom of negotiating for the type of society which would reflect their needs and interests. The irreversible nature of a British withdrawal strategy would be a major influence in convincing Loyalists that we were entering into a new situation which could not be changed by the traditional methods of Loyalist intransigence.

British withdrawal

As part of the military withdrawal, the RUC and UDR would be disarmed and disbanded.

The introduction of United Nations forces or European forces to supervise a British withdrawal or fill any alleged vacuum would only frustrate a settlement and must be avoided. Experience in other conflicts has shown that such a 'temporary' presence would become 'permanent' and the deployment would have a political bias. Their subsequent withdrawal would become a point of contention and there would be a re-run of the bloodbath-threat scenario. Similarly, there should be a real effort to avoid the introduction of forces from the Twenty-Six Counties.

The Constitutional Conference would be responsible for determining the nature and composition of an emergent national police service and the judiciary. There is absolutely no doubt in our minds that, if Britain was sincere about disengaging and committed to an orderly transference of power, this could be achieved with a minimum of disorder.

All political prisoners would be unconditionally released.

A cessation of all offensive military actions by all organizations would create the climate necessary for a peaceful transition to a negotiated settlement.

As part of the settlement, the British government must accept the responsibility for providing financial support by agreeing by treaty with the national government to provide economic subvention for an agreed period. Given the disastrous involvement of British rule in Ireland, reparations for an agreed period are the least contribution Britain could make to ensure an ordered transition to a national democracy and the harmonization of the economies, North and South.

The onus is on the British government to ensure a peaceful transition to a united and independent Ireland. The shape of that society is a matter for the Irish people. Only when Britain recognizes that right and initiates a strategy of decolonization along these lines will peace and reconciliation between Irish people and between Britain and Ireland be established.

Appendix 6
The BBC's Standing Instructions and Guidance for Journalists: 'Coverage of Matters Affecting Northern Ireland'

The document reproduced here – the BBC's standing instructions and guidance to journalists concerning the way in which they must report Northern Ireland issues – illuminates the manner and extent to which news coverage of the conflict in the province has been managed.

Standing instructions and guidance

The special circumstances of Northern Ireland required that the BBC's News and Current Affairs Guidelines be set out in particular detail and with somewhat greater formality than in other areas. The purpose of the Guidelines remains, here as elsewhere, to assist and not to inhibit the proper making of programmes. The present revision like earlier ones, seeks to draw upon the lessons of actual practice and experience.

Heads of Programme Output Departments in both Television and Radio are responsible for seeing that their staff understand and follow the Standing Instructions and Guidance and that their programme plans are communicated adequately – that is, in accordance with the Instructions – *upwards* so that they can be discussed at Directorate meetings like the Television Target Meeting, to CNI and, where necessary, DDG.

It must not be assumed that the advice and co-operation given to Network staff by Northern Ireland staff implies responsibility for the programme in its final form; that overall responsibility remains with the Network output departments.

Standing instructions

1   Referring up through Line Management

The BBC's system of delegated responsibility puts the onus on individual programme-makers to judge when to refer upwards in case of doubt or difficulty with regard to policy or the law. **The normal process of line management referral – from programme editors or producers, through Heads of Department and Network Controllers, to senior Directorate Management – is especially important in dealing with programmes affecting Northern Ireland.** Those involved in the referral process – from Editors and Heads of Department upwards – should keep a log of incidents and programme requests.

Although as programme-makers we wish to be judged by what we broadcast, we must recognize that the making of a programme is often itself a public activity and therefore one that may attract attention. This applies especially in Northern Ireland where our work comes under close and sometimes strongly partisan observation. Actions by BBC staff may lead, at any stage in the preparation of a programme, to public, political or paramilitary reaction. Referral enables senior and experienced professionals in the BBC to weigh the editorial value of programme material and programme-making activities against the physical, political and legal risks in a sectarian environment affected by terrorism.

Because the public perception of a programme can be significantly affected by the way it is promoted – in the press, in *Radio Times* and over BBC airwaves – the promotion of programmes affecting Northern Ireland must be referred. The Editors of *Radio Times* and *The Listener*, heads of Presentation Departments and Chief Publicity Officers carry responsibilities in their respective areas. They should consult the relevant output department Head and refer to CEP if necessary, as well as keeping CNI and their own senior line management informed; some instances will require specific clearance by Managing Directors.

2   Referring to Northern Ireland Staff

(a) **For all programme proposals other than on-the-day journalism Controller Northern Ireland must be consulted and his agreement sought on all programmes and items having**

a bearing on Ireland as a whole and Northern Ireland in particular. Programme proposals and responses to them should be confirmed in writing.

CNI does not have a right of veto, but in cases of disagreement the proposal shall be suspended until it has been referred to DDG and, if necessary, to DG for their ruling.

CNI will be the first point of contact on network programme proposals other than on-the-day journalism. In his absence, Head of Programmes, Northern Ireland (HPNI) and Editor, News and Current Affairs, Northern Ireland (ENCANI) will deputize, in that order – which corresponds to the delegation of responsibilities within BBC Northern Ireland.

CNI will, at his discretion, involve other members of his staff in the process of referral. Normally HPNI will be the point of reference for continuing consultation and advice on network programme proposals.

(b) For on-the-day journalism ENCANI will be the first contact point in all day-to-day matters of coverage for radio and television news bulletins and current affairs daily programmes and sequences.

ENCANI will nominate a senior member of his staff as an alternative point of contact in his absence.

Matters of particular urgency:

In news programmes ENCANI, together with ENCAR and ENCAT, will refer to their senior line management and CEP.

In daily current affairs programmes ENCANI will follow the same procedure together with ENCAR and ENCAT or other appropriate Head of Department.

Longer Term projects of daily current affairs programmes require referral to CNI, as under 2(a) above.

(c) **Consultation** in both on-the-day items and longer term projects, is a two-way process requiring the fullest possible disclosure of programme plans, upon which CNI, HPNI, ENCANI and other BBC Northern Ireland staff can form an opinion. Consultation is also a *continuing* process. On any longer term project, after the initial consultation at the outset of the proposal, CNI should be kept informed about its development and consulted about any significant change, incident or problem which may occur. He also needs to be kept aware of the transmission date envisaged, of the context in which the programme or item is being transmitted, and of how it is being billed, promoted and publicized.

CNI for his part will refer to Board of Management level as necessary.

3   Referring Proposals to Interview Members of Terrorist Organizations and those who are or may be associated with such organizations

The Head of Department [including, of course, ENCAT and ENCAR in their own areas of responsibility] with the programme editor or producer who has initiated the proposal, must make a fundamental judgement about the intended interviewee(s) and the subject matter of the interview. One of two referral procedures (a) and (b) follows from his judgement:

EITHER:

(a)   **Interviews with individuals who may be associated with terrorists or paramilitary organizations but who are active in legal political parties with seats on District Councils, in the Northern Ireland Assembly and/or at Westminster, and who are to be interviewed in connection with their legitimate activities.**

Such interviews are broadcast from time to time, for example, as part of BBC Northern Ireland's news and current affairs coverage of events and opinion in the province. Every such interview proposal, however, needs to be carefully assessed in terms of content and context. **Editor News and Current Affairs Northern Ireland (ENCANI) is the referral point for all network television or radio programmes proposing an interview in this category.**

This requirement – so far as longer term proposals are concerned – complements and in no way replaces the procedures set out in 2(a).

OR:

(b)   **Any other interviews with individuals who are members of or associated with terrorist or paramilitary organizations.**

These may not be sought or transmitted – two separate stages – without the prior permission of DDG and DG. This permission must be sought through CEP who will discuss each proposed interview with CNI.

The initiating programme editor or producer will first have

put the proposal to the Head of Department who, in addition to referring the matter to CEP, will have notified Senior Directorate Management and CNI.

WHEN IN DOUBT

Because of the difficulty of 'type-casting' potential interviewees in a political and legal environment which is both complex and variable there will inevitably be uncertainty, on occasions, as to which procedure – (a) or (b) – applies to a proposed interview. In such cases the initiating programme department will naturally seek advice from ENCANI and other Northern Ireland staff. In forming a judgement the Head of Department may refer to Senior Directorate Management as well as to CEP.

Some legal considerations relating to terrorism

In general there is no positive obligation placed upon a member of the public to volunteer information to the police. It can, however, be a criminal offence to provide misleading information or to obstruct the police in their duty. The professional rule that a journalist does not divulge his sources does not, however, confer immunity from criminal liability upon the journalist for failing to disclose information to a court of law when so required, and in rare instances in recent years journalists have been imprisoned for refusal to identify in court the source of information.

These general principles are, however, modified in Northern Ireland where there is a positive duty to inform the police where a person has committed a criminal offence punishable by five years or more imprisonment. The duty extends to providing information where any person knows or believes that such an offence has been, or may be, committed, and where such information might be of assistance in securing either the prevention of the crime or the prosecution of the offender (*sec. 5 Criminal Law Act (Northern Ireland) 1967*).

In relation to the whole of the United Kingdom (including Northern Ireland) a number of criminal offences are enacted by the Prevention of Terrorism (Temporary Provisions) Act 1976 relating to 'terrorism' in the whole of the United Kingdom – terrorism being defined as 'the use of violence for political ends, and includes any use of violence for the purpose of putting the public or any section of the public in fear'. Thus, under section II, if a person has information which he knows or believes might be of material assistance in either preventing an act of terrorism or in securing the apprehension or prosecution of any person for an offence connected with an act of terrorism he commits an offence if he fails without reasonable excuse to disclose that information as soon as reasonably practicable to the police, or, in Northern Ireland, to the armed forces.

There is also a number of other offences connected with terrorism in the United Kingdom (including Northern Ireland) enacted by the 1976 Act and the Northern Ireland Emergency Powers Act 1973. The principal offences which are likely to concern the journalist fall into the following broad categories and relate to dealings with 'proscribed organizations'. The Secretary of State for Northern Ireland has power to declare an organization to be within that category where it appears to him to be concerned in terrorism or promoting or encouraging it, and at present the Irish Republican Army and Irish National Liberation Army are the only proscribed organizations in the United Kingdom other than Northern Ireland. In Northern Ireland the proscribed organizations are the:

Irish Republican Army
Irish National Liberation Army
The Cumann na mBan
Fianna Eireann
Saor Eire
Ulster Freedom Fighters
The Red Hand Commando
Ulster Volunteer Force

These offences fall into the following broad categories:

Support for proscribed organizations

(a) belonging to a proscribed organization;
(b) wearing any item of dress or displaying any article showing support for a proscribed organization;
(c) inviting financial or other support for a proscribed organization;
(d) making or receiving any contribution in money or otherwise to the resources of a proscribed organization (e.g. the payment of any fees);

Meetings

(e) arranging or assisting in arranging, or addressing any meetings of three or more persons (public or private) knowing that the meeting is to support a proscribed organization or is to be addressed by a person belonging to such an organization;

Contributions towards acts of terrorism

(f) giving, lending or making available any money or property to any person knowing or suspecting that the money will or may be used in connection with the commission of acts of terrorism.

These are the main areas which Editors need to watch. **When providing coverage of affairs in or connected with Northern Ireland, Editors should seek specific advice from The Solicitor's Department on the legal implications in order to avoid or minimize the risks so far as practicable.**

Abbreviations

DG	Director General
DDG	Deputy Director General
CNI	Controller Northern Ireland
CEP	Controller Editorial Policy
ENCAR	Editor News and Current Affairs Radio
ENCAT	Editor News and Current Affairs Television

Appendix 7
Religion and Population in Northern Ireland: Past Trends and Future Prospects

This appendix is concerned with the share of Catholics in the Northern Ireland population. It describes the behaviour of this share since the first Census of Population in 1861; examines the factors which account for this behaviour; and considers what may happen to the share of Catholics in the future.

History: 1861–1981

Table A7.1 shows what has happened to the number of Catholics and non-Catholics (Protestants for short) in Northern Ireland since 1861. Figures for the pre-partition years refer to the six Irish counties (Antrim, Armagh, Down, Fermanagh, Londonderry and Tyrone) which now make up Northern Ireland. Information is derived from the decennial Census of Population which up to 1961 gave a fairly accurate picture of religious affiliations. Since then, however, there has been a sharp increase in both the number of people refusing to state their religion and the number failing to complete their census return. In each case, the increase is mainly political in origin, reflecting either a growing reluctance to reveal or divulge information about religious affiliation or else hostility to the very idea of a British-organized census. Such feelings are more widespread amongst Catholics than Protestants. Various efforts have been made to adjust the official census figures so as to estimate the true number of Catholics and Protestants. This is relatively easy for 1971 when the number of refusals was fairly small. It is more difficult for 1981, when approximately one person in five either refused to state their religion or failed to complete the census return. Among experts there is disagreement concerning both the total size of the Northern Ireland population and its religious composition. Estimates of the share of Catholics in 1981 range from 38.0 per cent (Compton, 1985), 38.3 per cent (Compton and Power, 1985) and 39.1 per cent (Eversley and Herr, 1985) to 42.5 per cent (Curran, 1984). On the evidence provided by these authors, the most reliable estimate seems to be that of Compton and Power, whose figure of 38.3 per cent is used in table A7.1.

Table A7.1 The religious composition of NI population, 1861–1981

		(*Thousands*)		
	(1)	*(2)*	*(3)*	*(4)*
	Catholics	*Non-Catholics*	*Total*	*Catholics as % of total*
1861	572	825	1,396	40.9
1871	534	825	1,359	39.3
1881	496	809	1,305	38.0
1891	448	788	1,236	36.3
1901	430	807	1,237	34.8
1911	430	820	1,251	34.4
1926	420	836	1,257	33.5
1937	428	851	1,280	33.5
1951	471	899	1,371	34.4
1961	498	927	1,425	34.9
1971	565	971	1,536	36.8
1981	588	947	1,535	38.3

Sources: For 1861–1961, NI Census of Population, as given in Compton (1985), table 1. For 1971–81, figures for total population are taken from Compton (1986) table 2; the religious breakdown is estimated using the shares given in Compton and Power (1985), table 2.

The main developments revealed by table A7.1 are as follows. In the nineteenth century there was a considerable fall in the Catholic population of Northern Ireland, from 572,000 in 1861 to 430,000 in 1901. This reflects the mass exodus of poor Catholic farmers from the land and their emigration in search of work. In the early twentieth century the number of Catholics stabilized; later, from the 1930s onwards, numbers began to increase fairly rapidly. This growth has continued up to the late 1980s, but even so there are only slightly more Catholics in Northern Ireland than there were in 1861. It has taken 60 years to reverse the effects of the nineteenth-century exodus of Catholics. Amongst Protestants the picture is rather different. The number of Protestants in Northern Ireland remained more or less constant throughout the nineteenth century and right up to the 1930s. Since then it has increased somewhat though on nothing like the scale observed amongst Catholics. The contrasting behaviour of the two populations is illustrated in figure A7.1(a).

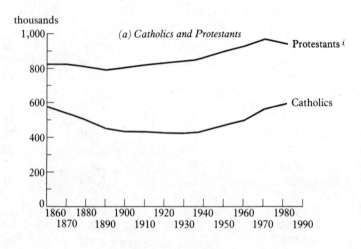

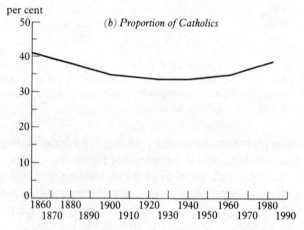

i includes all non-Catholics

Figure A7.1   Religious composition of NI Population, 1861–1981

The changes just described are reflected in the religious composition of the Northern Ireland population. Figure A7.1(b) shows what has happened to the share of Catholics in this population. During the nineteenth century the Catholic share fell rapidly; in the early twentieth century this share stabilized; finally during the interwar period it began to rise, at first slowly and then at an accelerating pace. From a peak recorded figure of 40.9 per cent in 1861 (the unrecorded figures for earlier years were almost certainly higher), the Catholic share fell to 33.5 per cent in 1937. Since then the figure has risen to 38–42 per cent, depending on which estimate one accepts. Thus, despite its rapid growth in recent years, the share of Catholics in the Northern Ireland population has only just reached the level achieved in 1861 when the first reliable statistics were collected. It is almost certainly well below their share in the earlier part of the nineteenth century, before the Great Famine and before statistics were compiled. In the late 1980s, the share of Catholics is increasing rapidly and there is debate as to whether or not they will eventually achieve a majority. This question is considered below.

The determinants of population growth

The growth of population in a particular region depends in the first instance on birth and death rates. Together these determine what is called the natural growth rate of population. This tells us by how much the population would change in the absence of migration into and out of the region concerned. To arrive at the actual growth rate of population, we must take into account the effects of migration. Emigration will either reduce the population – or slow down its growth – while immigration will have the opposite effect. These observations apply not just to the total population of a region, but also to particular subgroups. For example, what happens to the number of Catholics in the region depends both on the birth and death rates of Catholics and on the movement of Catholics into and out of the region. The same applies to Protestants. Thus, by considering birth and death rates within each religious group, together with migration behaviour, we can explain what has happened historically to the absolute number in each group and its share in the total population of the region. We can also predict what may happen in the future.

Let us now use the above ideas to analyse the changing share of Catholics in the Northern Ireland population. Table A7.2 shows the natural growth rate of each religious community in Northern Ireland.

Prior to 1961 the figures are estimates; moreover the table is incomplete as certain figures cannot be estimated with any precision. Even so, enough information is available for our purposes. The general picture revealed by this table is as follows. In the nineteenth century, Catholics had a lower birth rate than Protestants, presumably because they were poorer and married later; being poorer their death rate was also probably higher. As a result, the natural rate of increase was lower for Catholics than Protestants. However, this differential was reversed in the twentieth century. Protestants began to practise contraception so their birth rate began to fall. Amongst Catholics on the other hand, contraception remained unusual until quite recently, and moreover they began to marry at an earlier age. Because of these two features, the Catholic birth rate rose dramatically (see table A7.2). As a result, an enormous differential emerged between the two communities. By 1981 the natural rate of increase among Protestants had fallen to around 3 per 1,000 (=0.3% p.a.); among Catholics the natural rate of increase was 13 per 1,000 (=1.3% p.a.).

Ever since partition the natural rate of increase of Catholics has exceeded that of Protestants usually by an enormous margin. This differential is sometimes ascribed to social class. The argument runs as follows. In modern Western countries, the birth rate generally declines as one moves up the social scale. Lower-class families have a higher

Table A7.2   Natural increase of population in NI, 1861–1981

| | *(Rates per 1,000 of population)* | | |
	(1) Catholics	*(2)* Non-Catholics	*Difference (1)–(2)*
1861–1911	n.a.	n.a.	−2.0
1911–26	n.a.	n.a.	0.0
1926–37	8.0	6.0	2.0
1937–51	10.7	4.4	6.3
1951–61	15.9	6.2	9.7
1961–71	18.1	7.6	10.5
1971–81	13.1	3.1	10.0

Note: Figures for 1861–1937 are rough guesstimates made in the light of observations in Compton (1982); figures for 1937–61 are derived by averaging the relevant census figures as given in Compton (1982), table 2; figures for 1961–81 are derived from Compton (1985), table 5 (variant b) and table 9.

birth rate and a larger number of children; upper-class families have à lower birth rate and fewer children. Since Catholics are, on average, from a lower social class than Protestants, it is only to be expected that their birth rate is higher. This was the argument used by Prime Minister O'Neill in the 1960s when attempting to assuage Protestant fears of being outbred by Catholics. Hard-line Loyalists argued that the higher Catholic birth rate was a potential threat to the Protestant majority in Northern Ireland; that the only way to keep Catholic numbers down was to force them to emigrate. To this end, the hard-liners supported policies, such as job and housing discrimination, designed to make life unpleasant for Catholics and drive them out of the province. O'Neill rejected this line of argument. While accepting the need to keep down Catholic numbers, he claimed this could be done in a more humane fashion. Social reforms and the ending of discrimination, he argued, would eliminate Catholic poverty. As their poverty declined, Catholics would begin to behave like Protestants and practise contraception. Their birth rate would therefore decline. Thus, O'Neill argued that reforms would make Catholics better off and reduce their birth rate; hard-line opponents argued that reforms would have no effect on the Catholic birth rate. Who was correct? Although not absolutely conclusive, the evidence favours the hard-liners.

Table A7.3, which is based on the 1971 Census, gives information on family size by religion and social class. The figures given in this table show that upper-class Protestants had fewer children on average

Table A7.3 Average family size (children per family) in Northern Ireland: couples married 20–4 years in 1971

Socio-economic grouping	Catholics	Non-Catholics
Employers and managers	4.8	2.5
Professional workers	4.7	2.4
Other non-manual	4.6	2.5
Foremen and supervisors (manual)	4.8	2.6
Skilled manual	5.1	3.0
Semi-skilled manual	5.0	3.0
Unskilled manual	5.4	3.5
Farmers and farm managers	5.4	3.5
Agricultural labourers	5.0	3.7

Source: Compton (1986)

than lower-class Protestants. Amongst Catholics, however, family size was almost unrelated to social class: employers, managers and professionals had about as many children as farm labourers and unskilled manual workers. Thus, both rich and poor Catholics had very large families simply because they were Catholics. Although not absolutely conclusive, this evidence suggests that O'Neill was wrong. Reforms to improve the lot of the Catholic poor would not have altered their child-bearing habits significantly. During the period in question, Catholics of all incomes and all classes had very large families, and an improvement in their socio-economic status would not have reduced their birth rate noticeably. On the other hand, such reforms would have encouraged Catholics to remain in Northern Ireland instead of emigrating, thereby increasing the number of Catholics in the province. In their own terms, the hard-liners were correct. If the aim was to keep down the number of Catholics, enforced emigration was the only solution. A brutal answer, perhaps, but a logical one given their objective.

Emigration

For well over a century emigration has been a feature of life in Northern Ireland, for both Catholics and Protestants. However, because of their relative poverty and lack of employment opportunities the rate of emigration has been higher among Catholics. In the nineteenth century, the Catholic emigration rate was so high that, as we have seen, there was a large fall in the absolute number of Catholics living in the province. In the more recent past, however, this has not been the case. Catholic emigration, although considerable, has been insufficient to offset the extremely high Catholic birth rate, and the result has been a substantial increase in both the number of Catholics in Northern Ireland and their share in the total population. In the absence of emigration, of course, their numbers would have increased even faster and so too would their share.

The influence of emigration on the religious composition of Northern Ireland can be calculated as follows. Suppose there had been no emigration from Northern Ireland during the period 1926–81. Then, using the natural rates of increase shown in table A7.2, we can estimate how the number of Catholics and Protestants in Northern Ireland would have evolved over the period 1926–81. We can also estimate how emigration affected each religious community during this period. The results are shown in table A7.4.

Table A7.4   The impact of emigration, 1926–81

	(*Thousands*)	
	Catholics	*Non-Catholics*
(1) Population in 1926	420	836
(2) Natural increase 1926–81	431	289
(3) Hypothetical population in 1981		
(= line (1) + line (2))	851	1125
(4) Actual population in 1981	588	947
(5) Effect of emigration		
(= line (4) − line (3))	− 263	− 178

Let us go briefly through table A7.4. Line (1) shows the actual number of Catholics and Protestants in 1926. Lines (2) and (3) show the natural increase resulting from the excess of birth rates over death rates during the period 1921–81. These figures indicate how population in each community would have risen in the absence of emigration. The much higher natural growth rate of Catholics is clearly visible in these figures. In the absence of emigration, the Catholic population would have more than doubled over the period 1926–81, while the Protestant population would have risen by around a third. However, because of emigration the actual increase was less than these figures suggest. The natural increase in Catholics over the period 1926–81 was 431,000, of which 263,000 were siphoned off by emigration (including the future children of emigrants), leaving 168,000 at home to swell the number of Catholics within Northern Ireland. During the same period, the natural increase in Protestants was 289,000, of which 178,000 were siphoned off by emigration, leaving 111,000 at home to swell the number of Protestants. Comparing the two communities, we find that Catholics were more than twice as likely to emigrate as Protestants. Over the period as a whole, the annual emigration rate averaged around 6.7 per 1,000 for Catholics and 3.1 per 1,000 for Protestants (these figures include the future children of emigrants).

Thus, the higher birth rate of Catholics has been partially, though not completely, offset by their higher rate of emigration. In the absence of emigration the share of the Catholics in the Northern Ireland population would have risen even faster than it has done. Compton and Powers estimate that in 1981 the share of Catholics was

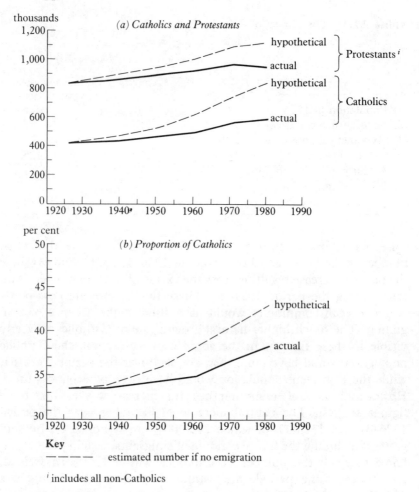

thousands

(a) Catholics and Protestants

hypothetical
actual
} Protestants [i]

hypothetical
actual
} Catholics

per cent

(b) Proportion of Catholics

hypothetical

actual

Key

— — — —   estimated number if no emigration

[i] includes all non-Catholics

Figure A7.2   Effects of emigration on NI population, 1926–81

38.3 per cent. Our estimates suggest that, if there had been no emigration over the entire period 1926–81, the share of Catholics would have been 43.1 per cent. This is still not a majority, but is well above the actual share.

The future

The share of Catholics in the population of Northern Ireland has been rising strongly in recent decades. The future behaviour of this share depends on what happens to birth rates, death rates and migration. Compton (1985) has estimated that, *with current birth and death rates and with no migration*, Catholics would achieve a majority of the population by 2026; moreover, a Catholic majority of the under 15 age group would emerge by the end of the century. However, as the same author points out, emigration rates are normally higher for Catholics than Protestants, which is a factor helping to keep down the Catholic share. In addition, Catholic birth rates are now falling quite rapidly as the use of contraceptives spreads amongst younger Catholics. Taking into account both factors, he predicts that the share of Catholics will rise more slowly in the future, eventually stabilizing at around 44 per cent as compared to 38.0 per cent (on his estimate) in 1981.

Compton's projection, although interesting, should be treated with caution for two reasons. Firstly, the present share of Catholics in Northern Ireland may be much higher than he estimates. Secondly, the Catholic birth rate may fall more slowly than he assumes, in which case the Catholic share will increase by a greater amount than he predicts. As an illustration, let us consider an alternative prediction under which Catholics do achieve an eventual majority. Suppose that Curran (1984) is correct in claiming that in 1981 Catholics were 42.5 per cent of the population, which is a considerably higher figure than Compton's estimate of 38.0 per cent. Moreover, suppose the Catholic share rises by 9.0 percentage points before stabilizing (as compared to the 6.0 points assumed by Compton). Under these assumptions, the Catholic share will eventually stabilize at 51.5 per cent and hence they will eventually be in the majority. The arithmetic of this alternative projection is laid out in table A7.5.

Table A7.5 Projected share of Catholics in the Northern Ireland population (per cent)

	Compton	*Alternative estimate*
Catholic share in 1981	38.0	42.5
Future increase in share	6.0	9.0
Ultimate share of Catholics	44.0	51.5

The alternative projection is, of course, purely illustrative and proves nothing. It is designed merely to show how much uncertainty there is regarding the future. Compton is probably right in claiming that Catholics will never achieve a majority of the adult population in Northern Ireland. However, the assumptions which underlie his projection could be wrong, and the Catholic share could behave according to our alternative projection, in which case the Catholics would eventually achieve a majority. Even if this does not happen, one thing is clear: the Catholic share will continue rising for some time to come, and the electoral position of Protestants will come under increasing threat.

Bibliography

Compton, P. A., 'Fertility, nationality and religion in Northern Ireland', in *Demography of Immigrants and Minority Groups in the United Kingdom*, ed. D. A. Coleman (London: Academic Press, 1982).

Compton, P. A., 'An evaluation of the changing religious composition of the population of Northern Ireland' (unpublished paper, 1985).

Compton, P. A., *Demographic Trends in Northern Ireland*, Northern Ireland Economic Council, Report no. 57, 1986.

Compton, P. A. and Power, J. P., 'Estimates of the religious composition of Northern Ireland local government districts in 1981 etc.' (unpublished paper, 1986).

Curran, F., Submission to the New Ireland Forum, New Ireland Forum (Dublin: Stationery Office, 1984).

Eversley, D. and Herr, V., *The Roman Catholic Population of Northern Ireland in 1981: a Revised Estimate* (Belfast: Fair Employment Agency, 1985).

Select Bibliography

The following bibliography provides a brief guide to further reading. Most of the books and reports listed are available either in bookshops or in public libraries. A few may be difficult to obtain but have been included because of their importance. The list has been chosen so as to give a reasonable cross-section of views and topics. Inevitably in such a brief selection, many important works are missing. However, some of the books listed here have extensive bibliographies of their own, which readers can consult as required. In addition two bibliographies, one extremely comprehensive, are included in the following list.

ADAMS, G., *The Politics of Irish Freedom* (Dingle: Brandon, 1986). Authoritative statement of the modern Republican case by the Sinn Féin MP for West Belfast.

BECKETT, J. C., *The Making of Modern Ireland 1906–1923*, 2nd edn (London: Faber and Faber, 1981). History of Ireland from the Conquest of Ulster to Partition. Impressive, scholarly account by a Northern Unionist.

BELL, G., *The Protestants of Ulster* (London: Pluto Press, 1976). Excellent and sympathetic brief history of the Protestants of Northern Ireland. The author is himself a Northern Protestant who supports the Republican cause.

BELL, G., *Troublesome Business* (London: Pluto Press, 1982). Critical analysis of British Labour Party policy on the Irish question. Short and readable.

BELL, G., *The British in Ireland: a Suitable Case for Withdrawal* (London: Pluto Press, 1984). A useful outline of the situation in Northern Ireland from a socialist-Republican perspective, urging the case for British withdrawal.

BENNETT REPORT, *Report of the Committee of Enquiry into Police Interrogation Procedures in Northern Ireland* (London: HMSO Cmnd 7497, 1979). Produced in response to evidence provided by Amnesty International documenting widespread ill treatment of suspects held in police custody in

Northern Ireland. Recommends revised methods of interrogation, including the installation of closed-circuit TV in all interview rooms.

BERESFORD, D., *Ten Men Dead* (London: Grafton Books, 1987). Well-written book on the Hunger Strike by the Guardian correspondent in Northern Ireland.

BEW, P., GIBBON, P., PATTERSON, H., *The State in Northern Ireland 1921–1972* (Manchester: Manchester University Press, 1979). Explicitly Marxist but strongly anti-Republican analysis of the state in Northern Ireland.

BEW, P., PATTERSON, H., *The British State and the Ulster Crisis* (London: Verso, 1985). Short history of the conflict in Northern Ireland from the mid-1960s. Concludes just before signing of the Anglo-Irish Agreement. Very hostile to Sinn Féin.

BOWYER BELL, J., *The Secret Army* (Dublin: Academy Press, 1979). Standard history of the IRA by an American historian. Covers military and political aspects. Includes brief but penetrating analysis of the split in the Republican movement in 1979 into the Provisional and the Official IRA. (The latter is now virtually defunct, though its former political wing continues as the 'Workers Party'.)

BOYD, A., *Have the Trade Unions Failed the North?* (Cork: Mercier Press, 1984). Anecdotal history of trade unions in Northern Ireland. Very critical of the unions from a Nationalist standpoint.

BOYLE, K., HADDEN, T., *Ireland: a Positive Proposal* (London: Penguin, 1985). Provides useful insight into the debate preceding the Anglo-Irish Agreement. Preoccupied with constitutional detail, at the expense of wider political factors.

BROAD, R. et al., *The Troubles: the Background to the Question of Northern Ireland*, 2nd edn (London: Thames/MacDonald Futura, 1982). A very impressive companion to the Thames TV series on Northern Ireland. Thoughtful, informative, extremely readable and well illustrated. Essential reading. Much superior to Robert Kee's *Ireland: a History*, also a companion to a television series.

BURTON, F., *The Politics of Legitimacy: Struggles in a Belfast Community* (London: Routledge & Kegan Paul, 1976). Study of political struggles in a Catholic working-class area of West Belfast. Describes problems the IRA faced in consolidating popular support in this area.

CAMERON REPORT, *Disturbances in Northern Ireland: Report of the Cameron Commission* (London: HMSO Cmd 532, 1969). Official inquiry into the origins of the civil disturbances. Documents discrimination in Northern Ireland and recommends changes in policing and administration. First official recognition of discrimination against Catholics. Of great historical importance.

CHAMBERS, G., SMITH, D. J., Equality and Inequality in Northern Ireland (PSI Occasional Paper 39) (London, Policy Studies Institute, 1987). A well researched report on the employment situation which appeared shortly before this book went to press. Strongly supports our economic analysis and contains extensive material, documenting and analysing discrimination in Northern Ireland.

COLLINS, T., *The Centre Cannot Hold: Britain's Failure in Northern Ireland* (Dublin: Bookworks, 1985). Well-produced, illustrated history and analysis of the Northern Ireland problem. Has a foreword by Sean McBride.

COOGAN, T. P., *The IRA*, 2nd edn (London: Pall Mall Press, 1987). History of the Irish Republican Army from its foundation up to recent times. Highly readable.

CORMACK, R., OSBORNE, R. D. eds, *Religion, Education and Employment* (Belfast: Appletree Press, 1983). Informative and thorough exploration of Catholic disadvantage in Northern Ireland. Contributors include most of the foremost authorities in this field.

COUGHLAN, A., *Fooled Again?* (Cork: Mercier Press, 1986). Nationalist critique of the Anglo-Irish Agreement.

CRONIN, S., *Irish Nationalism* (Dublin: Academy Press, 1980). History of Irish Nationalism by a one-time leader of the IRA. The author is now the US political correspondent of the Irish Times.

CURTIS, L., *Nothing But The Same Old Story* (London: Information on Ireland, 1984). Describes the roots and history of anti-Irish racism in Britain. An interesting and depressing book.

CURTIS, L., *Ireland: the Propaganda War* (London: Pluto Press, 1984). Meticulous analysis of the treatment of Ireland in the British media. Reveals the extent of distortion and censorship.

DANGERFIELD, G., *The Damnable Question* (London: Quartet, 1979). A warm and vivid account of Anglo-Irish relations in the years immediately leading up to partition. Written by an English author with strong Nationalist sympathies.

DE PAOR, L., *Divided Ulster* (London: Penguin, 1973). One of the best accounts of the conflict in Northern Ireland and its origins. Written from a broadly Nationalist perspective.

DEUTSCH, R. R., *Northern Ireland 1921–74: a Select Bibliography* (New York: Garland Publishing Inc., 1975). Useful short bibliography listing some of the main books, pamphlets and articles on Northern Ireland up to 1974. Describes briefly most of the works listed.

DEWAR, M. D., *The British Army in Northern Ireland* (London: Arms and Armour Press, 1985). First-hand account of the conflict in Northern Ireland by a Lieutenant Colonel in the British Army. Interesting and sophisticated.

DIPLOCK REPORT, *Report of the Commission to Consider Legal Procedures to Deal with Terrorist Activities of Northern Ireland* (London: HMSO Cmd 5185, 1972). Proposes measures to restrict legal rights in N. Ireland, of which the most important is abolition of trial by jury in the case of 'terrorist type' offences, and its replacement by trial by a single judge sitting alone. Following this report, the so-called Diplock courts were set up.

ELLIS, P. BERRESFORD ed., *James Connolly: Selected Writings* (London:

Penguin, 1973). Good selection of writings by Ireland's greatest socialist thinker and leader.

ELLIS, P. BERRESFORD, *Hell or Connaught* (London: Hamish Hamilton, 1975). History of Oliver Cromwell's brutal subjugation and colonization of Ireland.

FARRELL, M., *The Orange State*, 2nd edn (London: Pluto Press, 1980). Classic critical history of the Northern Ireland state. Clear and well argued. Essential reading.

FISK, R., *In Time of War: Ireland, Ulster and the Price of Neutrality 1939–45* (London: André Deutsch, 1983). Thorough history of Anglo-Irish relations during the second world war. Reveals how, in 1940, Britain offered Irish reunification in return for the use of military bases in the South. The offer was bitterly opposed by Northern Unionists. It was eventually rejected by the Southern government in the belief that Britain was not to be trusted, and would lose the war anyway.

FISK, R., *The Point of No Return* (London: André Deutsch, 1975). Account of the Protestant Ulster Workers Council strike which destroyed the power sharing executive in 1974. The author was Northern Ireland correspondent for the London *Times* during this period.

GALLAGHER, F., *The Indivisible Island* (London: Gollancz, 1957). Describes the origins, development and execution of partition. Contains an excellent chapter describing electoral 'gerrymandering' in Northern Ireland, including an explanation of the origin of this term.

GALLAGHER, T., O'CONNELL, J. eds, *Contemporary Irish Studies* (Manchester: Manchester University Press, 1983). Collection of essays on Ireland. Of main interest is that by John Whyte who argues that discrimination under the old Unionist regime did occur, but on a considerably lesser scale than is claimed by most Nationalists.

GARDINER REPORT, *Measures to Deal with Terrorism in Northern Ireland* (London: HMSO Cmnd 5847, 1975). Highly subjective and ill-informed account of paramilitary violence in Northern Ireland. Recommends the abolition of special category (political prisoner) status for paramilitary prisoners. The implementation of this recommendation led to the hunger strikes of 1980–1 during which ten Republican prisoners died.

GIFFORD, T., *Supergrasses: the Use of Accomplice Evidence in Northern Ireland* (London: Cobden Trust, 1984). Careful review of the whole supergrass episode – the quality of evidence in the main cases; the role of the police; the Diplock courts' handling of supergrass evidence, etc. Makes detailed recommendations for reform, in particular for prohibiting both trials and convictions in the Diplock courts on the basis of uncorroborated accomplice evidence.

GREER, S., WHITE, A., *Abolishing the Diplock Courts* (London: Cobden Trust, 1986). Makes a civil-libertarian case for abolition of these special non-jury courts.

HAMILL, D., *Pig in the Middle: the Army in Northern Ireland 1969–84* (London: Methuen, 1985). History of the conflict in Northern Ireland from the point of view of the British Army. Describes the evolution of security policy and the changing roles of the police and the Army.

HARVEY, S., REA, D., *The Northern Ireland Economy with Particular Reference to Industrial Development* (Newtownabbey: Ulster Polytechnic Innovation & Resource Centre, 1982). One of the few books cn Northern Ireland devoted exclusively to economic questions. Contains a good general survey of the economic situation and the evolution of government industrial and regional strategy.

HICKEY, J., *Religion and the Northern Ireland Problem* (Dublin: Gill & Macmillan, 1984). Interesting discussion of the role of religious beliefs in the Northern Ireland conflict.

HUNT REPORT, *Report of the Advisory Committee on the Police in Northern Ireland* (London: HMSO Cmd 535, 1969). Recommends disarming the RUC, abolishing the Ulster Special Constabulary (B Specials), and the formation of a locally recruited military force (the UDR) under the control of the British Army. All these recommendations were accepted at the time, though the RUC was later rearmed.

ISLES, K. S., CUTHBERT, N., *An Economic Survey of Northern Ireland* (Belfast: HMSO, 1957). Valuable source of statistical information. Gives detailed analysis of Northern Ireland's economy and its problems.

JACKSON, T. A., *Ireland Her Own* (1947) (London: Lawrence and Wishart, 1976). Reissued well-written Marxist history of Ireland.

KENNY, A., *The Road to Hillsborough* (Oxford: Pergamon, 1986). Deals concisely and clearly with the major developments leading up to the Anglo-Irish Agreement. The author is Master of Balliol College, Oxford.

LUSTIG, I., *State Building Failure in British Ireland and French Algeria* (Berkeley: University of California, 1986). Brief but fascinating study comparing British experience in Ireland with French experience in Algeria. Contains profound insights into the nature of settler colonialism.

MOLONEY, E., POLLACK, A., *Ian Paisley* (Dublin: Poolbeg Press, 1987). Biography of the most famous modern leader of militant Protestantism in Northern Ireland. Provides a good insight into Loyalist thinking. The authors have both worked in Belfast as journalists for the *Irish Times*.

MULLIN, C., *Error of Judgement* (Dublin: Poolbeg Press, 1987). A devastating account of the circumstances surrounding the arrest and conviction of six Irishmen for the 1974 Birmingham pub bombings.

NCCL, *Strip Searching* (London: NCCL, 1986). Report of an inquiry team which investigated the use of strip searching of women prisoners in Armagh gaol.

NEW IRELAND FORUM, *A Comparative Description of the Economic Structure and Situation, North and South* (Dublin: Stationery Office, 1983). One of many documents produced by the New Ireland Forum to accompany its main report. Provides a good general description of the two economies and their recent developments.

NEW IRELAND FORUM, *The Macroeconomic Consequences of Economic Policy, Planning, and Coordination in Ireland* (Dublin: Stationery Office, 1983). A study by a group of economists of the economic implications of various new constitutional arrangements for Ireland. Considers unification and other possibilities. Its conclusions are broadly in line with those of the present work.

NEW IRELAND FORUM, *Report* (Dublin: Stationery Office, 1983). Produced after lengthy public hearings and extensive research, this report outlines three different options for the future of Northern Ireland: a unified Ireland; a confederation of two Irish states; and 'joint authority' of Britain and the Republic over Northern Ireland. All three options were rejected by Mrs Thatcher in her famous 'Out, out, out' press conference. However, a very watered down version of joint authority was later embodied in the Anglo-Irish (Hillsborough) Agreement of 1985.

O'DOWD, L., ROLSTON, B., TOMLINSON, M., *Northern Ireland Between Civil Rights and Civil War* (London: CSE Books, 1980). Critical analysis of the role of the British state in Northern Ireland during the 1970s.

O'MALLEY, P., *The Uncivil Wars* (Belfast: Blackstaff Press, 1983). Wide-ranging examination of the issues at stake in Northern Ireland. Quotes extensively from interviews with leading figures from political and para-military organizations. Very interesting.

QUIGLEY REPORT, *Economic and Industrial Strategy for Northern Ireland: Report of a Review Team* (Belfast: HMSO, 1976). General description of the economy of Northern Ireland and analysis of policy options. One of the best works available on this topic. Written under a Labour government, it stresses the need for state investment both to create employment and to regenerate the local economy. Calls for the establishment of a state manu-facturing sector to create at least 1,500 jobs a year.

RANELAGH, J. O'BEIRNE, *A Short History of Ireland* (Cambridge: Cambridge University Press, 1983). A short and useful summary of Irish History from prehistoric times to the early 1970s.

ROLSTON, B. et al., *A Social Science Bibliography of Northern Ireland 1945–83* (Belfast: Queens University, 1983). A comprehensive bibliography listing nearly 6,000 books, pamphlets and articles written on Northern Ireland over the period 1945–83. Items are classified according to subject, but no descriptive notes are provided.

SCORER, C., HEWITT, P., SPENCER, S., *The Prevention Of Terrorism Act: the Case For Repeal*, rev. edn (London: NCCL, 1985). An account of the operation of the PTA, with its powers of summary exclusion from Britain, and detention for up to seven days without charge.

STALKER, J., *Stalker* (London: Harrap, 1988). Tells the inside story with great restraint. A bestseller in Ireland.

STANDING ADVISORY COMMISSION ON HUMAN RIGHTS, *Religious and Political Discrimination and Equality of Opportunity in Northern Ireland. Report on Fair Employment* (London: HMSO Cm 237). Companion to the PSI Report by Chambers and Smith (see above). Very sophisticated analysis of religious discrimination in Northern Ireland and the machinery for dealing with it. Criticizes the existing legal and institutional framework for tackling religious discrimination and makes a large number of far-reaching recommendations for strengthening this framework. A very thoughtful and useful publication.

STEWART, A. T. Q., *The Ulster Crisis* (London: Faber and Faber, 1967). Chronicles the formation and the activities of the illegal Ulster Volunteer Force up to 1914. Contains a moving epilogue describing the appalling casualties later suffered by these same Ulstermen in 1916 during the battle of the Somme. Easy to read account by a leading Unionist scholar.

STEWART, A. T. Q., *The Narrow Ground: Aspects of Ulster 1609–1969* (London: Faber and Faber, 1977). A Unionist view of Catholic–Protestant relations in Northern Ireland.

STRAUSS, E., *Irish Nationalism and British Democracy* (London: Methuen, 1951). A classic. Especially interesting on the economic background to partition.

TAYLOR, P., *Beating the Terrorists?* (London: Penguin, 1980). Investigation of serious police abuses of the interrogation system between 1976 and 1979. Taylor's original television programme on the subject triggered off an Amnesty Report and subsequently the official inquiry by the Bennett Committee.

TAYLOR, P., *Stalker* (London: Faber and Faber, 1987). Account of official Stalker inquiry into RUC killing of six unarmed suspected Republicans in 1982. Describes RUC attempts to conceal the truth and obstruct Stalker's investigation.

TEAGUE, P. ed., *Beyond the Rhetoric: Politics, the Economy and Social Policy in Northern Ireland* (London: Lawrence and Wishart, 1987). Collection of articles on Northern Ireland by authors of diverse political views. Useful up-to-date source of information.

VAN STRAUBENZEE REPORT, *Report and Recommendations of the Working Party on Discrimination in the Private Sector of Employment* (Belfast: HMSO, 1973). Chaired by a Tory MP, the working party produced a remarkably radical government document on the topic of religious discrimination. The report calls for such discrimination to be made illegal. It rejects rigid employment quotas on moral and practical grounds but strongly supports affirmative action programmes along the lines adopted in the United States to combat racial and sexual discrimination.

WALSH, D., *The Use and Abuse of Emergency Legislation in Northern Ireland* (London: The Cobden Trust, 1983). Detailed and painstaking account of the abuses of civil liberties that take place under the emergency legislation. Argues that the criminal justice system cannot be relied on to resolve conflicts which require a political solution.

Index

Standing Advisory Commission on
Human Rights 41
Stormont (Northern Ireland
Parliament) 16, 43
strikes, Unionist, against power
sharing 44
subsidies, industrial 82
Sunningdale agreement 44, 49,
129, 174, 175
supergrass system 56-7, 130, 131
synthetic fibres industry 79, 83-4

teachers
Catholic women as 107, 110, 119
increase in number of 73, 74
pupil-teacher ratio 90
Teevan, Tom 33-4
television censorship 66-7
Thatcher government
and the IRA hunger strikes 47-8
and the Northern Ireland
economy 87-8
tobacco firms 84
Tone, Theobald Wolfe 19-20
trade
in the Irish Republic 101-2
and Irish reunification 153
in Northern Ireland 97-9
trade unions
and Catholic employment 22, 34
in the Irish Republic 68

UDA (Ulster Defence Association)
143
Common Sense 8, 184, 185-8
and negotiated independence 138
and power sharing 7-8
UDI (unilateral declaration of
independence) 126, 138-9
UDR (Ulster Defence Regiment)
41, 45, 46, 62, 87, 121, 167
and British withdrawal 145, 147,
148

deaths in 61, 179
employment in 112
UFF (Ulster Freedom Fighters) 8
Ulster
definition of 13
partition of 24
Ulster Special Constabulary
(B Specials) 37-8, 39, 40, 41
Ulster Workers Council 44
unemployment
in the 1930s 71
in the 1980s 88, 91, 93, 98, 100
of Catholics and Protestants 74,
110-19
geography of 75, 112-15, 117
in the Irish Republic 100, 104
among men 89, 110, 111, 113,
114-15, 116, 117-19
and the Unionist government 72
among women 89, 110, 111, 113,
114
Unionist government 26-7, 28, 35,
41
economic policies of 72, 73, 76-9
Unionists
and the Anglo-Irish Agreement
129, 132, 135
and British withdrawal 143
definition of 12
and power sharing 44
united Ireland 4, 5-6, 126, 140-65
civil and religious liberties in
159-62
and the economy 152-8
and employment 158-9
guarantees 163-5
and the New Ireland Forum 49
United Irishmen, rising of (1789)
19-20
United Kingdom, definition of 14
United States 131, 157
in Vietnam 46
UVF (Ulster Volunteer Force) 24,
37, 143

Index by Isobel McLean